ABR: YOU CAN READ!

Adult Beginning Reader Program

Letters ~ Words ~ Let's Learn

A Basic Essentials English Literacy Program

by

Frederick J. Zorn, Ed.D.

Principal, Teacher, Adjunct Professor, Literacy Tutor

CCB Publishing
British Columbia, Canada

ABR: You Can Read! Adult Beginning Reader Program

Copyright © 2014 by Frederick J. Zorn, Ed.D.
ISBN-13: 978-1-77143-042-5
First Edition

Library and Archives Canada Cataloguing in Publication
Zorn, Frederick J., author
ABR : you can read! adult beginning reader program /
by Frederick J. Zorn. -- First edition.
Issued in print format.
ISBN 978-1-77143-042-5 (pbk.).
Additional cataloguing data available from Library and Archives Canada

Materials contained herein belong expressly to Dr. Frederick J. Zorn, are in the public domain, or are from the sources listed below. Some images have been adapted for space and context from the original. Appreciation is expressed to the following for permission to use images as part of this book. Note: Page numbers referenced below are the pages where the images appear within this book.
Authors and Editors: A Journey Through America, Elaine Kirn, ©1991.
        Images used on Pp. 273, 291, 330, 346, 351, 353.
Dover Publications, Inc.:
        Ready-to Use Illustrations of American Landmarks, Charles Hogart, ©1997.
        Images used on Pp. 338, 351, 356.
        Ready to Use, Illustrations of World-Famous Places, Charles Hogart, ©1993.
        Image used on P. 345.
Super Teacher Worksheets: Images used on Pp. x, 290.
Canstockphoto.com: Images used on
        Front cover, © lisafx, © monkeybusiness
        P. 1 © thorgal, © jonnya, © GeorgiosArt, © asafeliason, © sahua
        P. 141 © nenovbrothers, © freesoulproduction, © Toncsi47, © PixelsAway
        P. 275 © jminso679, © feedough, © 4774344sean, © Andres
        P. 286 © jelen80

Dr. Frederick J. Zorn may be contacted through CCB Publishing at: info@ccbpublishing.com

Publisher: CCB Publishing
               British Columbia, Canada
               www.ccbpublishing.com

Dedication and Acknowledgments

The ability to read is a precious gift. Family gave me books. Mom read to me and encouraged me in creative writing. Patient teachers used their expertise to help me learn. As a teacher and principal for 35 years, I learned from students, teachers, and professors. As a long time Literacy Tutor, I've been inspired by the courage and hard work of adults wanting to improve their reading skills. As a speaker and workshop leader at National Conferences, I learned from tutors and educators all over the country.

I dedicate this book to my parents, Samuel and Beatrice Hirsch Zorn, who instilled in me a love of learning, perseverance to accomplish, and enjoyment that comes from creating and helping others.

Thank you to all who inspired, encouraged, and helped me create this important work. May it be a useful, effective, and practical tool for those learning to read and for those helping others learn to read. This book and the illustrations I've commissioned are designed to respect adult maturity and facilitate meaningful learning. For me, each page is a work of love and belief that "YOU CAN READ!"

Best wishes!

P.S. Do let me hear from you!

Overview

ABR: You Can Read! is a basic essentials literacy curriculum and tutoring tool for use with adults at beginning reading levels. It covers sight and sound recognition of letters of the alphabet. It builds basic sight word banks. It covers a wide range of practical and academic sight vocabulary and concepts in context units. For ease of use, units are in one convenient volume with 3 main sections:

1. **Letters:** Build sight and sound recognition of the basic symbols of reading.
   - 26 letters   - (96 key words + 45 key Letter Ender words)
   - 5 Vowels (long / short)   - (90 key words)
   - Blended letters   - (131 Consonant / Vowel key words)

2. **Words:** Develop basic, practical and academic sight vocabulary & educational concepts.
   - Basic Sight Words / Phrases   - (253 key words)
   - Word / Pictures   - (138 key words)
   - 50 Word / Sound Families *(rhyming words)* - (500+ key words)
   - 29 Practical Literacy Units   - (1225 key words)

3. **Let's Learn:** Expand vocabulary and topic concepts. *(Use later in the term.)*
   - 31 Beyond Basics Units   - (750+ key words)
   - 18 Civics Units   - (200+ key words)

Profile of the Adult Beginning Reader

The Adult Beginning Reader is an adult with limited use of reading as a practical life skill. Limitations may be traced to learning difficulties, unsuccessful early learning experiences, and/or limited educational opportunities. Unlike younger learners, adults HAVE extensive life and language experiences to build on. *Note: Those with significant learning limitations may require specialized help.*

Learners may benefit by use of particular sensory learning styles:
- *Visual learning:*   Sight recognition and discrimination, use of pictures
- *Auditory learning:*   Hearing, sound recognition and discrimination, listening
- *Oral learning:*   Speech, repetition, discussion, responding
- *Tactile learning:*   Manipulating, touching, pointing, tracing, writing

Suggested Tutoring Session Guidelines

- **Term:**   6 – 9 months; 1 - 2 hour sessions, 1 - 2 x/week.
- **Group Size:** 2 – 5 members for optimal material coverage, peer support and interaction.
- **Lesson:**   Separate each session into 20 - 30 minute lessons from different sections.
  Use Letters and Basic Sight Words sections each session until completed.
  Add a story, writing exercise and/or visuals to supplement lessons.

Lesson Planning Suggestions:

Each session, include lessons from 2 or 3 different categories. *@20 - 30 minutes / lesson*

☐ **Letters:** Use in page order *(4 - 6 lessons)*. Repeat and review as needed.

☐ **Words: Basic Sight Words / Phrases:** 3 - 5 letter sets EACH session /any order.
 Improvement is a goal each lesson. Complete all sets. Repeat to achieve mastery.

☐ **Words: Word Pictures** *(1 - 2 lessons)*

☐ **Words: Word / Sound Families** Can select in each vowel section. *(3 - 5 lessons)*

☐ **Words: Practical Literacy** 1 mini-unit /session, any order.

☐ **Let's Learn:** 1 mini-unit /session, any order. *Use later in the term.*

◇ Note: Use *Word Attack, Grammar and Punctuation* skill lessons as needed.

Skills: Letters *Pp. 1 - 137*

☐ <u>26</u> letters are the basis of all words.

☐ Each letter has its own shape & sound (s).

☐ Each letter has an UPPER & lower case.

☐ 5 Letters are vowels: a, e, i, o, u.

☐ Other letters are consonants.

☐ Letters can BLEND & make new sounds.

◇ **Goal:** Build sight & sound recognition.

Skills: Basic Sight Words / Phrases

Use Words and/or Phrases unit. *Pp. 144 - 153*

☐ *250+ Basic Sight Words: Must know words* that make up much of all written material. **Final goal:** Mastery.

Unit: Word Pictures *Pp. 155 - 175*

◇ **Goal:** Build sight vocabulary.

Unit: Word / Sound Families

☐ Rhyming words. *Pp. 176 - 201*

◇ **Goal:** Learn sound patterns.

Units: Practical Literacy *Pp. 203 - 271*

☐ Important life skill words in context.

☐ Units help fill educational gaps.

◇ **Goal:** Learn words and concepts.

Units: Let's Learn *Pp. 275 - 358*

◇ **Goal:** Expand word study and learn academic concepts. *Do in later sessions.*

Skills: Word Attack *(See Index for units.)*

☐ **Word Endings:** Ex: *-s, -ed, -ing, -ion*

☐ **Compound Words:** Ex: *butterfly*

☐ **Contractions:** Ex: *don't*

☐ **Syllables:** Pronounce words in parts.

☐ **Root Word, Prefix, Suffix**

☐ **Homonyms**: Same sound; different meanings.

Skills: Grammar, Punctuation *(See Index.)*

☐ **Parts of Speech**: Noun, Pronoun, Adjective, Verb, Adverb, Preposition, Conjunction, Article, Interjection.

☐ **Punctuation Marks**: . ? ! , ; : " " ' ( )

☐ **Sentence, Subject, Predicate**

◇ Note: Use to aid reading / writing skills.

Techniques: Do Comfortable Reading

☐ One sentence or short selection only.

☐ Give prompts, cues, beginning sounds.

☐ Check correct place; have all point to it.

☐ When a task is tedious, change activity.

Techniques: Encourage Fluency

☐ Group words in meaningful phrases.

☐ Let eyes *wash over* a few words before reading out loud. Read in phrases.

☐ Use punctuation clues.

☐ Read with expression.

◇ *Key Words:* Pre-identify and pronounce.

Tutor Record of Lessons: Put date(s) covered

Letters:
_Alphabet; 26 Letters
- □ Recognition, order_____
- □ Upper/Lower Case_____
- □ Pronunciation_____
- □ Letter Shapes _____
- □ Letter Practice_____
- □ Same/Different_____
- □ Letter Discrimination_____
- □ 26 Letters: Sounds_____
- □ Consonants c / g_____
- □ Vowels - long, short_____
- □ Vowel Blenders_____
- □ Letter Enders_____
- □ Consonant Blenders_____

Words:
_Basic Sight Words
- □ a-g:_____
- □ h-p:_____
- □ q-v:_____
- □ w-z:_____

_Basic Sight Word Phrases
- □ a-g:_____
- □ h-p:_____
- □ q-v:_____
- □ w-z:_____

_Word Pictures
- □ a-o: _____
- □ p-z: _____

_Word / Sound Families
- □ a:_____
- □ e:_____
- □ i: _____
- □ o/u:_____

Practical Literacy: Words
(Stress key words and concepts)
- □ The Body_____
- □ Calendar_____
- □ National Observances_____
- □ Clothing_____
- □ Colors_____
- □ Compound Words_____
- □ Containers_____
- □ Contractions_____
- □ Directions/Opposites_____
- □ Family_____
- □ Fruits & Nuts _____
- □ Geometric Shapes_____
- □ Greeting Cards_____
- □ Homonyms_____
- □ Job Application_____
- □ Jobs: Occupations_____
- □ Mail (Letter, envelope)_____
- □ Menu_____
- □ Number Words_____
  - _Decimals, Fractions, Percent_____
  - _Roman Numerals _____
- □ Prepositions_____
- □ Signs _____
- □ Syllables_____
- □ Symbols_____
- □ Time_____
- □ Vegetables/Grains_____
- □ Vote_____

Tutor Record of Lessons: Put date(s) covered

- ☐ **Word Enders** _____
  - _Noun: -s, -es_____
  - _Noun: -er, -ful, -less_____
  - _Adjective: -er, -est_____
  - _Verb: -ed, -d_____
  - _Nouns: -ion, -ation, -ian_____
- ☐ **Functional Words: Chart**_____
- ☐ **Words of Praise**_____
- ☐ **Root Words:** (prefix, suffix)_____

Let's Learn: Beyond Basics
(Stress key words and concepts)
- ☐ **Birds**_____
- ☐ **Buildings: Furnishings** _____
- ☐ **Check**_____
- ☐ **Chemistry**_____
- ☐ **Citizen**_____
- ☐ **Food, Digestion** _____
- ☐ **Geography**_____
- ☐ **Grooming**_____
- ☐ **Health/Wellness:** _____
  - _Check Up_____
  - _Doctors _____
- ☐ **Ice Cream**_____
- ☐ **Mammals** _____
- ☐ **Measures**_____
- ☐ **Money: Coins, Bills** _____
- ☐ **Music: Instruments, Symbols**_____
- ☐ **Parts of Speech: Grammar**_____
  - _Noun, Pronoun, Adjective _____
  - _Verb, Adverb, Preposition _____
  - _Conjunction, Article, Interjection ___

- ☐ **Prescription, Labels**_____
- ☐ **Punctuation**_____
- ☐ **Sea Animals**_____
- ☐ **Solar System**_____
- ☐ **Sentence: Subject, Predicate** _____
- ☐ **Sports**_____
- ☐ **Table Setting**_____
- ☐ **Teeth**_____
- ☐ **Tools/Simple Machines**_____
- ☐ **United States:** _____
- ☐ **Weird Words:** _____

Let's Learn: Civics (Stress key terms)
- ☐ **U.S. Government: Branches**_____
- ☐ **Presidents** _____
- ☐ **Congress**_____
- ☐ **Supreme Court**_____
- ☐ **U.S. Beginnings**_____
- ☐ **Constitution** _____
- ☐ **Flag**_____
- ☐ **Pledge of Allegiance**_____
- ☐ **Patriotic Songs**_____
- ☐ **Statue of Liberty**_____
- ☐ **Gettysburg Address**_____

Literature Suggestions:
- ☐ *Fables* _____
- ☐ *Short Stories*_____
- ☐ *Fairy Tales* _____
- ☐ *Biographies*_____
- ☐ *Other*_____
- ☐ *Mechanics:*_____
  - _Fluency_____
  - _Comprehension_____
  - _Reading Pictures_____

ABR: YOU CAN READ! Adult Beginning Reader Program

Table of Contents

Letters - Words - Let's Learn

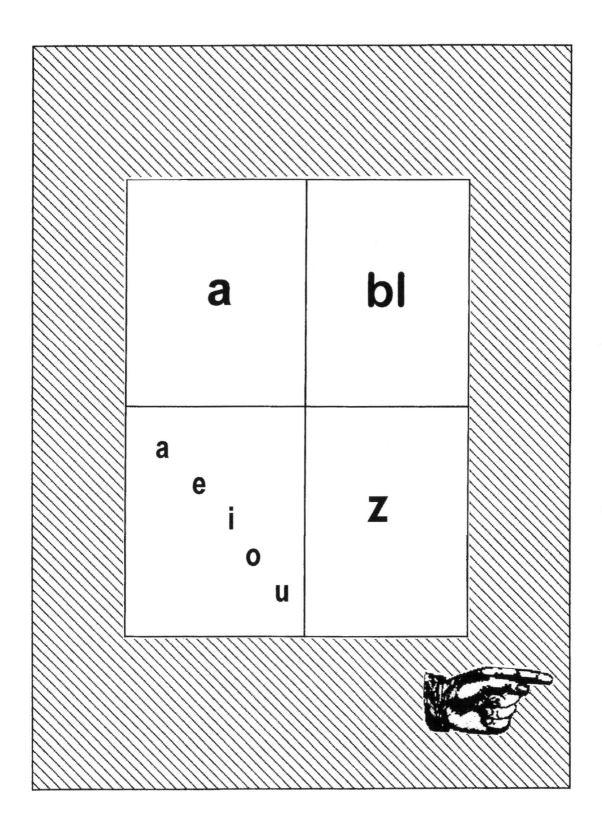

Writing: Marks for spoken language.

▢ 5,000 years ago, people began to leave records of events.

◇ Picture drawings: Caves, clay.

◇ Symbol drawings: Events, ideas instead of pictures.

- Egyptian Hieroglyphics
- Chinese Characters

▢ Letter symbols: Alphabet of sounds of a language.

◇ Phoenicians: 22 letters.

◇ Greek Alphabet: From the Phoenician alphabet.

◇ Roman/Latin Alphabet: From Greek and local alphabets.

Map: Mediterranean Sea Area   ■ Water   ▢ Land

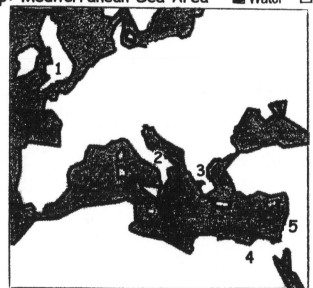

Key: 1. Britain   2. Rome   3. Greece   4. Egypt   5. Phoenicia

◇ English (Anglo-Saxon) Alphabet: From Latin & local alphabets.

- 26 letters (a-z); 43 spoken sounds (phonemes).

- Some letters have more than one sound.

- It's the base of many written languages today.

ABR: YOU CAN READ!
Adult Beginning Reader Program

Egyptian Hieroglyphics

ABC's

Chinese Symbols

Greek Alphabet

Hebrew Letters

Russian Alphabet

Section 1: Letters of the Alphabet

Letter Shapes   Same-Different   Letters (A-Z)

C & G   Vowels   Letter Enders   Consonant Blenders

by

Frederick J. Zorn, Ed.D.

Principal, Teacher, Adjunct Professor, Literacy Tutor

ABR Tips for Tutors: Letters of the Alphabet

Tutor: _Review the letters in alphabet order. (P. 4)
          _Note upper and lower case differences.
          _Note that manuscript and cursive letters differ.
          _Review Pronunciation Guide. (Pp. 6-7)
          _Discuss the importance of each letter as a basic symbol
              for reading.
          _Stress that each letter has at least one sound.
          _Note that letters make up words, words make up
              sentences, sentences make up paragraphs, and
              paragraphs make up books and other written matter.

Tutor: Note: Some letters have more than one sound.

Learner: _Name each letter of the alphabet in order.
Tutor: _Repeat each letter of the alphabet in order.
          _Group letters as you say them. (a-g, h-p, q-v, w-z)
          _Stress the key letter sound.
          _Show placement of tongue and lips for each letter.
          _Demonstrate long and short vowel sounds.
Learner: _Repeat after the tutor.

Tutor: Note: Some letters look very much alike.
          _a o c e   _f t l i k   _s z
          _b d p g q j   _m n u h r   _v w

Learning to recognize letters by sight and sound is a basic reading skill.

~ Enjoy learning to recognize and sound out the 26 Letters of the Alphabet! ~

© Frederick J. Zorn, 2014

Section 1: Letters of the Alphabet

Table of Contents

26 Letters of the Alphabet

A a	B b	C c	D d
E e	F f	G g	H h
I i	J j	K k	L l
M m	N n	O o	P p
Q q	R r	S s	T t
U u	V v	W w	X x
Y y	Z z		

Learning Concept: # Alphabet: Manuscript, Cursive

Letters of the Alphabet have 4 forms:
<u>Upper</u> & <u>Lower</u> Case / <u>Manuscript</u> *(print)* and <u>Cursive</u> *(writing)*

Manuscript: 26 letters of the Alphabet in print form.

Lower Case:

a b c d e f g h i j k l m

n o p q r s t u v w x y z

Upper Case:

A B C D E F G H I J K L M

N O P Q R S T U V W X Y Z

Upper Case: Capital Letters are used for names, places, months, first word of a sentence.

Cursive:

26 letters of the Alphabet in written form.

Lower Case:

a b c d e f g h i j k l m

n o p q r s t u v w x y z

Upper Case:

A B C D E F G H I J K L

M N O P Q R S T U V W X

Y Z

Note: Manuscript letters ARE usually used in all printed materials.

~ ABR Pronunciation Guide ~

Approximate Mouth, Teeth and Tongue Positions

Lips together

b   m   p   w

Upper teeth on lower lip

f   v

Stick tongue out between teeth

th

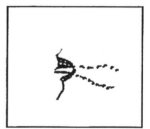

Tip of tongue to top of mouth above upper front teeth

d   n   l   t

Middle of tongue to top of mouth

ch   j   s   sh   y   z

Back of tongue to top of mouth

g (hard)   **k**

Open mouth and blow

h

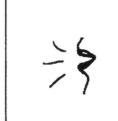

Stretch mouth wide

ā   **ē**   **ī**

Pucker lips

ō   **ū**

Open mouth;

tongue low, mid, or high

u   u   u
a (low front)   **e** (mid front)   **i** (high front)

u   u
o (low center)   **u** (mid center)

Key

-	Long vowel sound
u	Short vowel sound

7   © Frederick J. Zorn, 2014

Shapes:

Tutor: _Each letter (both upper and lower case) has its own shape.

_Some are lines: Horizontal, vertical, slanted; long, short.

_Some are curves: Circles, half-circles, open circles.

_Some are both lines and curves.

Note: Seeing shapes of letters is helpful in letter recognition.

Letter Practice:

Learner: _Practice tracing the letters and point out shapes.

_Concentrate on lower case letters.

Note: Most letters used in reading are lower case.

Same - Different:

Tutor: _Some letters look very much alike.

Learner: _Select letters that are the Same and/or Different.

Note: This is important sight recognition training.

Letter Discrimination:

Tutor: _Explain that some letters are built with the same shapes.

_Do each of the 5 letter sets separately.

Learner: _Identify how each letter in the set differs from the others.

Note: Refer to this section at any time as needed.

~ Enjoy learning to recognize the 26 Letters of the Alphabet! ~

ABR: YOU CAN READ!

Adult Beginning Reader Program

ABR Sight & Sound Guide to Letters of the Alphabet

Section I: **Letters**

Letter Recognition

Recognizing Visual Differences in Letters of the Alphabet

Shapes – Letter Practice – **Same-Different** – *Letter Discrimination*

by

Frederick J. Zorn, Ed.D.

Principal, Teacher, Adjunct Professor, Literacy Tutor

Upper Case Letters: Shapes

1. Some letters are lines:

2. Some letters are curves or lines and curves:

3. Note basic shapes: Lines, curves or lines and curves:

J i □   K i /   L i ☰

M i /   N i /   O ⬭

P i □   Q ⬭   R i /□

S □   T ☰   U i □

V /   W /   X /

Y /   Z / ☰

Lower Case Letters: Shapes

1. Some letters are lines:

2. Some letters are curves or lines and curves:

c   u   n   r   o

3. Note basic shapes: Some letters are lines, curves or lines and curves:

j   k   l

m   n   o

p   q   r

s   t   u

v   w   x

y   z

Letter Practice: Lower Case (Use as needed.)

1. a

2. b

3. c

4. d

5. e

6. f

7. g

8. h

9. i

10. j

11. k

12. I

13. m

14. n

15. o

16. p

17. q

18. r

19. S

20. t

21. U

22. V

23. W

24. X

25. Y

26. Z

Note: _ Letter writing practice is useful at any time.
_ Individual letters can be selected for practice when needed.
_ Lower case letters are the most used letters.
_ Make sure letters are printed not handwritten.
_ Letter lines can be used as long as needed.

Same - Different: Upper Case

Step 1: Look at the first letter in the row.
Step 2: Look at all the other letters in the row.
Step 3: Point to the letter that is <u>different</u> from the first letter.

1. A   V   A   A   A

2. B   B   B   B   D

3. B   E   B   B   B

4. C   C   O   C   C

5. D   B   D   D   D

17

6. D   D   D   P   D

7. E   E   F   E   E

8. H   H   F   H   H

9. M   M   M   M   W

10. N   N   M   N   N

11. O   O   Q   O   O

12. O   P   O   O   O

13. P   P   P   B   P

14. R   P   R   R   R

15. R   R   K   R   R

16. V   V   V   Y   V

17. W   V   W   W   W

18. W   W   M   W   W

Aa Bb Cc Dd Ee Ff Gg Hh Ii Jj Kk Ll Mm Nn Oo Pp Qq Rr Ss Tt Uu Vv Ww Xx Yy Zz

Same - Different: Lower case

Step 1: Look at the first letter in the row.
Step 2: Look at all the other letters in the row.
Step 3: Point to the letter that is <u>different</u> from the first letter.

1. a   a   a   o   a

2. b   b   p   b   b

3. d   d   b   d   d

4. e   e   e   o   e

5. f   t   f   f   f

6. g   g   g   p   g

7. g   g   q   g   g

8. h   n   h   h   h

9. l   l   l   i   l

10. m   m   n   m   m

11. n   n   n   u   n

12. n   m   n   n   n

13. p   p   q   p   p

14. p   b   p   p   p

15. r   r   r   r   n

16. s   s   s   c   s

17. t   t   f   t   t

18.   u   v   u   u   u

19.   v   v   y   v   v

20.   v   v   v   v   u

21.   w   w   w   v   w

22.   w   m   w   w   w

23.   z   z   s   z   z

Aa Bb Cc Dd Ee Ff Gg Hh Ii Jj Kk Ll Mm Nn Oo Pp Qq Rr Ss Tt Uu Vv Ww Xx Yy Zz

Letter Discrimination

Some letters are often confused in reading and printing.
Use the following exercise as needed to learn differences.

Set 1:	b	d	p	g	q	j

1. b

2. d

3. p

4. g

5. q

6. j

Set 2:   a   o   c   e   s

1. a

2. o

3. c

4. e

5. s

Set 3:   m   n   u   h   r

1. m

2. n

3. u

4. h

5. r

Set 4:   v   w

1.

2.

Set 5:   f   t   i   l

1.

2.

3.

4.

ABR Tips for Tutors: Letters of the Alphabet
Use the Alphabet Key Line at the top of each page.

Tutor: _Review the alphabet order.

              _Start unit with "A a" and go in order.

              _Do one letter at a time.

              _Complete the whole alphabet in one to two sessions.

              _For other units, review specific letters as needed.

_Where a letter has two sounds, do both.

Note: Reverse Color Ovals identify letters with two sounds.

Learner: _Name the letter.

              _'Read' each picture word on the page quickly.

Tutor: _Repeat each picture word on the page.

              _Stress the key letter sound.

Learner: _Repeat all picture words on the page.

              _Stress the key letter sound.

Note: *Letter Height Guides* (Ex: c̲ d̲ f̲ g̲ A̲ M̲) show how high or low a letter goes -- *top, middle, base, bottom line.* All sit on the base line; some go up and/or down; some go to the top. Useful for practicing letter printing.

Tutor: Note: Each letter with two picture sets has two sounds.

     _Vowels: a e i o u   (Long and short sounds)

     _Consonants: c g   (Hard and soft sounds)

Follow the same pattern for **Vowel** and **Consonant Blender lessons.**

~ Enjoy learning to recognize and sound out the 26 Letters of the Alphabet! ~

ABR: YOU CAN READ!

Adult Beginning Reader Program

ABR Sight & Sound Guide to Letters of the Alphabet

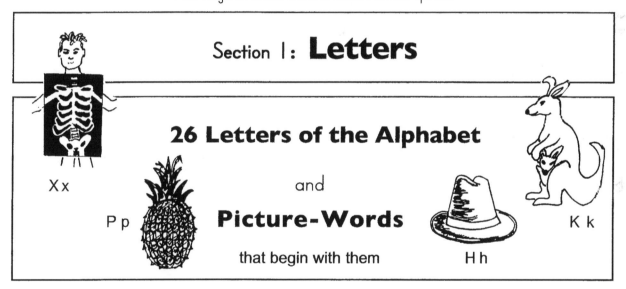

Section 1: **Letters**

26 Letters of the Alphabet

and

Picture-Words

that begin with them

X x

P p

H h

K k

by

Frederick J. Zorn, Ed.D.

Principal, Teacher, Adjunct Professor, Literacy Tutor

A̲a̲ Bb Cc Dd Ee Ff Gg Hh Ii Jj Kk Ll Mm Nn Oo Pp Qq Rr Ss Tt Uu Vv Ww Xx Yy Zz

apple

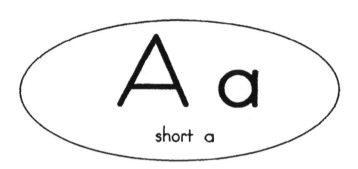

short a

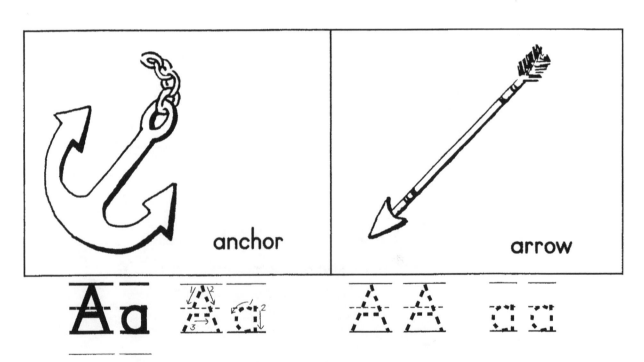

anchor

arrow

<u>Aa</u> Bb Cc Dd Ee Ff Gg Hh Ii Jj Kk Ll Mm Nn Oo Pp Qq Rr Ss Tt Uu Vv Ww Xx Yy Zz

ace

long a

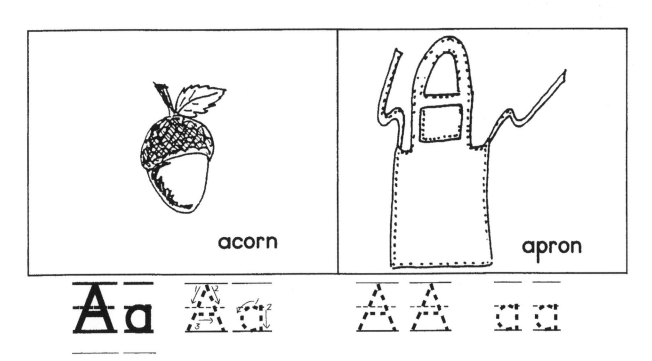

acorn

apron

© Frederick J. Zorn, 2014

Aa <u>Bb</u> Cc Dd Ee Ff Gg Hh Ii Jj Kk Ll Mm Nn Oo Pp Qq Rr Ss Tt Uu Vv Ww Xx Yy Zz

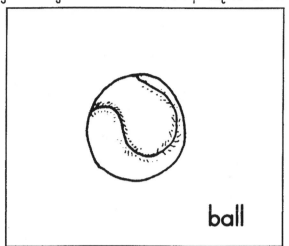

ball

B b

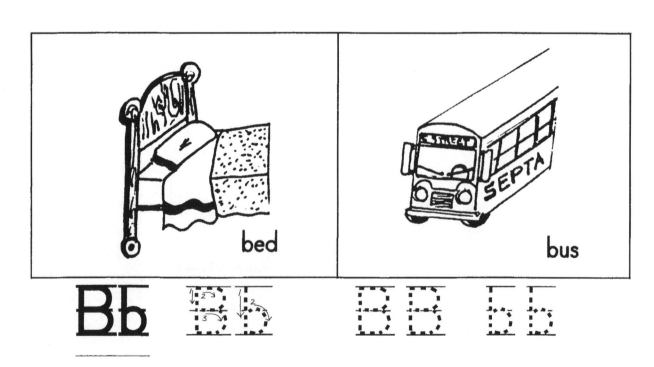

bed

bus

32

ABR: Letters: Word List

Note: Review words for each letter set without picture cues.

Total Alphabet Word List is at the end of the Letters Book.

Aa _apple

_anchor

_arrow

Aa _ace

_acorn

_apron

B b _ball

_bed

_bus

Aa Bb <u>Cc</u> Dd Ee Ff Gg Hh Ii Jj Kk Ll Mm Nn Oo Pp Qq Rr Ss Tt Uu Vv Ww Xx Yy Zz

cake

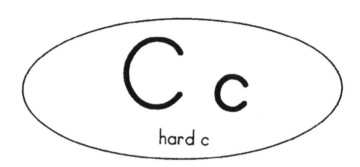

hard c

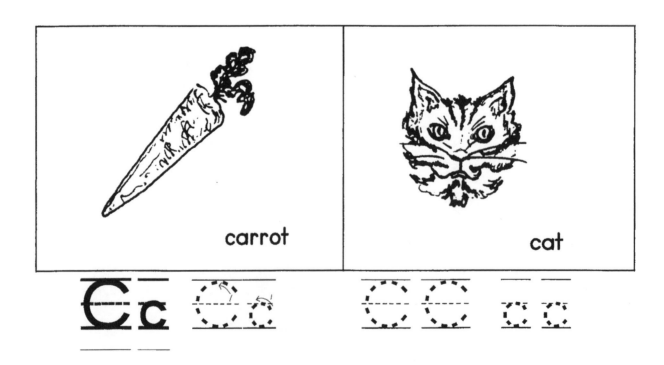

carrot

cat

Aa Bb <u>Cc</u> Dd Ee Ff Gg Hh Ii Jj Kk Ll Mm Nn Oo Pp Qq Rr Ss Tt Uu Vv Ww Xx Yy Zz

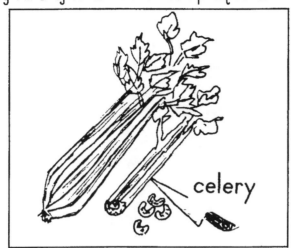

celery

soft c

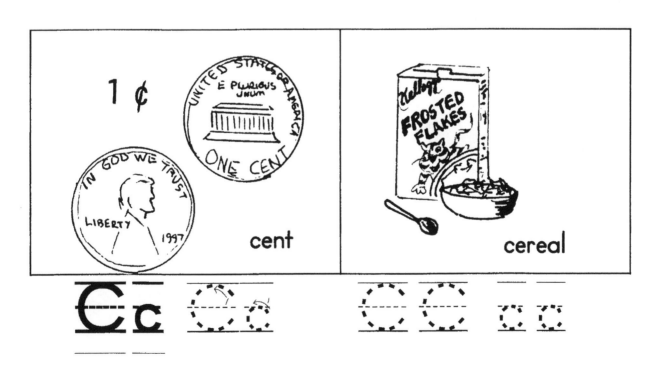

1 ¢

cent

cereal

© Frederick J. Zorn, 2014

Aa Bb Cc <u>Dd</u> Ee Ff Gg Hh Ii Jj Kk Ll Mm Nn Oo Pp Qq Rr Ss Tt Uu Vv Ww Xx Yy Zz

dog (Dalmation)

D d

donut

door

© Frederick J. Zorn, 2014

ABR: Letters: Word List

Note: Review words for each letter set without picture cues.

Total Alphabet Word List is at the end of the Letters Book.

Cc _cake

_carrot

_cat

Cc _celery

_cent

_cereal

Dd _dog

_donut

_door

Aa Bb Cc Dd <u>Ee</u> Ff Gg Hh Ii Jj Kk Ll Mm Nn Oo Pp Qq Rr Ss Tt Uu Vv Ww Xx Yy Zz

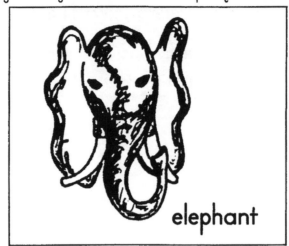

elephant

E e

short e

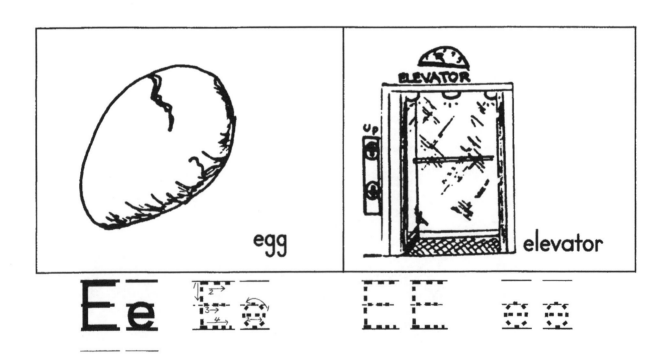

egg

elevator

Aa Bb Cc Dd <u>Ee</u> Ff Gg Hh Ii Jj Kk Ll Mm Nn Oo Pp Qq Rr Ss Tt Uu Vv Ww Xx Yy Zz

eagle

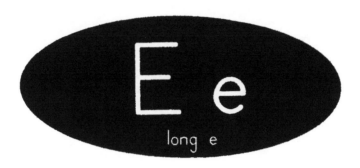

long e

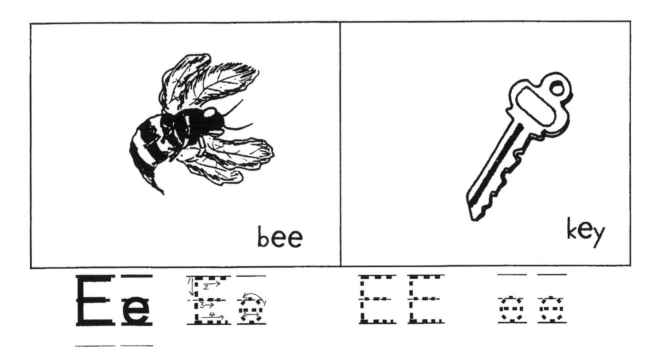

bee

key

© Frederick J. Zorn, 2014

Aa Bb Cc Dd Ee <u>Ff</u> Gg Hh Ii Jj Kk Ll Mm Nn Oo Pp Qq Rr Ss Tt Uu Vv Ww Xx Yy Zz

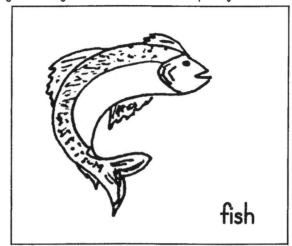

fish

F f

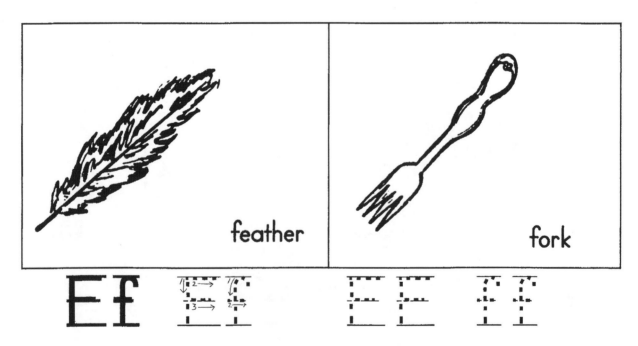

feather

fork

ABR: Letters: Word List

Note: Review words for each letter set without picture cues.

Total Alphabet Word List is at the end of the Letters Book.

Ee _elephant

_egg

_elevator

Ee _eagle

_bee

_key

Ff _fish

_feather

_fork

Aa Bb Cc Dd Ee Ff <u>Gg</u> Hh Ii Jj Kk Ll Mm Nn Oo Pp Qq Rr Ss Tt Uu Vv Ww Xx Yy Zz

goat

G g

hard g

girl

grapes

G g

© Frederick J. Zorn, 2014

Aa Bb Cc Dd Ee Ff <u>Gg</u> Hh Ii Jj Kk Ll Mm Nn Oo Pp Qq Rr Ss Tt Uu Vv Ww Xx Yy Zz

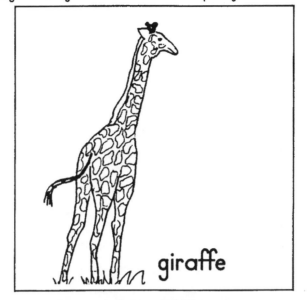

giraffe

G g
soft g

gingerbread

© Frederick J. Zorn, 2014

Aa Bb Cc Dd Ee Ff Gg <u>Hh</u> Ii Jj Kk Ll Mm Nn Oo Pp Qq Rr Ss Tt Uu Vv Ww Xx Yy Zz

hammer

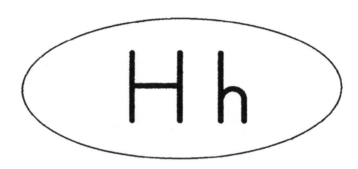

H h

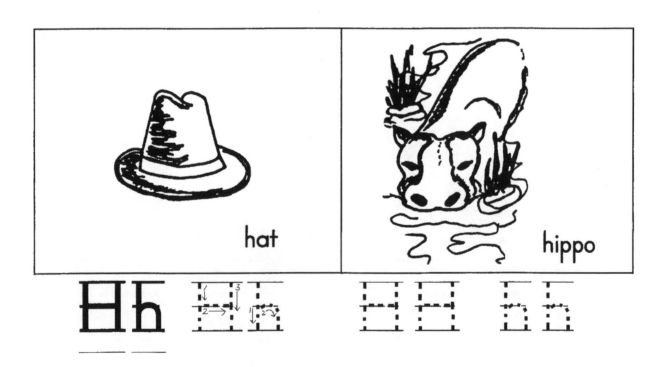

hat

hippo

© Frederick J. Zorn, 2014

ABR: Letters: Word List

Note: Review words for each letter set without picture cues.

Total Alphabet Word List is at the end of the Letters Book.

Gg _ goat
_ girl
_ grapes

Gg _ giraffe
_ gingerbread

H h _ hammer
_ hat
_ hippo

Aa Bb Cc Dd Ee Ff Gg Hh <u>Ii</u> Jj Kk Ll Mm Nn Oo Pp Qq Rr Ss Tt Uu Vv Ww Xx Yy Zz

igloo

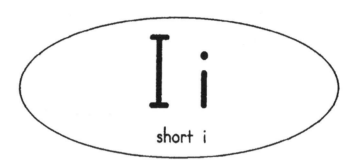

I i

short i

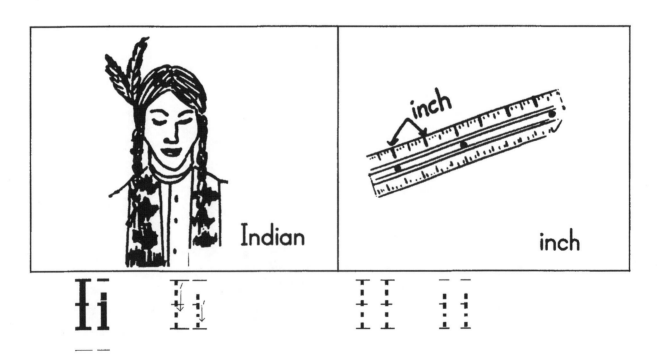

Indian

inch

inch

Aa Bb Cc Dd Ee Ff Gg Hh I̲i̲ Jj Kk Ll Mm Nn Oo Pp Qq Rr Ss Tt Uu Vv Ww Xx Yy Zz

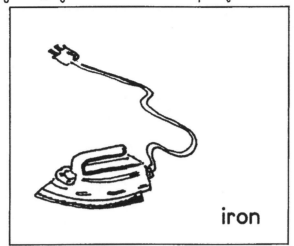

iron

I i

long i

ice cream (cone)

dinosaur

47

© Frederick J. Zorn, 2014

Aa Bb Cc Dd Ee Ff Gg Hh Ii J̲j̲ Kk Ll Mm Nn Oo Pp Qq Rr Ss Tt Uu Vv Ww Xx Yy Zz

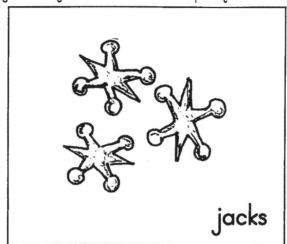

jacks

Jj

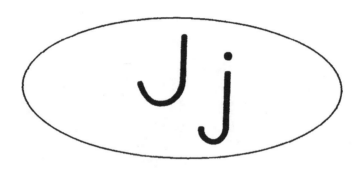

jar (jam)   jukebox

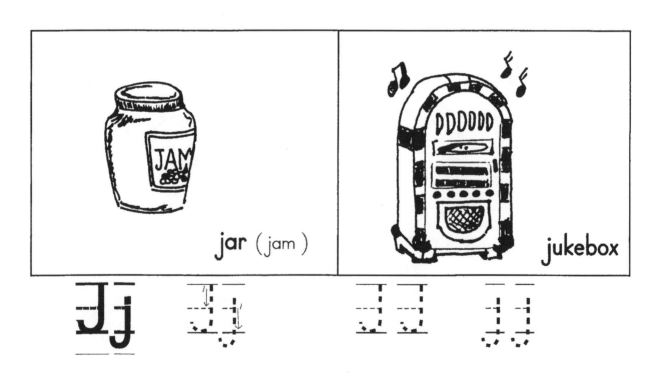

ABR: Letters: Word List

Note: Review words for each letter set without picture cues.

Total Alphabet Word List is at the end of the Letters Book.

I i _igloo

_Indian

_inch

I i _iron

_ice cream

_dinosaur

J j _ jacks

_ jar (jam)

_ jukebox

Aa Bb Cc Dd Ee Ff Gg Hh Ii Jj <u>Kk</u> Ll Mm Nn Oo Pp Qq Rr Ss Tt Uu Vv Ww Xx Yy Zz

kangaroo

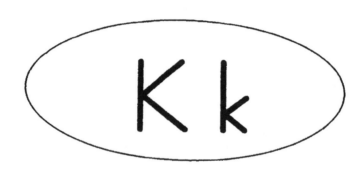

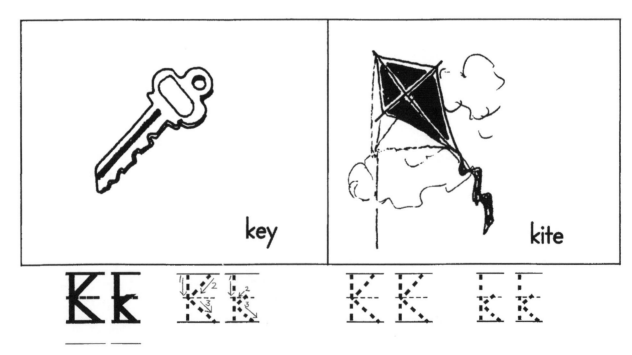

key

kite

© Frederick J. Zorn, 2014

Aa Bb Cc Dd Ee Ff Gg Hh Ii Jj Kk <u>Ll</u> Mm Nn Oo Pp Qq Rr Ss Tt Uu Vv Ww Xx Yy Zz

ladder

L l

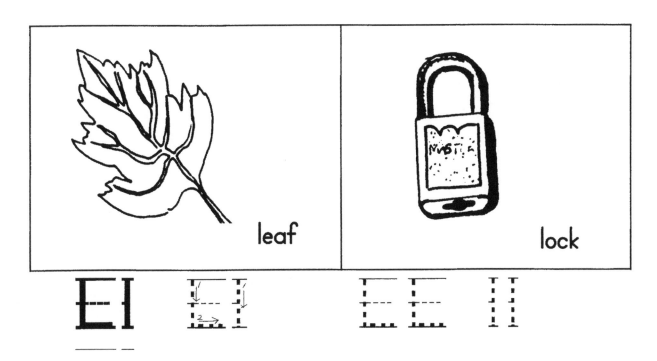

leaf

lock

Aa Bb Cc Dd Ee Ff Gg Hh Ii Jj Kk Ll <u>Mm</u> Nn Oo Pp Qq Rr Ss Tt Uu Vv Ww Xx Yy Zz

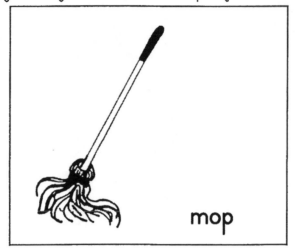

mop

M m

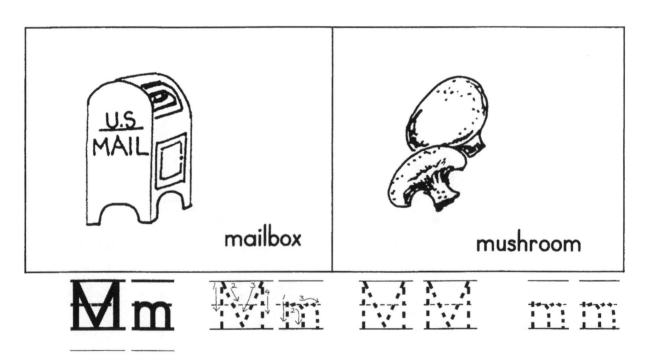

mailbox

mushroom

Aa Bb Cc Dd Ee Ff Gg Hh Ii Jj Kk Ll Mm <u>Nn</u> Oo Pp Qq Rr Ss Tt Uu Vv Ww Xx Yy Zz

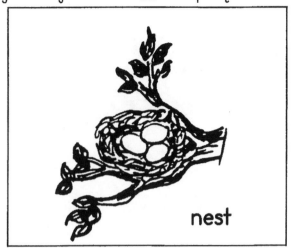

nest

Nn

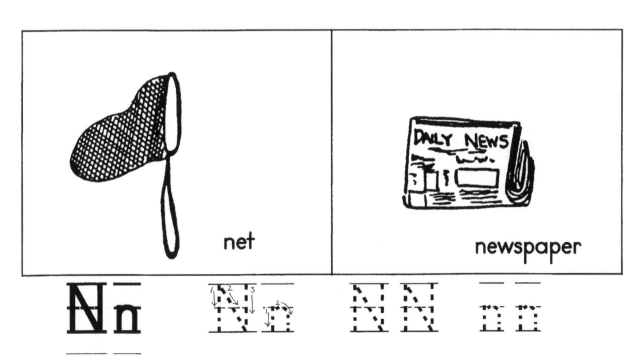

net

newspaper

Aa Bb Cc Dd Ee Ff Gg Hh Ii Jj Kk Ll Mm Nn <u>Oo</u> Pp Qq Rr Ss Tt Uu Vv Ww Xx Yy Zz

owl

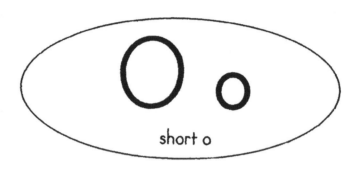

short o

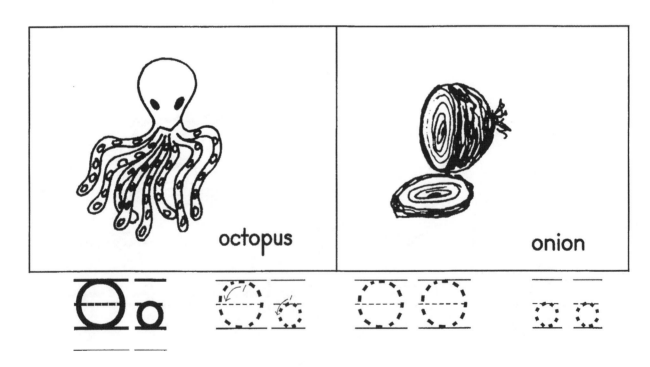

octopus

onion

Aa Bb Cc Dd Ee Ff Gg Hh Ii Jj Kk Ll Mm Nn <u>Oo</u> Pp Qq Rr Ss Tt Uu Vv Ww Xx Yy Zz

goat

long o

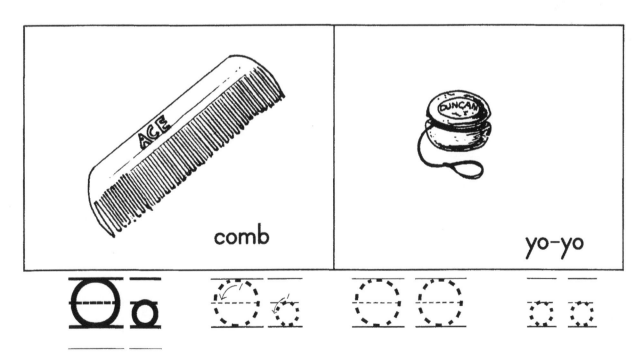

comb

yo-yo

© Frederick J. Zorn, 2014

Aa Bb Cc Dd Ee Ff Gg Hh Ii Jj Kk Ll Mm Nn Oo P̲p̲ Qq Rr Ss Tt Uu Vv Ww Xx Yy Zz

pineapple

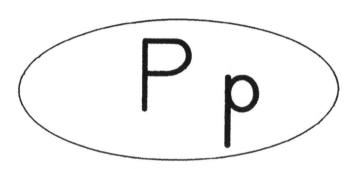

P p

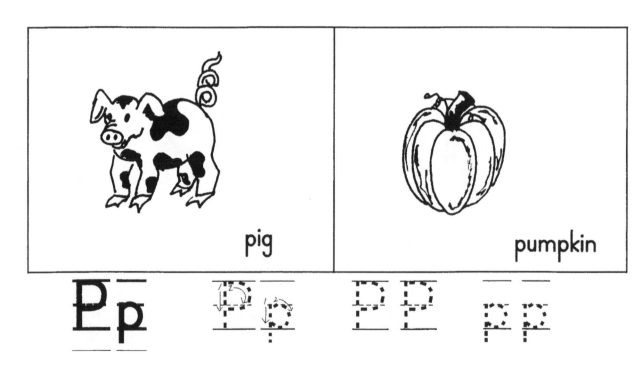

pig

pumpkin

© Frederick J. Zorn, 2014

Aa Bb Cc Dd Ee Ff Gg Hh Ii Jj Kk Ll Mm Nn Oo Pp <u>Qq</u> Rr Ss Tt Uu Vv Ww Xx Yy Zz

question mark

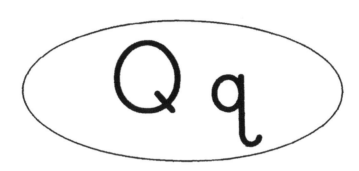

quarter

queen

Aa Bb Cc Dd Ee Ff Gg Hh Ii Jj Kk Ll Mm Nn Oo Pp Qq <u>Rr</u> Ss Tt Uu Vv Ww Xx Yy Zz

ring

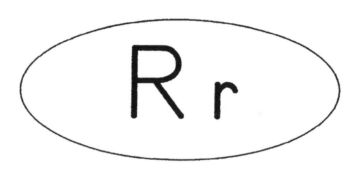

R r

rabbit

radio

Aa Bb Cc Dd Ee Ff Gg Hh Ii Jj Kk Ll Mm Nn Oo Pp Qq Rr S̲s̲ Tt Uu Vv Ww Xx Yy Zz

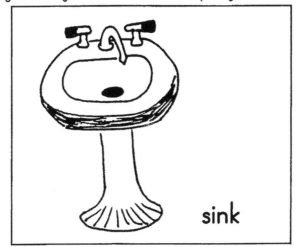

sink

S s

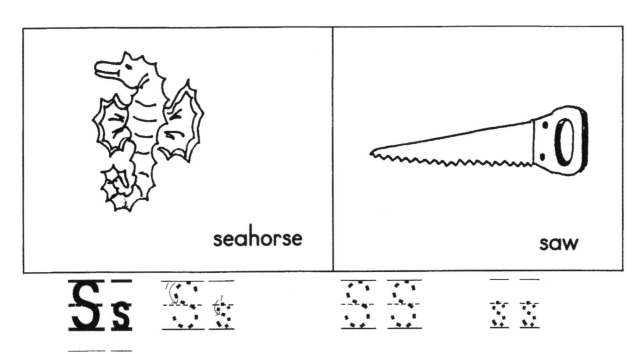

seahorse

saw

Aa Bb Cc Dd Ee Ff Gg Hh Ii Jj Kk Ll Mm Nn Oo Pp Qq Rr Ss T̲t̲ Uu Vv Ww Xx Yy Zz

turtle

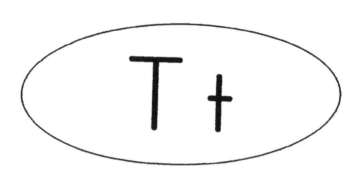

T t

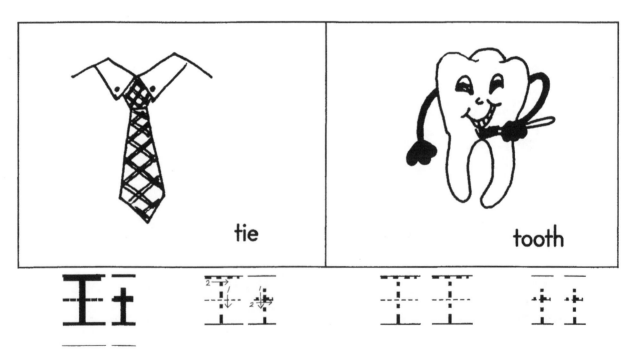

tie

tooth

© Frederick J. Zorn, 2014

ABR: Letters: Word List

Note: Review words for each letter set without picture cues.

Total Alphabet Word List is at the end of the Letters Book.

Kk _kangaroo
_key
_kite

Ll _ladder
_leaf
_lock

Mm _mop
_mailbox
_mushroom

Nn _nest
_net
_newspaper

Oo ŏ _owl
_octopus
_onion

Oo ō _goat
_comb
_yo-yo

Pp _pineapple
_pig
_pumpkin

Qq _question mark
_quarter
_queen

Rr _ring
_rabbit
_radio

Ss _sink
_seahorse
_saw

Tt _turtle
_tie
_tooth

Aa Bb Cc Dd Ee Ff Gg Hh Ii Jj Kk Ll Mm Nn Oo Pp Qq Rr Ss Tt <u>Uu</u> Vv Ww Xx Yy Zz

umbrella

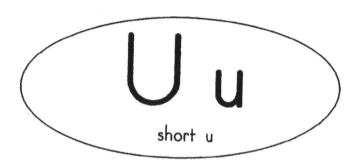

short u

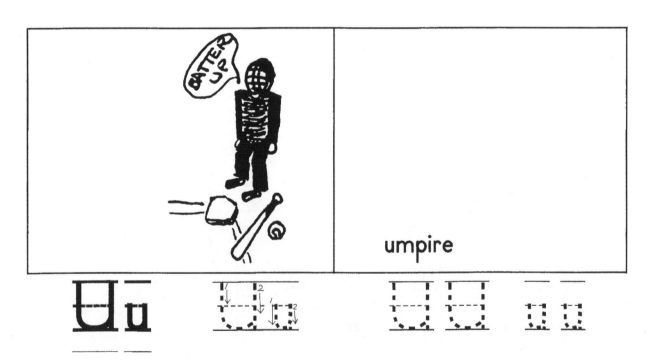

umpire

Aa Bb Cc Dd Ee Ff Gg Hh Ii Jj Kk Ll Mm Nn Oo Pp Qq Rr Ss Tt <u>Uu</u> Vv Ww Xx Yy Zz

unicorn

long u

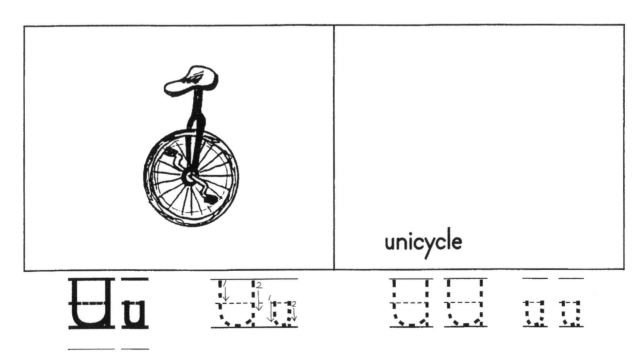

unicycle

Aa Bb Cc Dd Ee Ff Gg Hh Ii Jj Kk Ll Mm Nn Oo Pp Qq Rr Ss Tt Uu <u>Vv</u> Ww Xx Yy Zz

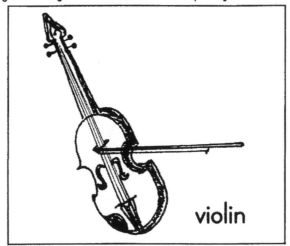

violin

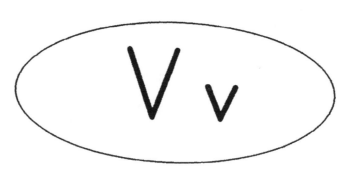

V v

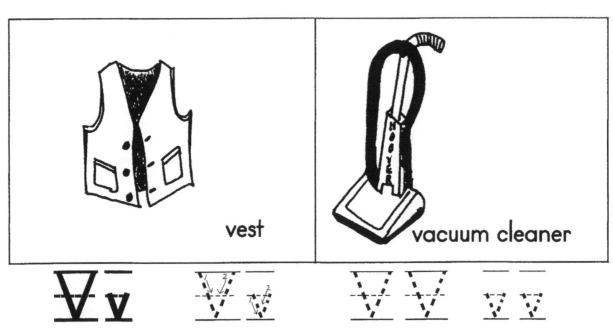

vest

vacuum cleaner

Aa Bb Cc Dd Ee Ff Gg Hh Ii Jj Kk Ll Mm Nn Oo Pp Qq Rr Ss Tt Uu Vv <u>Ww</u> Xx Yy Zz

watch

W w

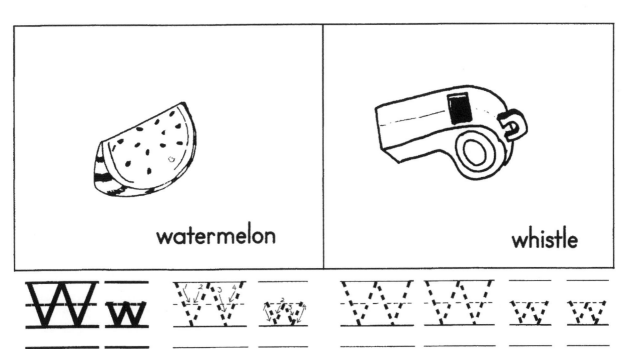

watermelon

whistle

Aa Bb Cc Dd Ee Ff Gg Hh Ii Jj Kk Ll Mm Nn Oo Pp Qq Rr Ss Tt Uu Vv Ww <u>Xx</u> Yy Zz

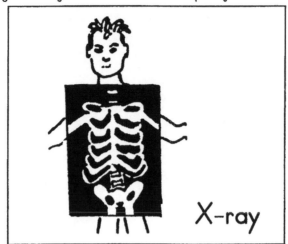

X-ray

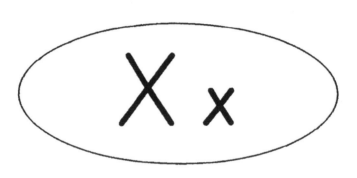

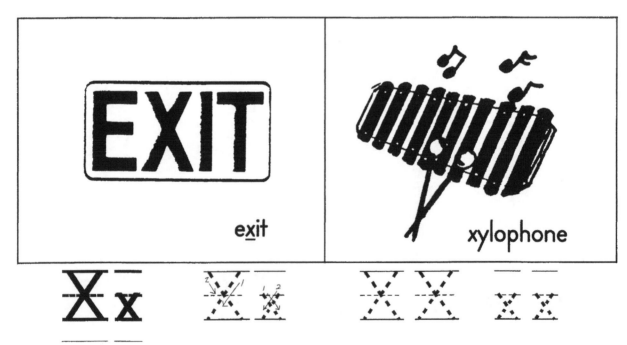

exit

xylophone

ABR: Letters: Word List

Note: Review words for each letter set without picture cues.

Total Alphabet Word List is at the end of the Letters Book.

Uu _umbrella

_umpire

Uu _unicorn

_unicycle

Vv _violin

_vest

_vacuum

Ww _watch

_watermelon

_whistle

Xx _X-ray

_exit

_xylophone

Aa Bb Cc Dd Ee Ff Gg Hh Ii Jj Kk Ll Mm Nn Oo Pp Qq Rr Ss Tt Uu Vv Ww Xx <u>Yy</u> Zz

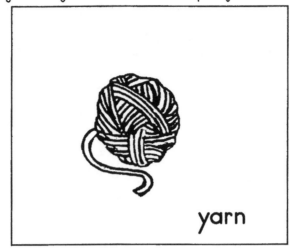

yarn

Y y

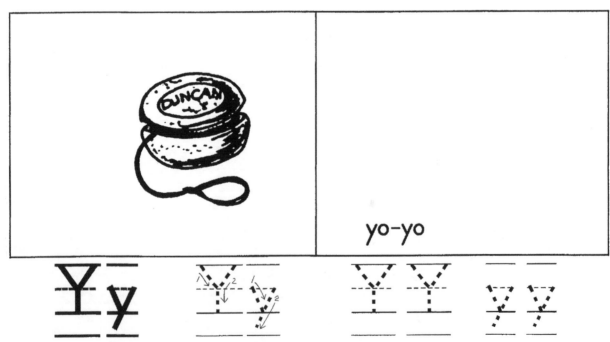

yo-yo

Aa Bb Cc Dd Ee Ff Gg Hh Ii Jj Kk Ll Mm Nn Oo Pp Qq Rr Ss Tt Uu Vv Ww Xx <u>Yy</u> Zz

y as *e*

baby

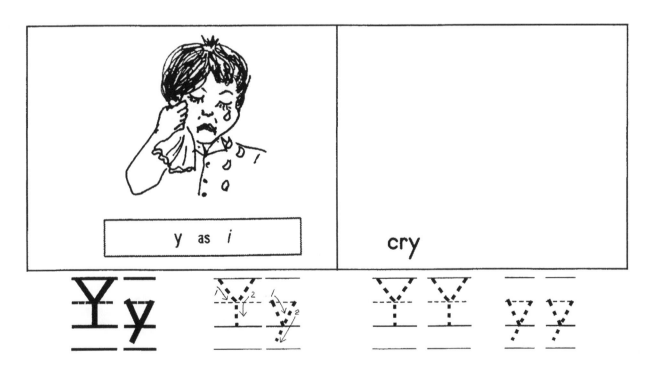

y as *i*

cry

© Frederick J. Zorn, 2014

Aa Bb Cc Dd Ee Ff Gg Hh Ii Jj Kk Ll Mm Nn Oo Pp Qq Rr Ss Tt Uu Vv Ww Xx Yy <u>Zz</u>

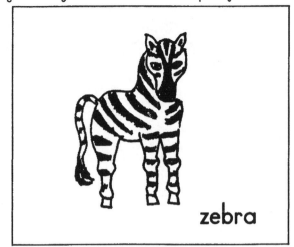

zebra

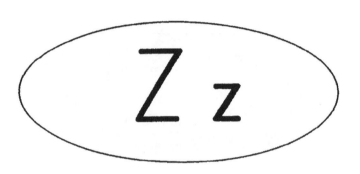

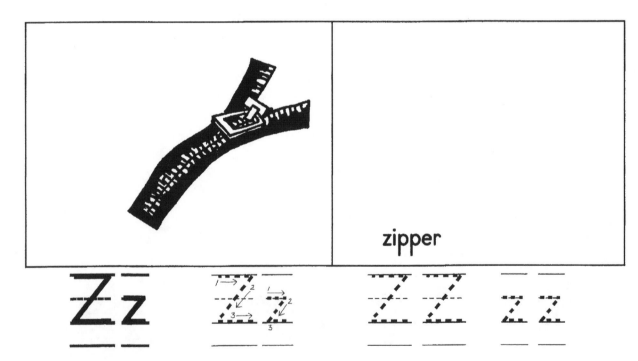

zipper

© Frederick J. Zorn, 2014

ABR: Letters: Word List

Note: Review words for each letter set without picture cues.

Total Alphabet Word List is at the end of the Letters Book.

Yy _yarn

_yo-yo

Yy _baby

_cry

Zz _zebra

_zipper

ABR: Letters: Alphabet Word List

Aa
_apple
_anchor
_arrow

_ace
_acorn
_apron

Bb
_ball
_bed
_bus

Cc
_cake
_carrot
_cat

_celery
_cent
_cereal

Dd
_dog
_donut
_door

Ee
_elephant
_egg
_elevator

_eagle
_bee   _key

Ef
_fish
_feather
_fork

Gg_goat
_girl   _grapes

_giraffe
_gingerbread

Hh
_hammer
_hat
_hippo

Ii
_igloo
_Indian
_inch

_iron
_ice cream
_dinosaur

Jj
_ jacks
_ jar (jam)
_ jukebox

Kk
_kangaroo
_key
_kite

Ll _ladder
_leaf
_lock

Pp _pineapple
_pig
_pumpkin

Uu _umbrella
_umpire

_unicorn   _unicycle

Mm _mop
_mailbox
_mushroom

Qq _question mark
_quarter
_queen

Vv _violin
_vest
_vacuum

Nn _nest
_net
_newspaper

Rr _ring
_rabbit
_radio

Ww _watch
_watermelon
_whistle

Oo _owl
_octopus
_onion

Ss _sink
_seahorse
_saw

Xx _X-ray
_xylophone

_goat
_comb
_yo-yo

Tt _turtle
_tie
_tooth

Yy _yarn _yo-yo
_baby _cry

Zz _zebra
_zipper

ABR: YOU CAN READ!

Adult Beginning Reader Program

ABR Sight & Sound Guide to Letters of the Alphabet

Section 1: **Letters**

Consonants C & G: Double Sounds

Hard and **Soft**

C

and

G

by

Frederick J. Zorn, Ed.D.

Principal, Teacher, Adjunct Professor, Literacy Tutor

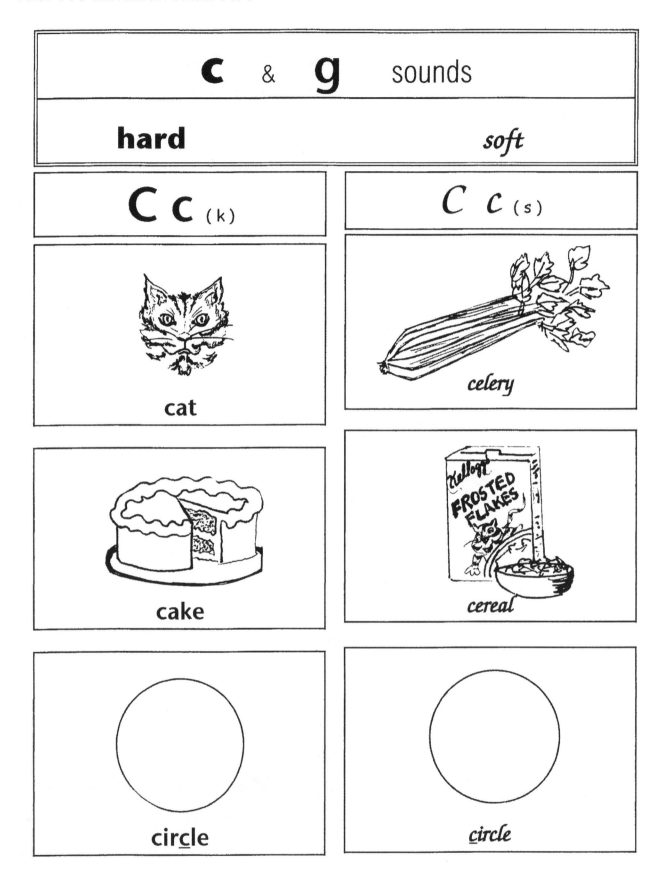

c & **g** sounds

hard   *soft*

C c (k)   *C c* (s)

cat

celery

cake

cereal

cir<u>c</u>le

<u>c</u>ircle

hard	soft

G g (g)	*G g* (j)

goat

giraffe

pig

page

5 Vowels and 21 Consonants
Make up all the letters of the Alphabet

The 5 vowels are:

A a

E e

I i

O o

U u

The 21 consonants are:

B b   C c   D d

F f   G g   H h

J j   K k   L l

M m   N n   P p

Q q   R r   S s

T t   V v   W w

X x   Y y   Z z

ABR: YOU CAN READ!

Adult Beginning Reader Program

ABR Sight & Sound Guide to Letters of the Alphabet

Section 1: **Letters**

Vowels

a   e   i   o   u

Short Sound

An Open Mouth

~

Long Sound

The Name of the Letter

by

Frederick J. Zorn, Ed.D.

Principal, Teacher, Adjunct Professor, Literacy Tutor

ABR Tips for Tutors: Vowels

Tutor: _Review the *Vowel-Consonant Chart*. (Page 78)
_There are 5 vowels: *a e i o u.*
_Every word has at least one vowel in it.
_Vowels vary their sounds. Most consonants have one sound.
_Demonstrate "long" - *mouth is long; says the vowel's name.*
_Demonstrate "short" - *mouth is open.*

Learner: _Name the vowel.
_'Read' each picture word on the page quickly.
Tutor: _Repeat each picture word on the page.
_Stress the vowel sound.
Learner: _Repeat all picture words on the page.
_Stress the vowel sound.

Tutor: _Use Key Words Chart (P. 92) to check word retention.

Tutor: Note:
_Each vowel has two Picture Sets: Long and short sound.
_Vowels: **a e i o u.**
_"y" is sometimes in the vowel section because it can have different sounds.

Note: Each syllable (part of a word) has a vowel.

~ Enjoy learning to recognize and sound out vowels! ~

Vowel Sounds

Short ͧ	Long ¯

ͧ **a** cat

¯ **a** cake

ͧ **e** bed

¯ **e** bee

ͧ **i** fish

¯ **i** kite

ͧ **o** mop

¯ **o** goat

ͧ **u** umbrella

¯ **u** unicorn

<u>Aa</u> Bb Cc Dd Ee Ff Gg Hh Ii Jj Kk Ll Mm Nn Oo Pp Qq Rr Ss Tt Uu Vv Ww Xx Yy Zz

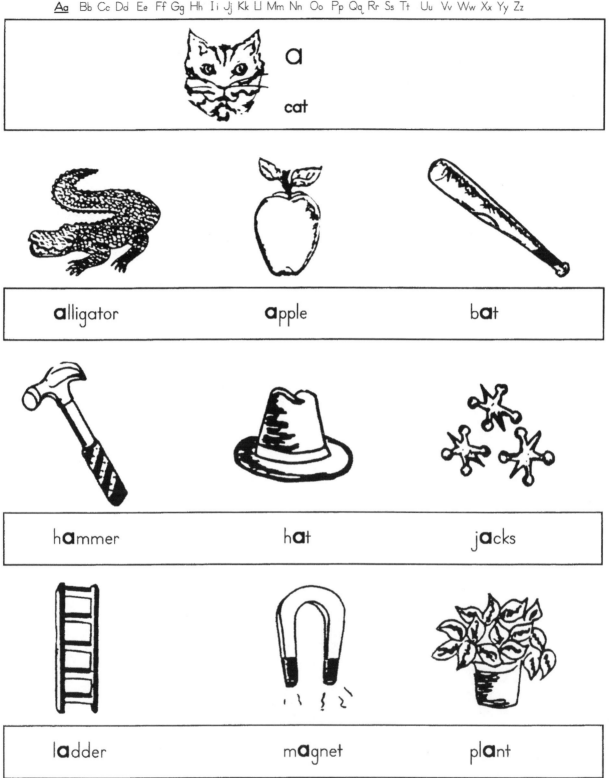

a

cat

alligator

apple

bat

hammer

hat

jacks

ladder

magnet

plant

Aa Bb Cc Dd Ee Ff Gg Hh Ii Jj Kk Ll Mm Nn Oo Pp Qq Rr Ss Tt Uu Vv Ww Xx Yy Zz

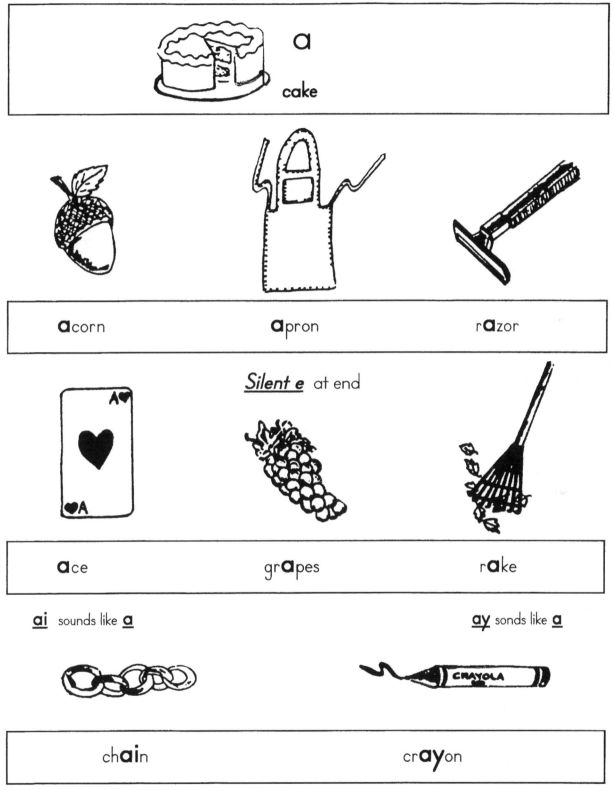

a

cake

acorn   apron   razor

Silent e at end

ace   grapes   rake

ai sounds like a   ay sonds like a

chain   crayon

Aa Bb Cc Dd **Ee** Ff Gg Hh Ii Jj Kk Ll Mm Nn Oo Pp Qq Rr Ss Tt Uu Vv Ww Xx Yy Zz

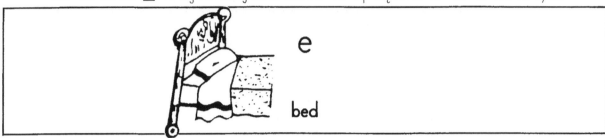

e

bed

dr**e**ss   **e**lephant   h**e**met

l**e**mon   t**e**nt   v**e**st

   **ea** sounds like e

f**ea**ther   sw**ea**ter

84   © Frederick J. Zorn, 2014

Aa Bb Cc Dd **Ee** Ff Gg Hh I i Jj Kk Ll Mm Nn Oo Pp Qq Rr Ss Tt Uu Vv Ww Xx Yy Zz

e
bee

ee:

ch**ee**se   qu**ee**n   tr**ee**

ea:

eagle   l**ea**f   s**ea**l

ey sounds like e   (**y** sounds like e)

k**ey**   turk**ey**   (bab**y**)

Aa Bb Cc Dd`Ee Ff Gg Hh <u>Ii</u> Jj Kk Ll Mm Nn Oo Pp Qq Rr Ss Tt Uu Vv Ww Xx Yy Zz

i

fish

igloo
indian
inch

hippo
pig
ship

six
windmill

86

Aa Bb Cc Dd Ee Ff Gg Hh **Ii** Jj Kk Ll Mm Nn Oo Pp Qq Rr Ss Tt Uu Vv Ww Xx Yy Zz

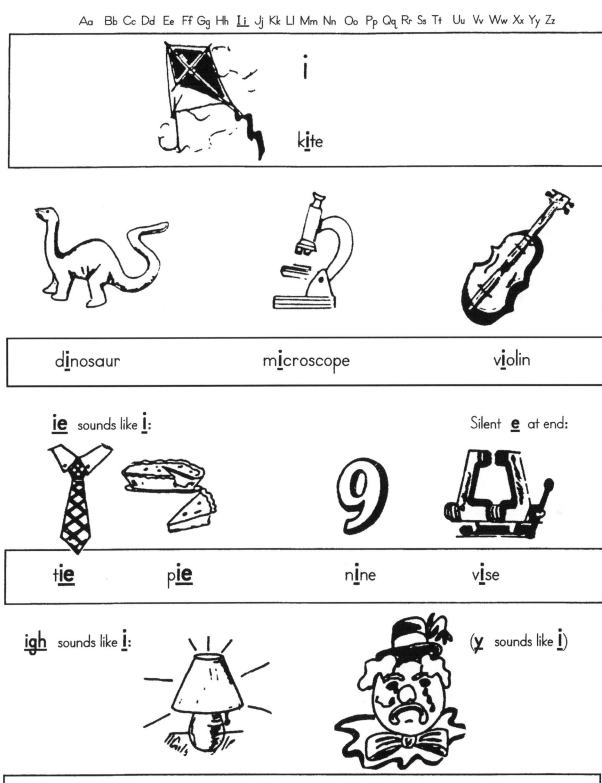

i

k**i**te

d**i**nosaur   m**i**croscope   v**i**olin

ie sounds like **i**:   Silent **e** at end:

t**ie**   p**ie**   n**i**ne   v**i**se

igh sounds like **i**:   (**y** sounds like **i**)

l**i**ght   cr**y**

Aa Bb Cc Dd Ee Ff Gg Hh Ii Jj Kk Ll Mm Nn **Oo** Pp Qq Rr Ss Tt Uu Vv Ww Xx Yy Zz

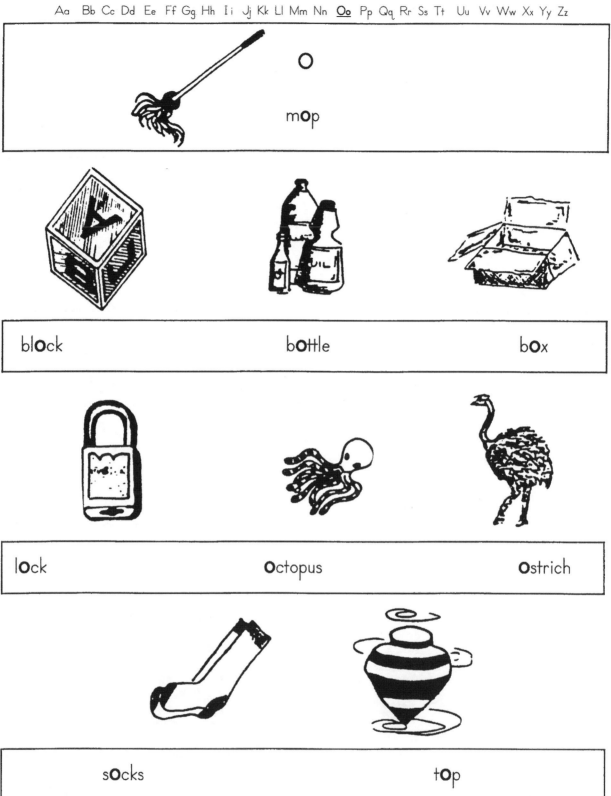

mOp

block

bOttle

bOx

lOck

Octopus

Ostrich

sOcks

tOp

Aa Bb Cc Dd Ee Ff Gg Hh Ii Jj Kk Ll Mm Nn **Oo** Pp Qq Rr Ss Tt Uu Vv Ww Xx Yy Zz

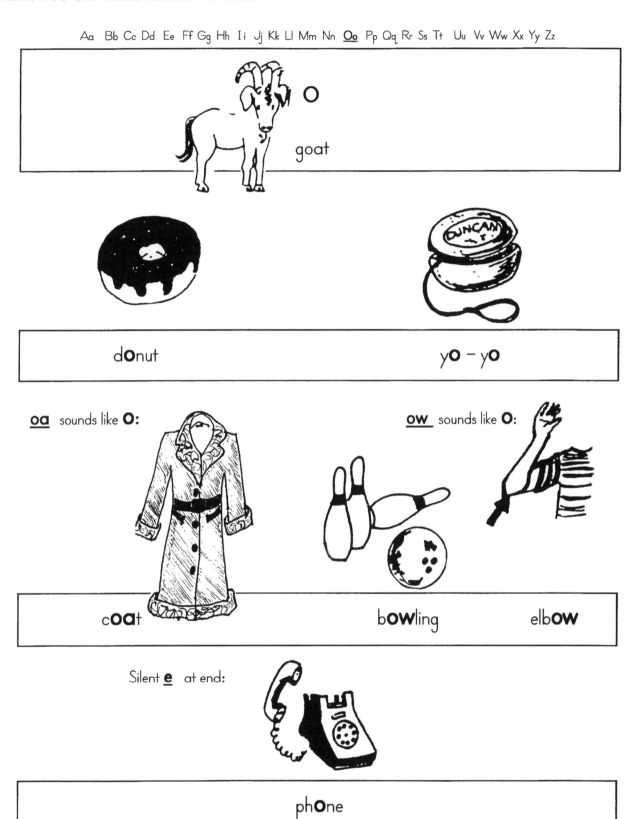

O

goat

d**O**nut   y**O** – y**O**

oa sounds like **O**:   **ow** sounds like **O**:

c**oa**t   b**ow**ling   elb**ow**

Silent **e** at end:

ph**O**ne

Aa Bb Cc Dd Ee Ff Gg Hh Ii Jj Kk Ll Mm Nn Oo Pp Qq Rr Ss Tt <u>Uu</u> Vv Ww Xx Yy Zz

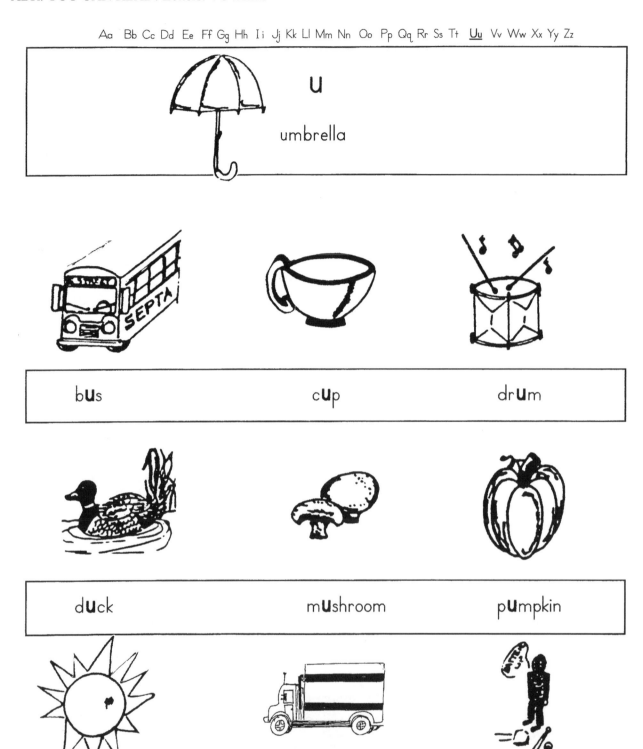

u

umbrella

bus   cup   drum

duck   mushroom   pumpkin

sun   truck   umpire

Aa Bb Cc Dd Ee Ff Gg Hh Ii Jj Kk Ll Mm Nn Oo Pp Qq Rr Ss Tt <u>Uu</u> Vv Ww Xx Yy Zz

u

unicorn

r**u**ler   **u**nicycle   United States

<u>ui</u> sounds like **u**:

s**ui**t

<u>ue</u> sounds like u: <u>ew</u> sounds like u:

blue   **new**

bl**ue**   n**ew**

Vowels: **Key Words**

Aa   **cat**
_alligator
_apple
_bat
_hammer
_hat
_jack
_ladder
_magnet
_plant

Ee **bee**	
_cheese	ee sounds like e
_queen	"
_tree	"
_eagle	ea sounds like e
_leaf	"
_seal	"
_key	ey sounds like e
_turkey	ey sounds like e
_baby	y sounds like e

Oo   **mop**
_block
_bottle
_box
_lock
_octopus
_ostrich
_socks
_top

Aa **cake**	
_acorn	
_apron	
_razor	
_ace	
_grapes	silent e at end
_rake	silent e at end
_chain	ai sounds like a
_crayon	ay sounds like a

I i   **fish**
_igloo
_Indian
_inch
_hippo
_pig
_ship
_six
_windmill

Oo **goat**	
_donut	
_yo-yo	
_coat	oa sounds like o
_bowling	ow sounds like o
_elbow	
_phone	silent e at end

Uu **umbrella**	
_bus	_cup
_drum	_duck
_mushroom	
_pumpkin	_sun
_truck	_umpire

Ee **bed**	
_dress	
_elephant	
_helmet	
_lemon	
_tent	
_vest	
_feather	ea sounds like e
_sweater	ea sounds like e

I i **kite**	
_dinosaur	
_microscope	
_violin	
_tie	ie sounds like i
_pie	ie sounds like i
_nine	*Silent e*
_vise	"
_light	igh sounds like i
_cry	y sounds like i

Uu **unicorn**	
_ruler	
_unicycle	
_United States	
_suit	ui sounds like u
_blue	ue sounds like u
_new	ew sounds like u

92

Vowel Blenders

Note: *Vowels: a e i o u (y)*

Two vowels together:
- ☐ **One** vowel sounds its name.
- ☐ The other vowel is silent.

Two vowels together:
- ☐ **Make a new compound sound.**

First Vowel Speaks:	Long sound
☐ **ai**	- r**ai**n
☐ **ay**	- d**ay**
☐ **ea**	- **ea**t
☐ **ee**	- f**ee**t
☐ **eo**	- p**eo**ple
☐ **ei**	- **ei**ther (*)
☐ **ey**	- mon**ey**
☐ **ie**	- p**ie**
☐ **oa**	- b**oa**t
☐ **oe**	- t**oe**
☐ **ou**	- s**ou**l
☐ **ue**	- bl**ue**
☐ **ui**	- s**ui**t

Both Vowels Blends:	Long sound
☐ **au**	- h**au**l
☐ **ei**	- **ei**ght
☐ **oi**	- c**oi**n
☐ **oo**	- s**oo**n
☐ **ou**	- **ou**t
☐ **oy**	- b**oy**

To Do: Underline Vowel Blenders

_about	_mountain
_bought	_noise
_enjoy	_oil
_famous	_peach
_health	_room
_join	_weather

Second Vowel Speaks:	Long sound
☐ **ea**	- gr**ea**t
☐ **ei**	- **ei**ther (*)
☐ **ie**	- ch**ie**f
☐ **ou**	- y**ou**

Answers:

_ ab**ou**t	_ m**ou**ntain
_ b**ou**ght	_ n**oi**se
_ enj**oy**	_ **oi**l
_ fam**ou**s	_ p**ea**ch
_ h**ea**lth	_ r**oo**m
_ j**oi**n	_ w**ea**ther

* Note: Can be pronounced both ways.

93

© Frederick J. Zorn, 2014

ABR Tips for Tutors: Letter Enders
Use the Alphabet Key Line at the top of each page.

Tutor: _Review the alphabet letter order.

              _Explain that a letter at the end of a word is
                      pronounced the same anywhere in a word.

              _*Letter Enders* are letters at the end of a word.

              _Do letter blocks in order.

              _Pronounce end letter distinctly.

              _The whole set can be done in one lesson.

Learner: _Name the letter.

              _'Read' each picture word in the box quickly.

Tutor: _Repeat each picture word.

              _Stress the end letter sound; pronounce distinctly.

Learner: _Repeat all picture words in the box.

Tutor: _Use Letter Enders Words Chart (P. 104) to check word
            retention.

Letter Sounds Exercise: Reminders:

  Tutor: _Most consonants keep their same sounds.

            _A letter can be at the beginning, middle or end of a word.

            Note: Vowels have more than one sound.

~ Enjoy learning to recognize and sound out the Letters of the Alphabet! ~

ABR: YOU CAN READ!

Adult Beginning Reader Program

ABR Sight & Sound Guide to Letters of the Alphabet

Section 1: **Letters**

Letter Enders

Letters of the Alphabet at the End of Words

and

Picture-Words

that end with them

by

Frederick J. Zorn, Ed.D.

Principal, Teacher, Adjunct Professor, Literacy Tutor

Aa Bb Cc Dd Ee Ff Gg Hh Ii Jj Kk Ll Mm Nn Oo Pp Qq Rr Ss Tt Uu Vv Ww Xx Yy Zz

Ending Sounds

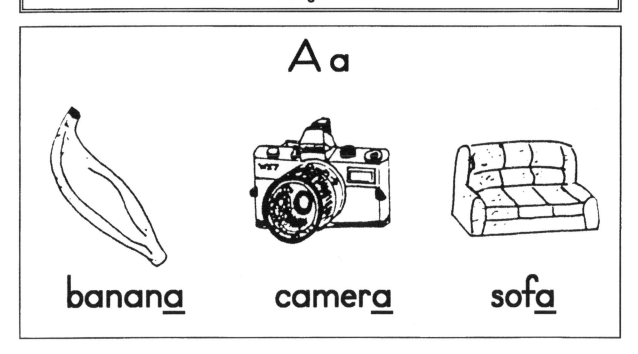

A a

banan<u>a</u>   **camer<u>a</u>**   **sof<u>a</u>**

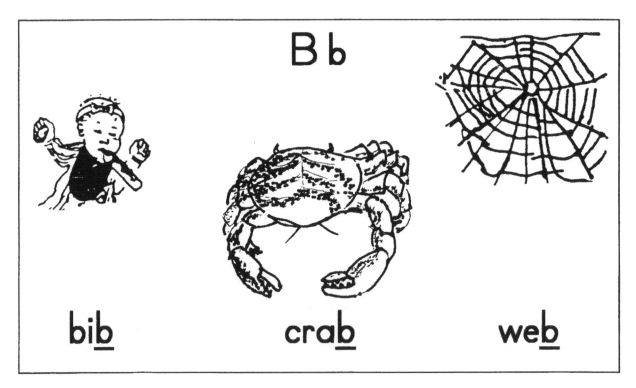

B b

bi<u>b</u>   **cra<u>b</u>**   **we<u>b</u>**

Aa Bb Cc Dd Ee Ff Gg Hh Ii Jj Kk Ll Mm Nn Oo Pp Qq Rr Ss Tt Uu Vv Ww Xx Yy Zz

Ending Sounds

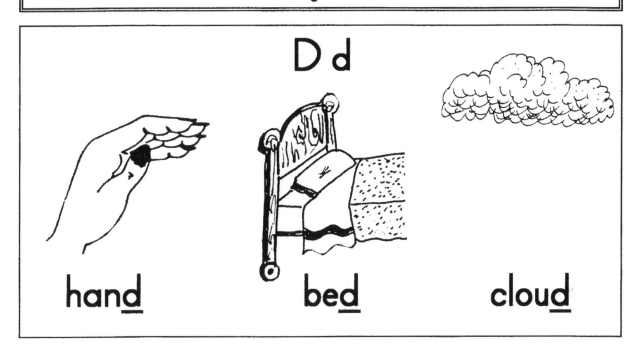

D d

hand   bed   cloud

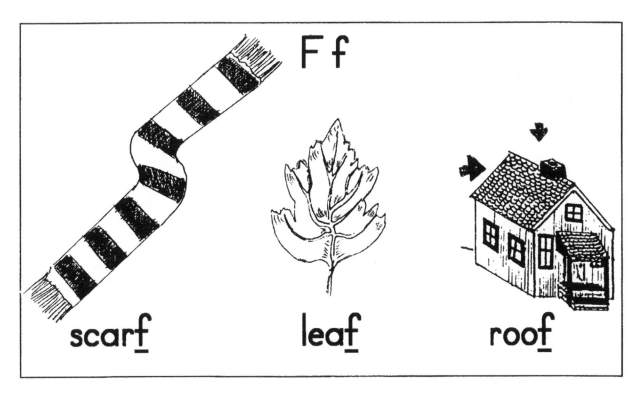

F f

scarf   leaf   roof

Aa Bb Cc Dd Ee Ff Gg Hh Ii Jj Kk Ll Mm Nn Oo Pp Qq Rr Ss Tt Uu Vv Ww Xx Yy Zz

Ending Sounds

G g

egg   flag   pig

K k

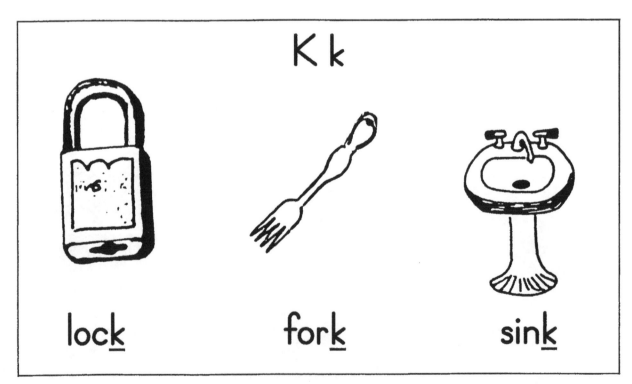

loc<u>k</u>   for<u>k</u>   sin<u>k</u>

Aa Bb Cc Dd Ee Ff Gg Hh Ii Jj Kk Ll Mm Nn Oo Pp Qq Rr Ss Tt Uu Vv Ww Xx Yy Zz

Ending Sounds

L l

ba**ll**   ow**l**   sai**l**

M m

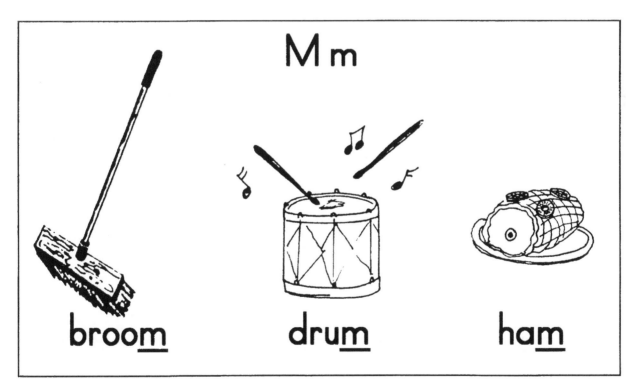

broo**m**   dru**m**   ha**m**

Aa Bb Cc Dd Ee Ff Gg Hh Ii Jj Kk Ll Mm Nn Oo Pp Qq Rr Ss Tt Uu Vv Ww Xx Yy Zz

Ending Sounds

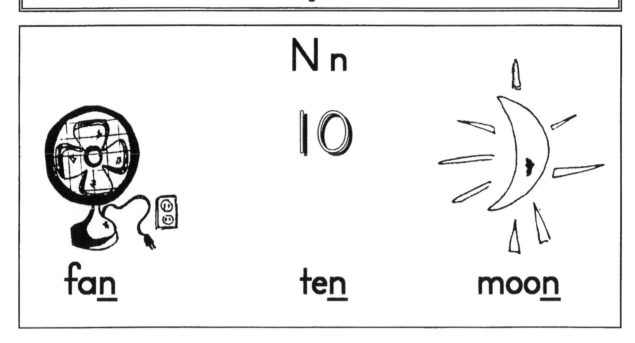

N n
10

fan   ten   moo<u>n</u>

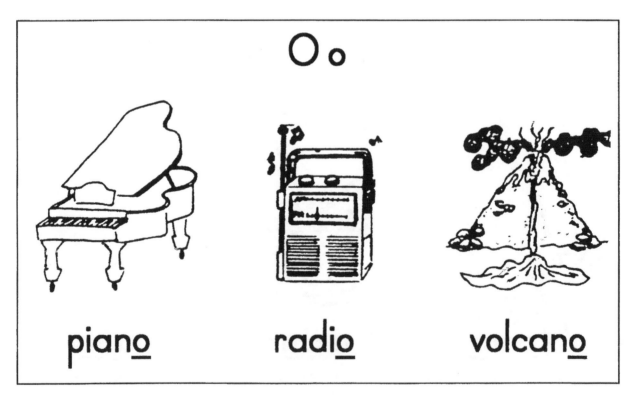

O o

pian<u>o</u>   radi<u>o</u>   volcan<u>o</u>

Aa Bb Cc Dd Ee Ff Gg Hh Ii Jj Kk Ll Mm Nn Oo Pp Qq Rr Ss Tt Uu Vv Ww Xx Yy Zz

Ending Sounds

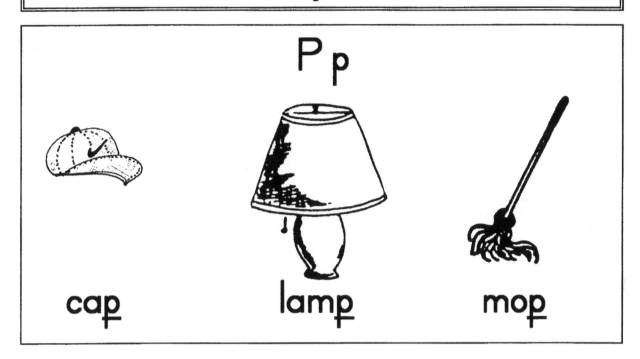

cap   lamp   mop

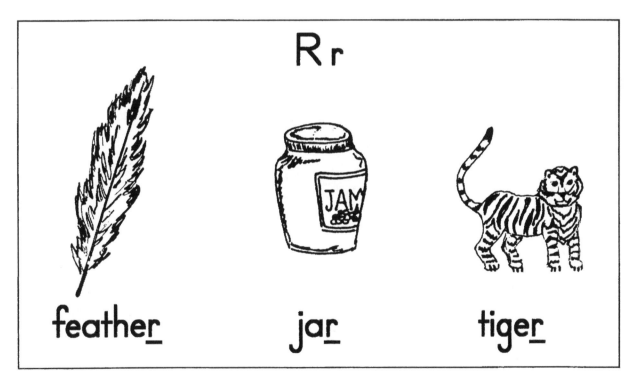

feather   jar   tiger

Aa Bb Cc Dd Ee Ff Gg Hh Ii Jj Kk Ll Mm Nn Oo Pp Qq Rr Ss Tt Uu Vv Ww Xx Yy Zz

Ending Sounds

S s

bus   dress   grapes

T t

foot   goat   hat

Aa Bb Cc Dd Ee Ff Gg Hh Ii Jj Kk Ll Mm Nn Oo Pp Qq Rr Ss Tt Uu Vv Ww Xx Yy Zz

Ending Sounds

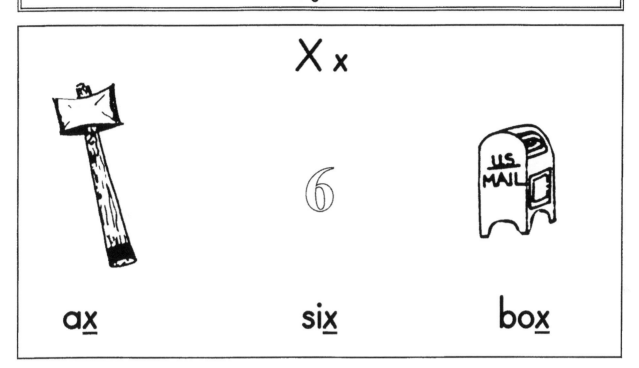

X x

6

ax   six   box

Words - letter enderS

Aa
_banana
_camera
_sofa

Kk
_lock
_fork
_sink

Pp
_cap
_lamp
_mop

Bb
_bib
_crab
_web

Ll
_ball
_owl
_sail

Rr
_feather
_jar
_tiger

Dd
_hand
_bed
_cloud

Mm
_broom
_drum
_ham

Ss
_bus
_dress
_grapes

Ff
_scarf
_leaf
_roof

Nn
_fan
_ten
_moon

Tt
_foot
_goat
_hat

Gg
_egg
_flag
_pig

Oo
_piano
_radio
_volcano

Xx
_ax
_six
_box

ABR: YOU CAN READ!

Adult Beginning Reader Program

ABR Sight & Sound Guide to Letters of the Alphabet

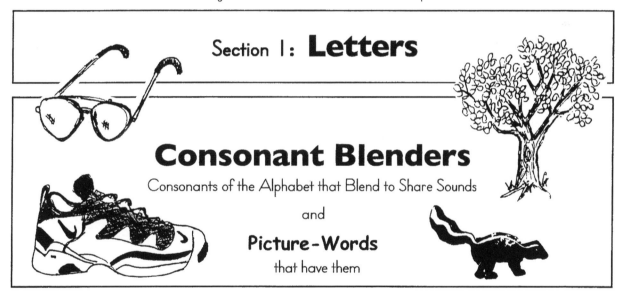

Section 1: **Letters**

Consonant Blenders

Consonants of the Alphabet that Blend to Share Sounds

and

Picture-Words

that have them

by

Frederick J. Zorn, Ed.D.

Principal, Teacher, Adjunct Professor, Literacy Tutor

ABR Tips for Tutors: **Consonant Blenders**
Two or more consonants sounded together

Tutor: Explain that Consonant Blenders can:
   _Blend letters and make a new sound.
   _Blend letters and you hear both sounds.
   _Blend letters and you hear only one of the sounds.
   Note: Blenders can be at the beginning, middle, or end of a word.

Learner: _Identify each word/picture on the page.
Tutor: _Repeat each word/picture on the page.
            _Stress the Blender sound.
Learner: _Do all the words on the page quickly.
   Note: Entire Blenders Unit can be done in one lesson.

Learner: Use your senses:
   _Visual: Look at one Blender set and its pictures.
   _Auditory: Hear and repeat the Blender sound.
   _Speech: Pronounce each slowly and carefully.
               Comment on interesting words.
   _Tactile: Point to each picture as you identify it.

Tutor: _Use the Word List when Blenders are finished. (Pp. 135-7)
            _Check for word recognition.
            _Use Blenders Chart to review Blender sounds. (P. 107)
            _Note that vowels can also blend. (P. 93)
   Note: Blender sound mastery is the goal.

Note: Review the 26 letters in the Alphabet and the sound each has as needed.

~ Enjoy Blending Letters! ~

Consonant Blenders: Blended letter sounds

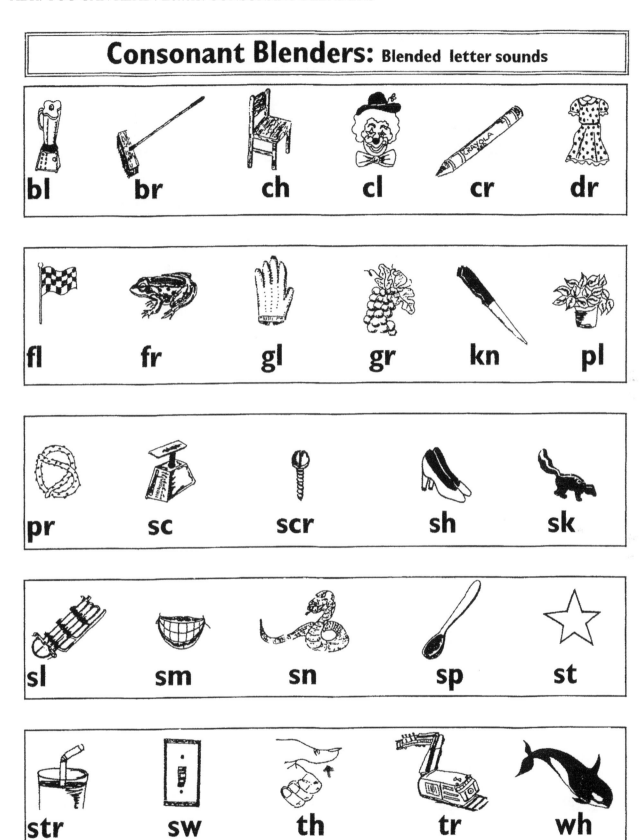

bl   br   ch   cl   cr   dr

fl   fr   gl   gr   kn   pl

pr   sc   scr   sh   sk

sl   sm   sn   sp   st

str   sw   th   tr   wh

blackboard

blender

bl

block

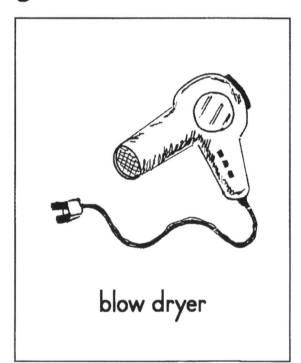

blow dryer

108

branch

brick

br

broom

brush

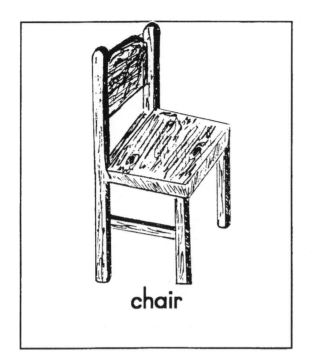

chair

chicken

ch

cheese

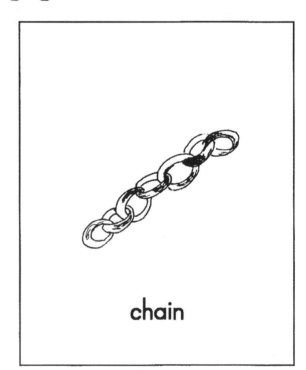

chain

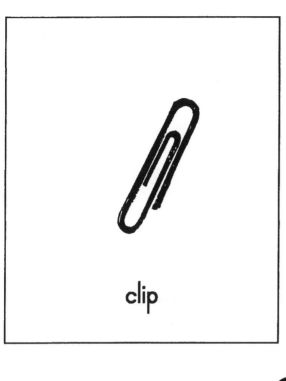

clip

clock

cl

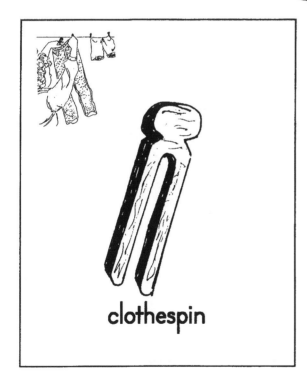

clothespin

clown

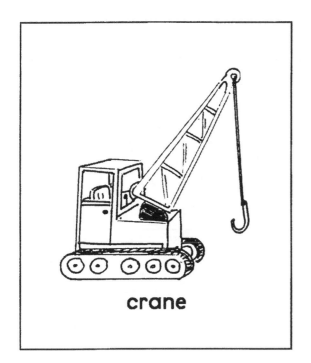

crane

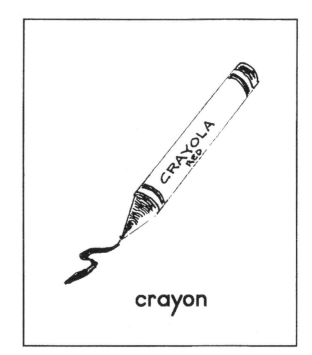

crayon

cr

crown

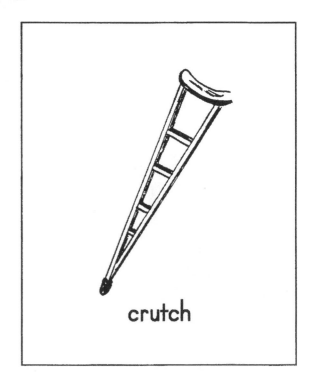

crutch

dress

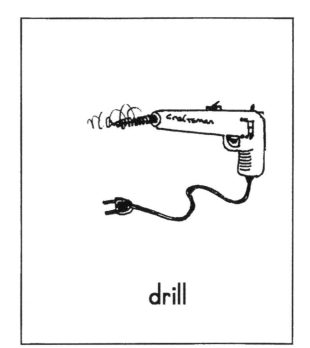

drill

dr

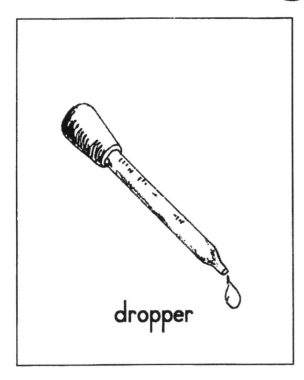

dropper

drum

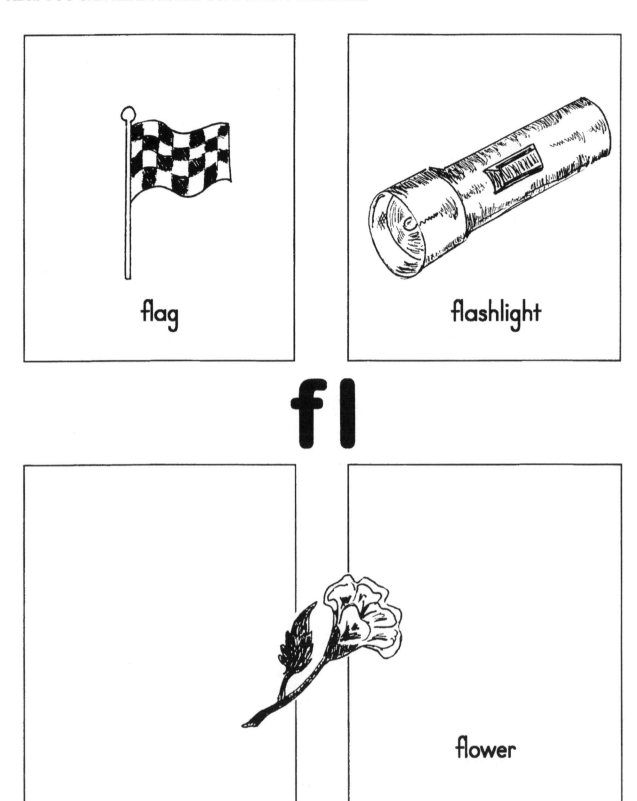

flag

flashlight

fl

flower

fraction

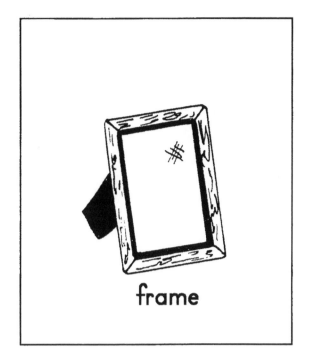

frame

fr

frog

fruit

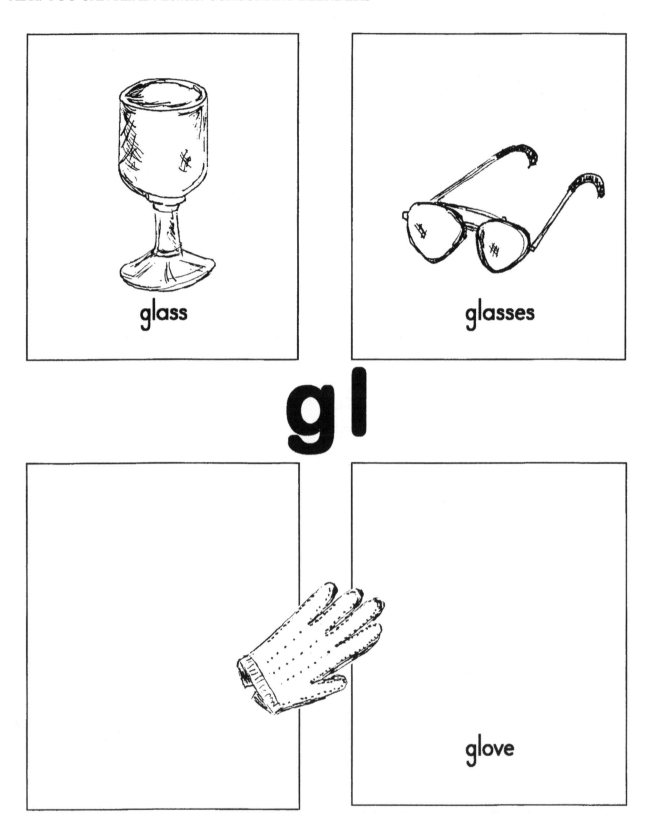

glass

glasses

gl

glove

graduate

grapes

gr

grave

knapsack

(backpack)

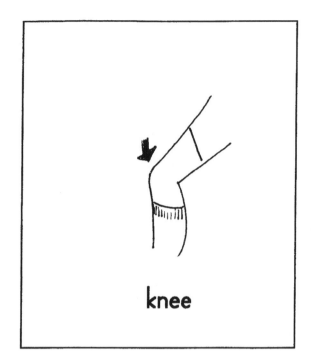

knee

kn

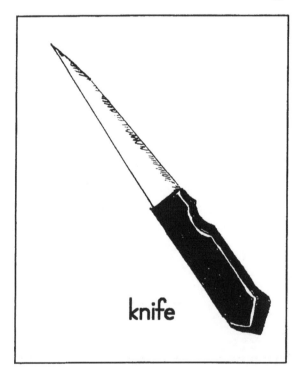

knife

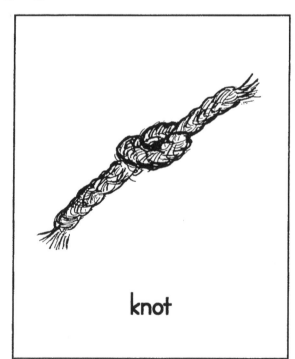

knot

plant

plaque

pl

playground

pliers

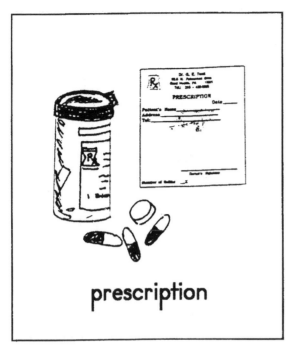

prescription

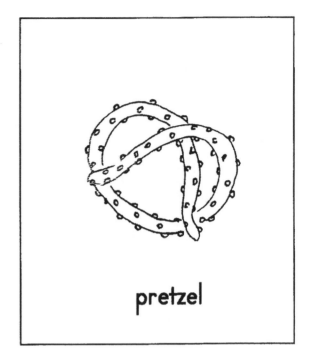

pretzel

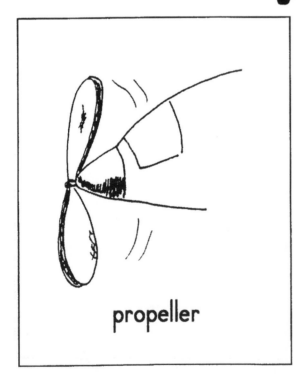

propeller

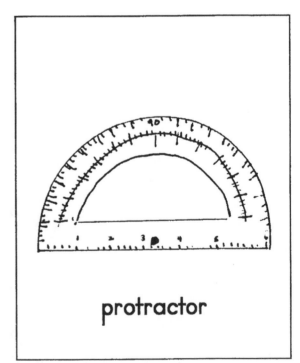

protractor

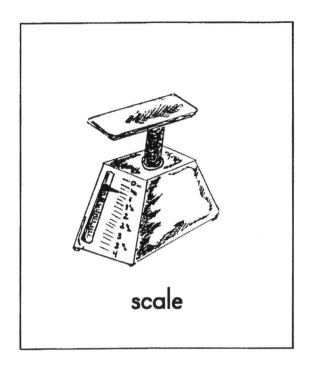

scale

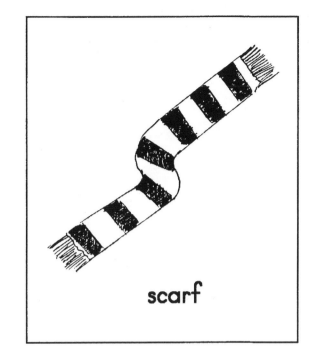

scarf

scarecrow

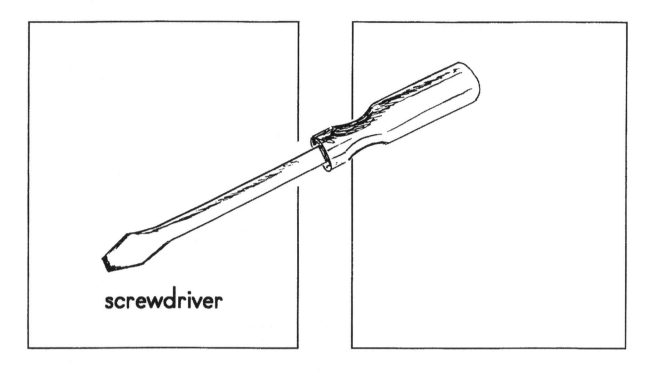

screwdriver

scr

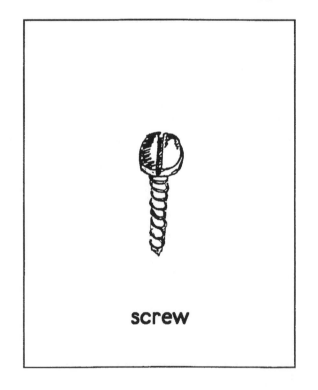

screw

scribble

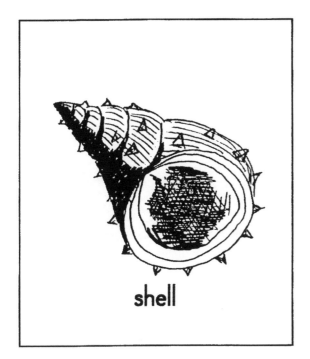

shell

ship

sh

shoes

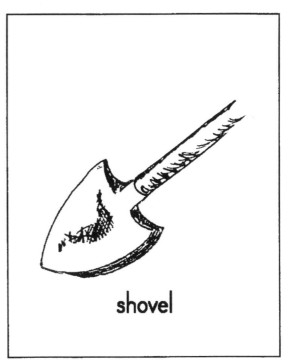

shovel

skate

skillet

sk

skunk

desk

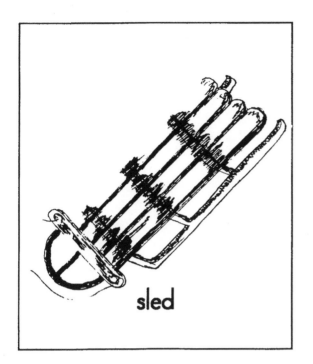

sled

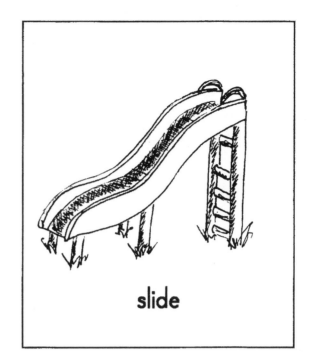

slide

sl

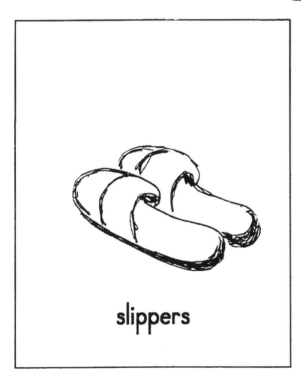

slippers

slots

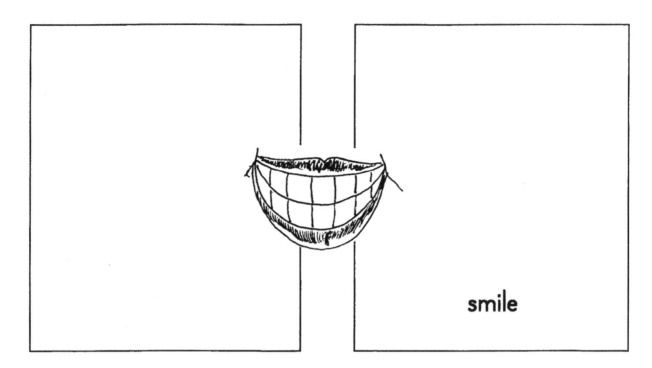

smile

sm

smoke

snake

sneaker

sn

snowman

spider

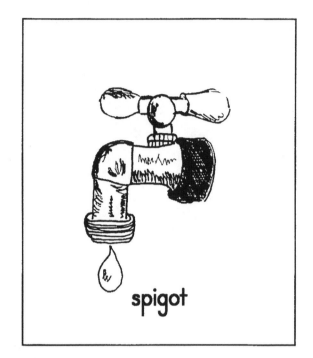

spigot

sp

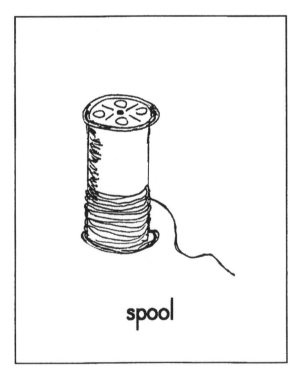

spool

spoon

stamp

star

st

stop

stump

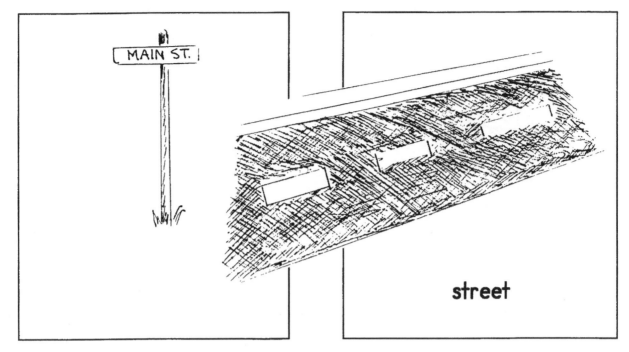

street

str

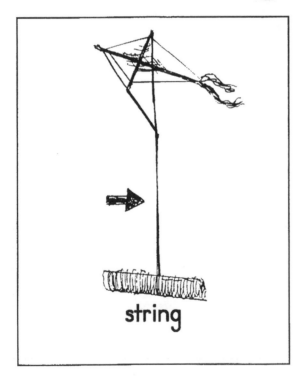

string

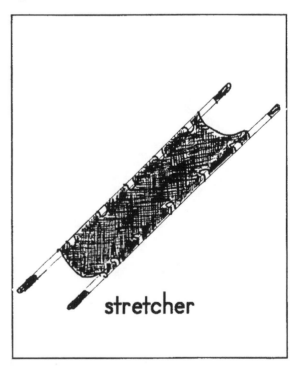

stretcher

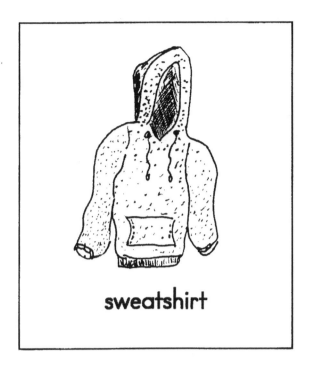

sweatshirt

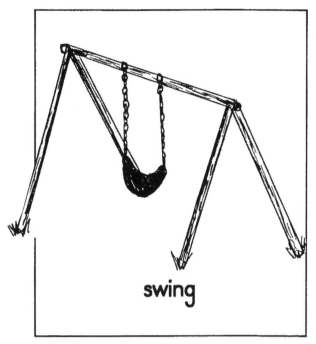

swing

sw

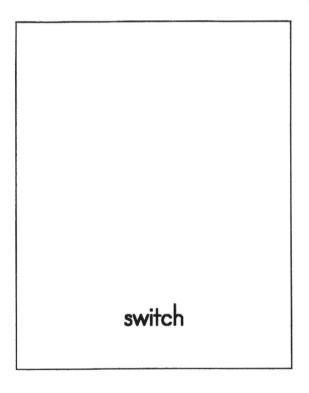

switch

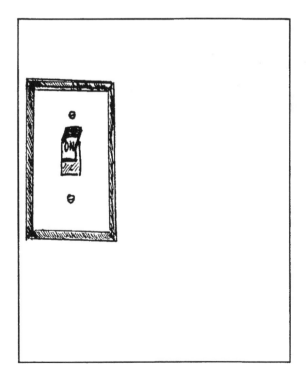

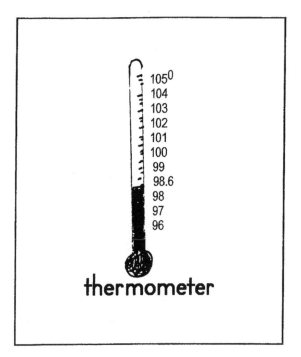

thermometer

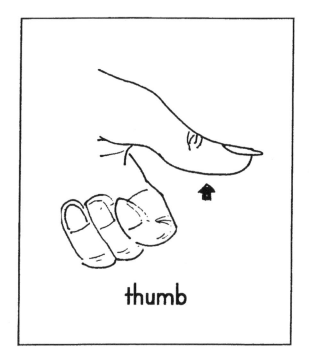

thumb

th

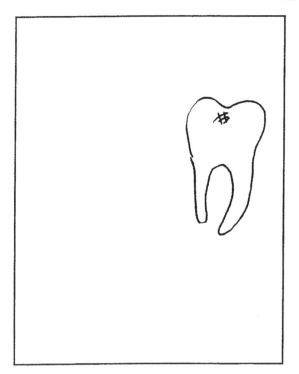

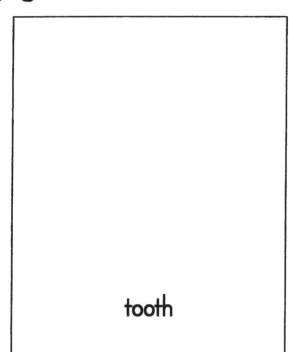

tooth

tree

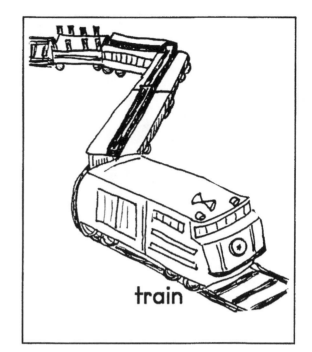

train

tr

triangle

truck

whale

wheelbarrow

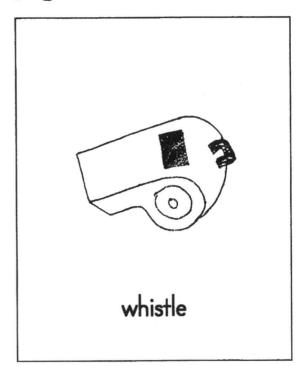

whistle

Consonant Blenders: Word List

b l

_ blackboard
_ blender
_ block
_ blow dryer

cr

_ crane
_ crayon
_ crown
_ crutch

gl

_ glass
_ glasses
_ glove

br

_ branch
_ brick
_ broom
_ brush

dr

_ dress
_ drill
_ dropper
_ drum

gr

_ graduate
_ grapes
_ grave

ch

_ chair
_ chicken
_ cheese
_ chain

fl

_ flag
_ flashlight
_ flower

kn

_ knapsack (backpack)
_ knee
_ knife
_ knot

cl

_ clip
_ clock
_ clothespin
_ clown

fr

_ fraction
_ frame
_ frog
_ fruit

pl

_ plant
_ plaque
_ playground
_ pliers

pr	sk	sp
_ prescription	_ skate	_ spider
_ pretzel	_ skillet	_ spigot
_ propeller	_ skunk	_ spool
_ protractor	_ desk	_ spoon

sc	sl	st
_ scale	_ sled	_ stamp
_ scarf	_ slide	_ star
_ scarecrow	_ slippers	_ stop
	_ slots	_ stump

scr	sm	str
_ screwdriver	_ smile	_ street
_ screw	_ smoke	_ string
_ scribble		_ stretcher

sh	sn	sw
_ shell	_ snake	_ sweatshirt
_ ship	_ sneaker	_ swing
_ shoes	_ snowman	_ switch
_ shovel		

136

th

_ thermometer
_ thumb
    _ tooth

t r

_ tree
_ train
_ triangle
_ truck

w h

_ whale
_ wheelbarrow
_ whistle

Blenders: **Let's Read!**

_1. which wheel

_2. gray sky

_3. sharp tooth

_4. brown drum

_5. green frog

_6. crown from France

_7. small shell

_8. chicken on a chair

_9. short spoon

_10. shell on a ship

_11. blue mask

_12. flower flag

_13. thick thumb

_14. small brush

_15. sticky stamp

_16. clock on a block

_17. scarecrow's scarf

_18. fish fry

_19. crab and snail

_20. elephant on a truck

_21. matched patch

_22. white wheel

_23. clown with a skate

_24. glue on a glove

_25. sweet grapes

_26. pretty prize

_27. shining star

_28. gray sky

_29. blue whale

_30. tricky triangle

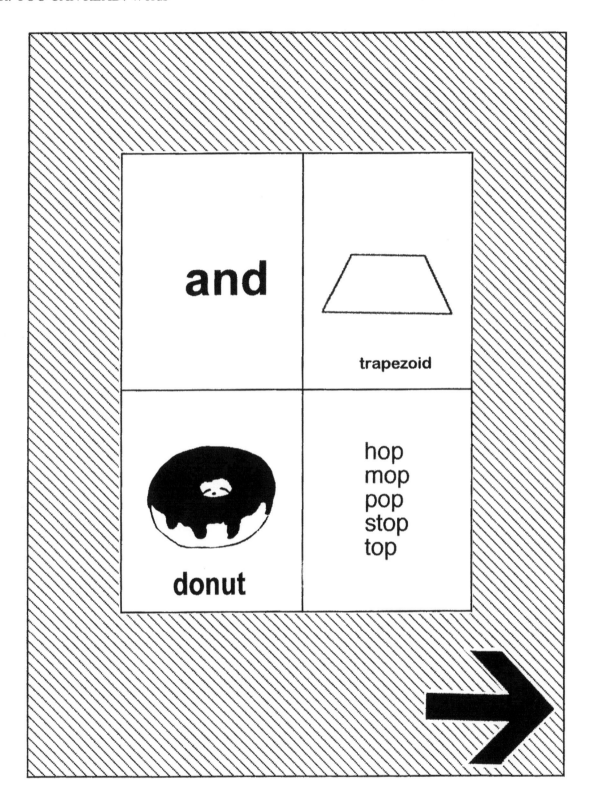

and

trapezoid

donut

hop
mop
pop
stop
top

ABR: YOU CAN READ!

Adult Beginning Reader Program

Section 2: Words

250+ Basic Sight Words   Sight Word Phrases   Word Pictures

Word / Sound Families   Practical Literacy Units

by

Frederick J. Zorn, Ed.D.

Principal, Teacher, Adjunct Professor, Literacy Tutor

Tips for Tutors: Learning Words

Alphabet Review: All words are made up of letters.
□ Review letter visual recognition: *Upper and Lower Case.*
□ Review letter sounds: *consonants, vowels, blenders.*

Basic Sight Words / Phrases:
□ With practice and repetition, mastery is an important goal.
□ The 253 'little' words make up much of all reading material.
□ Do all words in letter sets (words that start with the same letter).
□ Select letter sets in any order.

Word / Sound Families:
□ Use to build letter and word recognition -- both sight and sound.

Word - Pictures: Use pictures as cues to printed words.
□ Share ideas about pictures to build oral vocabulary and concepts.
□ Then work on words without the picture cues.

Practical Literacy Units: Words in context.
□ Most words included are familiar in speech and understanding.
□ Reviewing words in context units helps bridge educational gaps.
□ Assist with beginning word sounds as needed.
□ Talk about the topic to expand vocabulary and information.
□ Find books, pictures, and stories that relate.
□ Word attack lessons are important for building reading skills:
Compound Words (Pp. 216-7), Contractions (Pp. 220-1), Syllables (Pp. 250-3),
Word Enders (Pp. 264-7), Root Words (P. 271).

Section 2: Words

Table Of Contents

ABR Tips for Tutors: **Basic Sight Words**

These 250+ Basic Sight Words make up much of all reading material.

Technique: Approximately 20 minutes / lesson.

- ☐ *Tutor:* Give each learner an alphabetized Basic Sight Words list.
- ☐ *Tutor:* Use the learner's copy. *Learner:* Use an unmarked copy.
- ☐ Do lesson in rounds. Note improvement each time.

Round 1: *Select one letter of the alphabet.*

Learner: _'Read' each word in that set quickly.

_Move from word to word without prompts.

_Skip any word not immediately recognized.

Tutor: _Check off each word read correctly.

Round 2: *Tutor:* Read each word in the set distinctly.

Learner: _Repeat after <u>each</u> word. In a group, all repeat.

Round 3: *Learner:* Again read the letter set quickly.

Tutor: _Circle each word mastered (both new and those checked in the first round),

---

Note improvement.

_Continue with other letter sets

Sight Word Phrases: Follow the same procedures.

_Can be used instead of Sight Words or for additional practice.

Reminder: *Use a line marker under words when reading.*

~ Enjoy Learning To Read! ~

ABR: YOU CAN READ!

Adult Beginning Reader Program

ABR Sight & Sound Guide to Word Recognition

Section 2: **Words**

ABR: **Basic Sight Words**

~ 250+ Basic Sight Words ~

– Much of all reading material is made up of these Basic Sight Words. –

by

Frederick J. Zorn, Ed.D.

Principal, Teacher, Adjunct Professor, Literacy Tutor

253 ABR Basic Sight Words: Make up much of all reading material.

A
_a
_about
_after
_again
_all
_always
_am
_an
_and
_any
_are
_around
_as
_ask
_at
_ate
_away

B
_back
_be
_because
_been
_before
_best
_better
_big
_black
_blue
_both
_bring
_brown
_but
_buy

_by

C
_call
_came
_can
_car
_carry
_city
_clean
_cold
_come
_could
_cut

D
_day
_did
_do
_does
_done
_don't
_down
_draw
_drink
_drive

E
_each
_eat
_eight
_end
_every

F
_fall
_far

_fast
_find
_first
_five
_fly
_for
_found
_four
_friend
_from
_full
_funny

G
_gave
_get
_give
_go
_going
_goes
_good
_got
_green
_grow

H
_had
_has
_hat
_have
_he
_help
_her
_here
_him
_his

_hold
_hot
_how
_hurt

I
_I
_if
_in
_into
_is
_it
_it's

J
_jump
_just

K
_keep
_kind
_know

L
_last
_laugh
_left
_let
_light
_like
_little
_live
_long
_look

M
_made

_make
_many
_me
_may
_more
_move
_Mr.
_Mrs.
_much
_must
_my

N

_name
_near
_never
_new
_next
_night
_no
_not
_now
_number

O

_of
_off
_old
_on
_once
_one
_only
_open
_or
_other
_our
_out
_over

_own

P

_part
_people
_pick
_place
_plant
_play
_please
_pretty
_pull
_put

R

_ran
_read
_red
_ride
_right
_round
_run

S

_said
_saw
_say
_see
_seven
_shall
_she
_show
_sing
_sit
_six
_sleep
_small
_so

_some
_soon
_star
_start
_stop

T

_take
_tell
_ten
_thank
_that
_the
_their
_them
_then
_there
_these
_they
_thing
_think
_this
_they're
_those
_three
_to
_too
_today
_together
_top
_try
_two

U/V

_under
_up
_upon
_us

_use
_very

W

_walk
_want
_warm
_was
_wash
_water
_way
_we
_well
_went
_were
_what
_wheel
_when
_where
_which
_white
_who
_why
_will
_wish
_with
_work
_would
_write

Y

_year
_yellow
_yes
_you
_your
_you're

ABR: YOU CAN READ!

Adult Beginning Reader Program

ABR Sight & Sound Guide to Word Recognition

Section 2: **Words**

ABR: **Basic Sight Words Phrases**

~ 250+ Basic Sight Words in Phrases ~

– Much of all reading material is made up of these Basic Sight Words. –

by

Frederick J. Zorn, Ed.D.

Principal, Teacher, Adjunct Professor, Literacy Tutor

Basic Sight Word Phrases
250+ ABR Basic Sight Words in Phrases

A

___ 1. **about now**

___ 2. **as good as new**

___ 3. **any more of it**

___ 4. **all for one**

___ 5. **around here**

___ 6. **are you near by**

B

___ 7. **been here much**

___ 8. **be kind**

___ 9. **best friend**

___ 10. **big wheel**

___ 11. **black and blue**

___ 12. **bring it here**

___ 13. **but only if**

C

___ 14. **call first**

___ 15. **carry him**

___ 16. **clean with water**

___ 17. **come back**

___ 18. **could you**

___ 19. **cut it out**

D

___ 20. **do you live here**

___ 21. **does it hurt**

___ 22. **don't drink**

___ 23. **don't open it**

___ 24. **drive over**

E

___ 25. **eat last**

___ 26. **eight came over**

___ 27. **every little thing**

F

___ 28. **fall on it**

___ 29. **far out**

___ 30. **find him for me**

___ 31. **from here on in**

G

___32. **get some sleep**

___33. **get up now**

___34. **give it to her**

___35. **go away**

___36. **good work**

___37. **got one**

___38. **grow a plant**

H - I

___39. **has a brown top**

___40. **have many more**

___41. **he ran after it**

___42. **he saw them**

___43. **help each other**

___44. **here goes seven**

___45. **hot or cold**

___46. **hold off**

___47. **how much is made**

___48. **I am better**

___49. **I ask because**

___50. **I always did**

___51. **I ate an *apple***

___52. **I gave before**

___53. **if I can**

___54. **in there**

___55. **it's full today**

J - K

___56. **jump over it**

___57. **just say no**

___58. **keep going**

___59. **keep it up**

___60. **know how**

L

___61. **last night**

___62. **left or right**

___63. **long ride**

___64. **look at the city**

M

___65. **make me laugh**

___66. **me first**

___67. **Mr. and Mrs.**

___68. **must we**

___69. **my place**

N

___	70.	**new year**
___	71.	**never again**
___	72.	**not this way**

O

___	73.	**on our way**
___	74.	**once upon a *time***
___	75.	**over there**
___	76.	**own up to it**

P

___	77.	**people want that**
___	78.	**pick it up**
___	79.	**play together**
___	80.	**please ride there**
___	81.	**pull over**
___	82.	**put five into this**

R

___	83.	**read fast**
___	84.	**red light**
___	85.	**red, white & blue**
___	86.	**round it out**
___	87.	**run and jump**

S

___	88.	**see you**
___	89.	**shall we draw it**
___	90.	**she is so pretty**
___	91.	**sing out**
___	92.	**sit down**
___	93.	**six and four = ten**
___	94.	**small one**
___	95.	**so what**
___	96.	**start it up soon**

T

___	97.	**take your hat off**
___	98.	**tell it like it is**
___	99.	**tell them why**
___	100.	**thank you**
___	101.	**their name is**
___	102.	**then move over**
___	103.	**they're green**
___	104.	**think before**
___	105.	**those two**
___	106.	**three more**
___	107.	**too much**

continued

| ___108. | **top show** |
| ___109. | **try and stop me** |

U-V

___110.	**under these**
___111.	**up there**
___112.	**use it with me**

| ___113. | **very good** |

W

___114.	**walk it off**
___115.	**warm it up**
___116.	**was it found**
___117.	**wash up**
___118.	**well**
___119.	**were they funny**
___120.	**what a day**
___121.	**what now**
___122.	**when will you**
___123.	**where is the car**
___124.	**which part**

___125.	**wish on a star**
___126.	**who had it last**
___127.	**who is next**
___128.	**why buy both**
___129.	**would she go**
___130.	**write us soon**

Y

___131.	**yes you may**
___132.	**yellow fly**
___133.	**you're good**
___134.	**you did it fast**
___135.	**you go *girl***
___136.	**you let it go**
___137.	**you said it**
___138.	**your number is**

~

| ___139. | **the end** |

ABR: YOU CAN READ!

Adult Beginning Reader Program

ABR Sight & Sound Guide to Word Recognition

Section 2: **Words**

Word - Pictures

Building Sight Word Vocabulary Using Picture Cues.

by

Frederick J. Zorn, Ed.D.

Principal, Teacher, Adjunct Professor, Literacy Tutor

ABR: Tips for Tutors: Word / Pictures

Includes many words already in the learner's spoken vocabulary.

Learner: _Use Picture Cues to help recognize words in print.
_Point to the word and say it.
_Sound out initial letter of the word as needed.

Tutor and Learner: Talk about words of interest.
_This expands knowledge and builds verbal skills.
_Share experiences and expertise.
_Write or draw about words to increase word recognition.

Tutor and Learner: Use Words Checklist (P. 157).
_Can use before and/or after each letter set.
_Learner can check the picture if unsure of a word.
_Mastery is not necessary; practice with words is.

Tutor and Learner:
_Do as many letter sets per lesson as is productive.
_Do sentence sets (Pp. 174-175) after entire unit is done.

Note: Whole Word-Pictures Unit can be done as one lesson.

ENJOY!

Word Pictures: WORDS CHECKLIST

a
___ alligator
___ anchor
___ apple
___ aquarium
___ arrow
___ ax

b
___ baby
___ balloon
___ banana
___ baseball
___ bed
___ bicycle
___ bridge
___ bus
___ butterfly

c
___ cactus
___ camera
___ candle
___ comb
___ computer
___ corn

d
___ deer
___ doctor
___ dog
___ donut
___ door
___ duck

e
___ egg
___ elbow
___ elephant
___ elevator
___ elf
___ Eskimo

f
___ fan
___ feather
___ fence
___ fish
___ foot
___ fork

g
___ gas
___ gear
___ girl
___ goat
___ golf
___ guitar

h
___ hair
___ hammer
___ harp
___ hat
___ head
___ helmet
___ hippo
___ horse
___ house

i - j
___ igloo
___ Inch
___ Indian
___ jar
___ jacks
___ jukebox

k
___ kangaroo
___ key
___ kite

l
___ ladder
___ lamp
___ leaf
___ lemon
___ lobster
___ lock

m
___ magnet
___ mailbox
___ merry-go-round
___ microscope
___ monkey
___ mop

n - o
___ nest
___ net
___ newspaper
___ octopus
___ onion
___ owl

p - q
___ peanut
___ pear
___ piano
___ pie
___ pig
___ pineapple
___ pitcher
___ pizza
___ pumpkin
___ quarter
___ queen
___ question mark

r
___ rabbit
___ radio
___ rake
___ razor
___ refrigerator
___ ring

s
___ sandwich
___ saw
___ seahorse
___ sink
___ snake
___ sofa
___ sun
___ sailboat
___ seal

t
___ table
___ telephone
___ tent
___ tie
___ tiger
___ tooth
___ top
___ tree
___ turtle

u
___ umbrella
___ umpire
___ Uncle Sam

v
___ vacuum cleaner
___ van
___ vest
___ violin
___ vise
___ volcano

w
___ wagon
___ watch
___ watermelon
___ well
___ window
___ windmill

x - y - z
___ X-ray
___ xylophone
___ yarn
___ yo-yo
___ zebra
___ zipper

A a

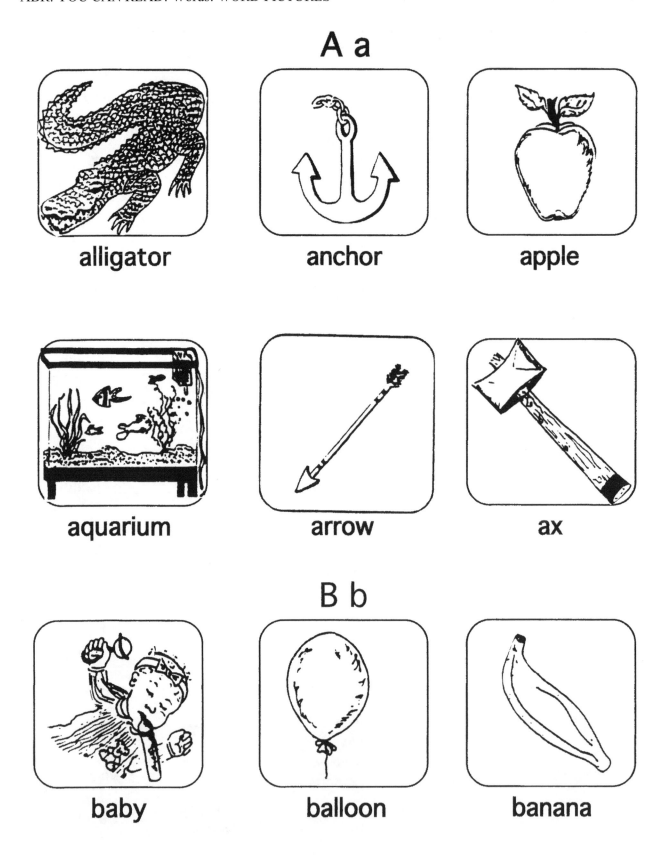

alligator

anchor

apple

aquarium

arrow

ax

B b

baby

balloon

banana

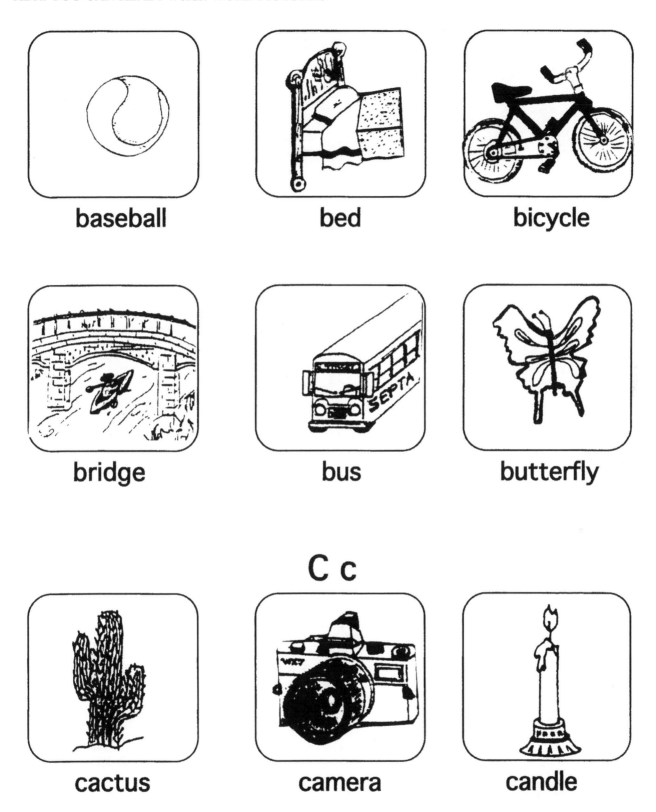

baseball

bed

bicycle

bridge

bus

butterfly

C c

cactus

camera

candle

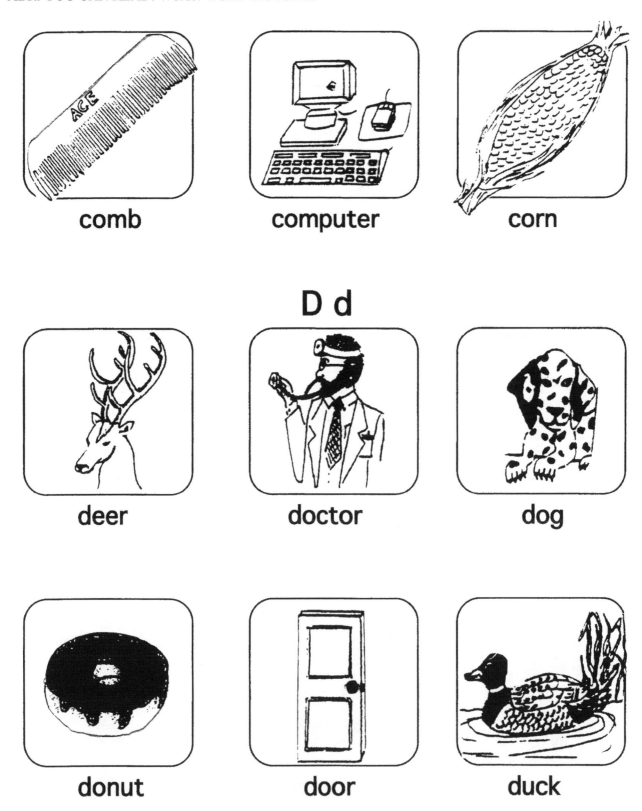

comb

computer

corn

D d

deer

doctor

dog

donut

door

duck

E e

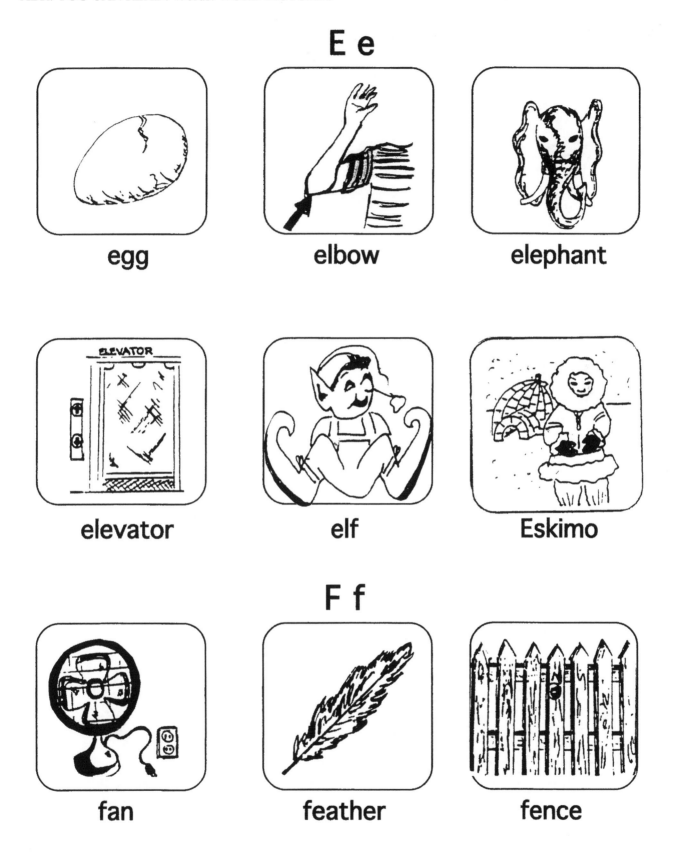

egg

elbow

elephant

elevator

elf

Eskimo

F f

fan

feather

fence

fish   foot   fork

G g

gas   gear   girl

goat   golf   guitar

H h

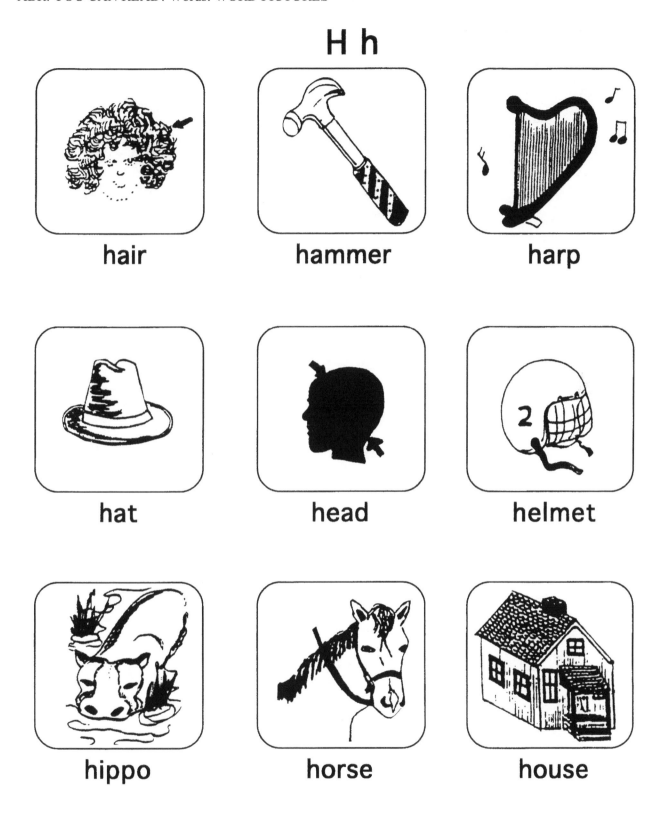

hair	hammer	harp
hat	head	helmet
hippo	horse	house

I i

igloo

inch

Indian

J j

jar

jacks

jukebox

K k

kangaroo

key

kite

L l

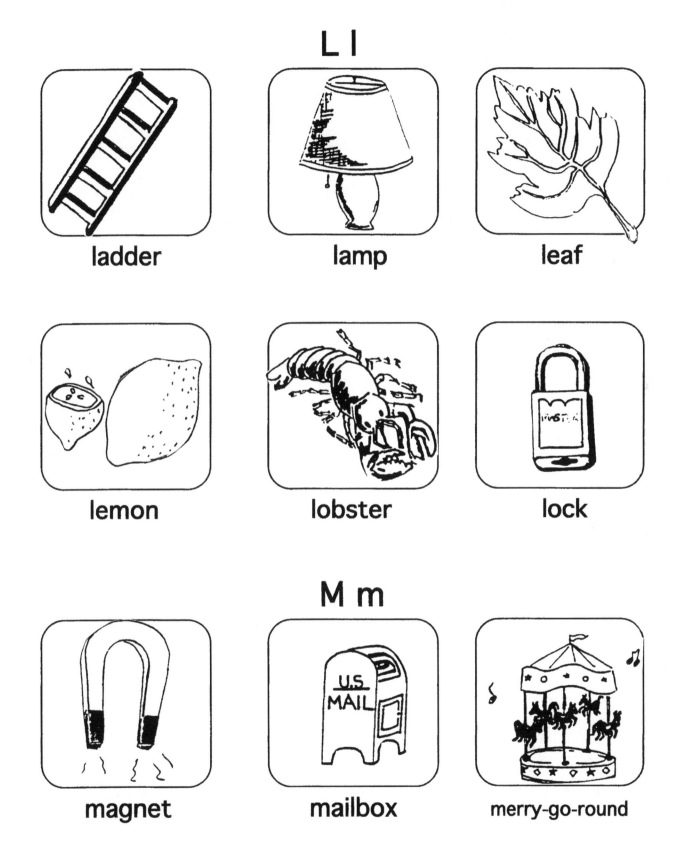

ladder

lamp

leaf

lemon

lobster

lock

M m

magnet

mailbox

merry-go-round

microscope

monkey

mop

N n

nest

net

newspaper

O o

octopus

onion

owl

P p

peanut	pear	piano
pie	pig	pineapple
pitcher	pizza	pumpkin

Q q

quarter

queen

question mark

R r

rabbit

radio

rake

razor

refrigerator

ring

S s

sandwich

saw

seahorse

sink

snake

sofa

sun

sailboat

seal

T t

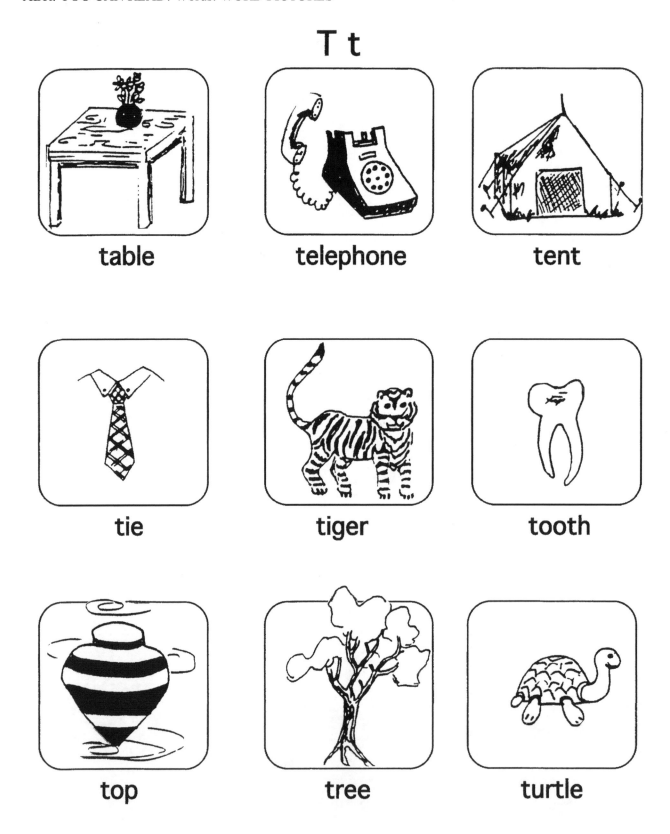

table telephone tent

tie tiger tooth

top tree turtle

U u

umbrella

umpire

Uncle Sam

V v

vacuum cleaner

van

vest

violin

vise

volcano

W w

wagon

watch

watermelon

well

window

windmill

X x

x-ray

xylophone

Y y

yarn

yo-yo

Z z

zebra

zipper

Word - Pictures: **Sentences**
Refer to Word - Pictures and Basic Sight Words as needed

Letter	Word - Picture	Sentence
A a	_alligator	_1. The alligator is big.
	_anchor	_2. Put the anchor in the water.
	_apple	_3. The apple is red.
	_aquarium, fish	_4. An aquarium has fish.
	_ax, tree	_5. Cut the tree with an ax.
B b	_bed, door	_6. The bed is by the door.
	_bicycle	_7. I can ride a bicycle.
	_bridge, bus	_8. Take a bus over the bridge.
	_butterfly, leaf	_9. The butterfly is on a leaf.
C c D d	_candle, elbow	_10. The candle is near your elbow.
	_computer	_11. Put a lamp by the computer.
	_doctor, donut	_12. The doctor ate a donut.
	_dog, sofa	_13. The dog is on the sofa.
E e	_elephant, duck	_14. I saw an elephant and a duck.
	_elevator, rake	_15. Take the rake off the elevator.
	_elf, hat	_16. The elf has a funny hat.
	_Eskimo, igloo	_17. The Eskimo lives in an igloo.
F f	_fan, table	_18. Put the fan on the table.
	_foot, fence, girl	_19. A girl has her foot in the fence.
	_fork, pear	_20. Eat the pear with a fork.
G g H h	_guitar, harp	_21. Do you play the guitar or harp?
	_helmet, head	_22. Put a helmet on your head!
	_hippo, zebra	_23. Did you see the zebra or hippo?
	_horse, wagon	_24. A horse can pull a wagon.
I i J j	_inch, magnet	_25. Move the magnet over an inch.
	_ jacks, jar	_26. Can you open a jar of jacks?

K k L l	_kangaroo, tent	_27.	A kangaroo went in the tent.
	_kite	_28.	Go fly a kite!
	_ladder, saw	_29.	Take the saw up the ladder.
	_lock, key	_30.	Try the key in the lock.
M m	_microscope	_31.	Look at it under a microscope.
	_monkey, peanut	_32.	I gave the monkey a peanut.
	_mop, vacuum	_33.	Use a mop and vacuum cleaner.
N n O o	_net	_34.	Get the net!
	_newspaper	_35.	Read the newspaper.
	_octopus	_36.	An octopus has 8 legs.
	_onion, sandwich	_37.	Put onion in my sandwich.
P p	_piano, violin	_38.	I play the piano and violin.
	_pie, lemon	_39.	Eat the lemon pie.
	_pig, van	_40.	The pig ran next to the van.
	_pineapple, sink	_41.	Put the pineapple on the sink.
	_pitcher	_42.	Water is in the pitcher.
Q q R r	_question mark	_43.	Put a question mark at the end.
	_queen, ring	_44.	The queen has a big ring.
	_rabbit, deer	_45.	The rabbit ran from the deer.
	_radio	_46.	Turn on the radio.
S s T t	_snake, grapes	_47.	The snake ate the grapes.
	_seal, sailboat	_48.	I saw a seal from the sailboat.
	_telephone	_49.	Use the telephone to find out.
	_tiger, sun	_50.	The tiger sits in the sun.
U u V v	_umbrella	_51.	Take your umbrella today.
	_umpire, vest	_52.	The umpire had a vest on.
	_volcano, house	_53.	The house is near a volcano.
W w	_watch, tie	_54.	No watch and tie for the X-ray!
Y y	_yo-yo, top	_55.	I have a toy top and yo-yo.
Z z	_zipper, vise	_56.	Hold the zipper in the vise.

ABR: Tips For Tutors: Word / Sound Families

Lesson: _20-30 minutes.

_Work on one Word / Sound Family at a time (a, e, i, o, u).

Goal: _Learn to see each letter and hear each sound in a word.

Note: Not necessary to use all lessons in a Vowel Family.

Tutor: Explain that each Word / Sound Family set:

_Has rhyming words with the same vowel sound.

_Gets new words by changing consonants. (Ex: <u>c</u>at, <u>f</u>at, <u>map</u>.)

Note: Review letter sounds: vowels (a, e, i, o, u), consonants, blenders.

Learner: _Develop skill in learning to read new words.

_See the small difference a vowel or consonant can make.

_Gain practice with hearing vowel sounds.

Method:

Tutor: _Select a Word / Sound Family (a, e, i, o, u).

Learner: _Select a Word / Sound Family set. (Rhyming group).

_"Read" the Picture Cue. ("What word is it?)

_Then read that list of words quickly.

_Read sentences that go with it. *They are tricky!*

Note: All words rhyme in each Word / Sound Family rhyme set.

Refer back to the picture cue as needed.

Tutor: _Go on to other Word / Sound Family rhyme sets.

_Repeat the same procedure.

Note: Move quickly. Mastery is not necessary; practice is.

Enjoy!

ABR: YOU CAN READ!

Adult Beginning Reader Program

ABR Sight & Sound Guide to Word Recognition

Section 2: **Words**

Word / Sound Families

Rhyming Vowel Words

Sight and sound words to build reading skill.

Seeing and hearing small differences in words.

by

Frederick J. Zorn, Ed.D.

Principal, Teacher, Adjunct Professor, Literacy Tutor

Lesson 1: **a t**

b **a t**	m **a t**
c **a t**	N **a t**
ch **a t**	P **a t**
f **a t**	r **a t**
fl **a t**	s **a t**
h **a t**	th **a t**

Lesson 1: **a t**

_1. **Is a hat on the cat?**

_2. **Chat with Pat.**

_3. **Pat sat on the hat.**

_4. **The hat was flat.**

_5. **A fat rat is on a mat.**

Lesson 2: **a d** **a b**

b **a d**	c **a b**
D **a d**	d **a b**
gl **a d**	g **a b**
h **a d**	j **a b**
m **a d**	l **a b**
p **a d**	n **a b**
s **a d**	t **a b**

Lesson 2: **a d** **a b**

_1. **Dad had a cab at the lab.**

_2. **A cab had an ad on a tab.**

_3. **Dad is mad and sad.**

_4. **To nab and jab is bad!**

_5. **Did he gab in the lab?**

_6. **Is Dad glad or sad?**

_7. **Did dad dab the pad?**

Lesson 3: **a p**

c **a p**	n **a p**
cl **a p**	r **a p**
g **a p**	sl **a p**
l **a p**	t **a p**
m **a p**	z **a p**

Lesson 3: **a p**

_1. **Dad had a map on his lap.**

_2. **Pat had a nap with a cap.**

_3. **Dad had a gap on his lap.**

_4. **Tap the cap. Slap! Zap!**

_5. **Rap and clap for Dad!**

REVIEW: Lesson 1 - 3

_1. **Dad had a cat on his lap.**

_2. **The cat was fat and bad.**

_3. **Dad had a cap on the cat.**

REVIEW: Lesson 1 - 3

_4. **Dad had the bat and map on his lap with the cat.**

_5. **Dad had a nap in a cab.**

_6. **Dad was glad to gab.**

Lesson 4: **a ck**

b **a ck**	r **a ck**
bl **a ck**	s **a ck**
cr **a ck**	st **a ck**
j **a ck**	t **a ck**
p **a ck**	Z **a ck**

Lesson 4: **a ck**

_1. **Go back, Zack, with a rack and jack!**

_2. **Pack a snack in a black sack.**

_3. **Tack the crack on the rack.**

Lesson 5: **a n**　　**a m**

c **a n**	cl **a m**
D **a n**	d **a m**
f **a n**	h **a m**
J **a n**	j **a m**
m **a n**	P **a m**
p **a n**	r **a m**
r **a n**	S **a m**
t **a n**	sl **a m**
v **a n**	y **a m**

Lesson 5: **a n**　　**a m**

_1. **Pam ran to Dan and Jan.**
_2. **Jan had jam in a tan van.**
_3. **A man had a fan and a can.**
_4. **Sam had a ham.**
_5. **Jan had jam on a yam?**
_6. **Did Sam slam Dan with a pan?**

Lesson 6: **a g**

b **a g**	n **a g**
br **a g**	r **a g**
fl **a g**	t **a g**
g **a g**	w **a g**

Lesson 6: **a g**

_1. **Sam had a rag in a bag.**
_2. **A tag on the flag is a gag.**
_3. **I brag about the flag.**
_4. **The tag is not a rag.**
_5. **Nan is not a nag.**

REVIEW: Lesson 4 - 6
_1. **Nan had Dad in a hat.**
_2. **Nan and Sam had jam.**

REVIEW: Lesson 4 - 6
_3. **It was a gag from Pat.**
_4. **Nat had ham in a pan.**
_5. **He had a bat. Slam!**

Lesson 7: **a ll**

b **a ll**  m **a ll**

c **a ll** sm **a ll**

f **a ll** t **a ll**

h **a ll** w **a ll**

Lesson 7: **a ll**

_1. **Call the mall!**

_2. **Did the ball fall on the wall.**

_3. **The wall in the hall is tall.**

_4. **The ball is small.**

_5. **That is all at the mall!**

Lesson 8: **a r** ark, art

b **a r** d **a rk**

c **a r** m **a rk**

f **a r** p **a rk**

j **a r** sh **a rk**

t **a r** c **a rt**

st **a r** st **a rt**

Lesson 8: **a r** **a rk, a r t**

_1. **The star is in the dark.**

_2. **Park the cart far from a bar.**

_3. **Start the car and mark the jar.**

REVIEW: Lesson 7 - 8 Different sounds of a.

_1. **Jack was tall at the mall.**

_2. **Is the ball in the car?**

REVIEW: Lesson 7 - 8 Different sounds of a.

_3. **A dark car has it all.**

_4. **Is the hall far from the park?**

Lesson 9: **a k e** *Long a*

b **a ke**   m **a ke**

c **a ke**   sh **a ke**

f **a ke**   t **a ke**

J **a ke**   w **a ke**

l **a ke**

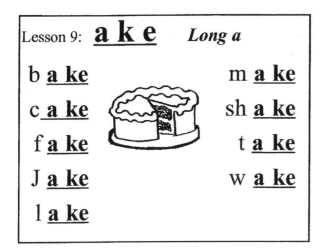

Lesson 9: **a k e** *Long a*

_1. **Wake Jake at the lake.**

_2. **Wake Jake with a shake.**

_3. **Bake a fake cake.**

Lesson 10: **a y** *Long a*

b **a y**   M **a y**

cl **a y**   pl **a y**

d **a y**   R **a y**

h **a y**   s **a y**

J **a y**   t o d **a y**

K **a y**   w **a y**

Lesson 10: **a y** *Long a*

_1. **Is Jay to play with clay today?**

_2. **Ray is at the bay.**

_3. **The hay is for May.**

_4. **Pay Kay on the way, Jay!**

Lesson 11: **a i n** *Long a*

p **ai n**   ch **ai n**

r **ai n**   dr **ai n**

br **ai n**   tr **ai n**

Lesson 11: **a i n** *Long a*

_1. **The chain is a pain.**

_2. **Drain the rain from the train.**

182   © Frederick J. Zorn, 2014

Lesson 12:   *Long a*

a t e   **a c e**

d **a t e**   f **a c e**

g **a t e**   l **a c e**

l **a t e**   p **a c e**

pl **a t e**   pl **a c e**

r **a t e**   r **a c e**

sk **a t e**   sp **a c e**

st **a t e**   tr **a c e**

Long a

Lesson 12: **a t e   a c e**

_1. **Lace the skate at the gate.**

_2. **Don't be late for the date.**

_3. **Place a plate in the space.**

_4. **Set a pace for the race.**

_5. **Face the gate for the race.**

REVIEW: Lesson 9 - 12   *Long a*

_1. **Will Jay bake cake today?**

_2. **Did Ray see a fake lake?**

REVIEW: Lesson 9 - 12   *Long a*

_3. **Take the cake to the place.**

_4. **Shake Jay at the bay.**

_5. **Pay Kay to wake Ray.**

Lesson 1: **e d**   **ea d** *

b **e d**	ah **ea d**
E d	br **ea d**
f **e d**	h **ea d**
fl **e d**	r **ea d**
l **e d**	thr **ea d**
r **e d**	
sh **e d**	
T **e d**	
w **e d**	

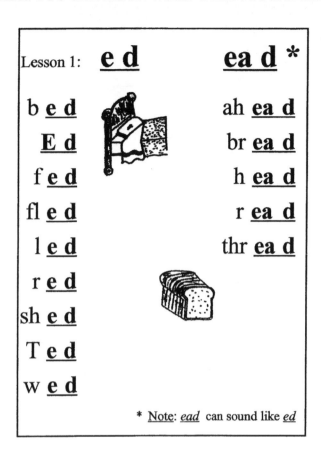

* Note: *ead* can sound like *ed*

Lesson 1: **e d**   **ea d** *

_1. **Ted led Ned to a red bed.**
_2. **Ed saw thread in a bread.**
_3. **Ted fed and read to Ed.**

Lesson 2: **e p**   **elt**

p **e p**	b **e lt**
r **e p**	f **e lt**
st **e p**	kn **e lt**
y **e p**	m **e lt**

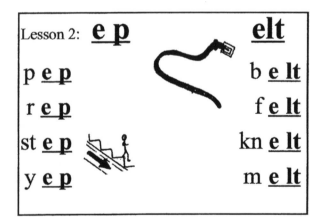

Lesson 2: **e p**   **elt**

_1. **Ed had a red belt.**
_2. **He had pep in his step. Yep!**
_3. **He felt it melt when he knelt.**

Lesson 3: **e n**   **e nd**

B **e n**	b **e nd**
d **e n**	l **e nd**
h **e n**	m **e nd**
K **e n**	s **e nd**
m **e n**	
p **e n**	
t **e n** wh **e n**	

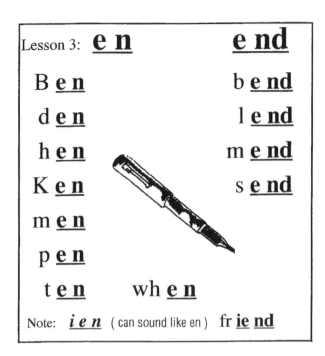

Note: **i e n** (can sound like en) fr **ie nd**

Lesson 3: **e n**   **e nd**

_1. **Ben had a hen in the den.**
_2. **Lend a friend a pen.**
_3. **Send ten men to Ken?**
   When?
_4. **Can Ken bend the pen?**

Lesson 4: **e t**

b **e t**	p **e t**
g **e t**	s **e t**
l **e t**	v **e t**
m **e t**	w **e t**
n **e t**	y **e t**

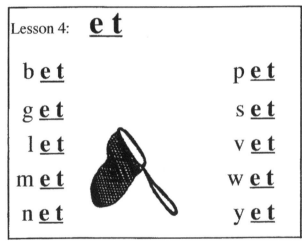

Lesson 4: **e t**

_1. **I met a pet at the vet.**
_2. **Get the pet a net.**
_3. **Let the vet wet the pet.**

Lesson 5: **e ll**

b **e ll**	sp **e ll**
f **e ll**	t **e ll**
s **e ll**	w **e ll**
sh **e ll**	y **e ll**

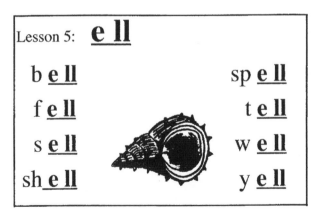

Lesson 5: **e ll**

_1. **I fell on a shell at the well.**
_2. **I didn't yell!**
_3. **Tell me how to spell** *"sell."*
_4. **Did you yell to tell me to**
   sell the bell?

185

Lesson 6: **e st**

b **e st**   r **e st**

n **e st**   t **e st**

p **e st**   v **e st**

Lesson 6: **e st**

_1. **This is my best vest.**

_2. **Rest for the test.**

_3. **The pest was in the nest.**

REVIEW: Lesson 1 - 6

_1. **Ben met Ed at the vet.**

_2. **A friend then went to the well.**

_3. **See the best bread yet?**

_4. **He let the bell bend.**

_5. **He knelt and felt wet.**

_6. **Did he get to mend the red belt?**

_7. **Ken had the best vest yet.**

Lesson 7: **Long e**

e   **ey**

b **e**   sh **e**   k **ey**
h **e**   w **e**
m **e**

Lesson 7: **Long e**

e   **ey**

_1. **We have the key.**

Lesson 8: **Long e**

ee   **ea**

b **ee**   p **ea**
f **ee**   s **ea**
s **ee**   t **ea**
fr **ee**   b **ea** d
kn **ee**   l **ea** d
tr **ee**   r **ea** d
thr **ee**   **ea** t
d **ee** d   m **ea** t
f **ee** d   n **ea** t
s **ee** d   tr **ea** t
f **ee** t   wh **ea** t
sw **ee** t

Lesson 8: **Long e**

ee   **ea**

_1. **We see a key by the sea.**
_2. **Did the bee see my knee?**
_3. **We had sweet tea for three.**
_4. **Feed a meal of meat, wheat
    and sweet tea for free.**

REVIEW: Lesson 7 - 8 _Long e_
_1. **Treat me to a free tea.**
_2. **Meat for three is a neat
    deed to see.**
_3. **Read to me about the sea.**

Lesson 1: **id**　　**ip**

b **id**	d **ip**
d **id**	h **ip**
h **id**	l **ip**
k **id**	r **ip**
l **id**	sh **ip**
r **id**	sl **ip**
S **id**	tr **ip**
sl **id**	z **ip**

Lesson 1: **id**　　**ip**
1. Slip the lid to Sid.
2. Zip the lid for a dip.
3. Did the kid get rid of the slip?
4. Did Sid bid for the ship?
5. Sid hid a rip on the trip.

Lesson 2: **in**　　**im**

b **in**	br **im**
f **in**	d **im**
p **in**	h **im**
sk **in**	J **im**
sp **in**	r **im**
th **in**	sl **im**
t **in**	T **im**
w **in**	wh **im**

Lesson 2: **in**　　**im**
1. Spin the pin on the tin in the bin!
2. Did Tim trim the brim with a pin?
3. Is Jim slim or thin?
4. Did Tim win on a whim?

Lesson 3: **i g**   **i t**

b **i g**	b **i t**
d **i g**	f **i t**
f **i g**	h **i t**
p **i g**	k **i t**
r **i g**	l **i t**
w **i g**	qu **i t**
	s **i t**
	spl **i t**

Lesson 3: **i g**   **i t**

_1. **Did the pig dig for a fig?**
_2. **Did the wig sit on the rig?**
_3. **Split the big pit or quit.**
_4. **Hit it a bit to fit the kit.**

Lesson 4: **i ng**   **i nk**

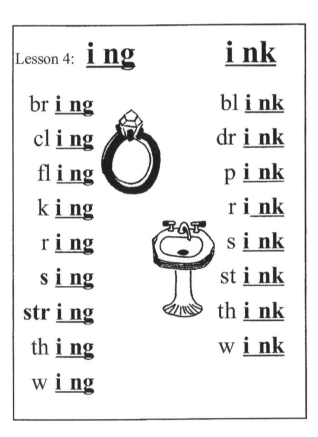

br **i ng**	bl **i nk**
cl **i ng**	dr **i nk**
fl **i ng**	p **i nk**
k **i ng**	r **i nk**
r **i ng**	s **i nk**
s **i ng**	st **i nk**
str **i ng**	th **i nk**
th **i ng**	w **i nk**
w **i ng**	

Lesson 4: **i ng**   **i nk**

_1. **The king had a big string.**
_2. **Bring the thing or I sing.**
_3. **Did Tim fling the ring?**
_4. **The king had a sling.**
_5. **Did she cling to the pink thing?**

Lesson 5: **i ll**

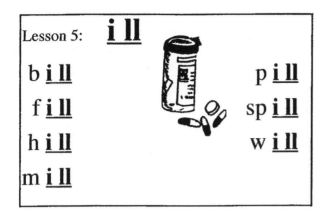

b **i ll**　　　　　　p **i ll**

f **i ll**　　　　　　sp **i ll**

h **i ll**　　　　　　w **i ll**

m **i ll**

Lesson 5: **i ll**

_1. **Did the pill fill the bill?**

_2. **Was the mill on a hill?**

REVIEW: Lessons 1 - 5

_1. **Did Sid bring a pig in a mill?**

_2. **Will Tim hit a wing tip?**

_3. **The fig has a thin skin.**

REVIEW: Lessons 1 - 5

_4. **He bit his lip on the ship.**

_5. **Did he blink when he quit the rink?**

Lesson 6: *Long i*

i ke　　　　**ice**

b **i k e**　　　　m **i c e**

h **i k e**　　　　n **i c e**

l **i k e**　　　　r **i c e**

M **i k e**　　　　sp **i c e**

str **i k e**　　　　tw **i c e**

Long i

Lesson 6: **i ke**　　　**ice**

_1. **Mike hid on a bike hike.**

_2. **I like nice rice and spice.**

_3. **Mike saw mice twice.**

Lesson 7:   *Long i*

i te	**ight**
b <u>i t e</u>	f <u>i ght</u>
k <u>i t e</u>	l <u>i ght</u>
qu <u>i t e</u>	n <u>i ght</u>
sp <u>i t e</u>	r <u>i ght</u>
wr <u>i t e</u>	s <u>i ght</u>
	t <u>i ght</u>

Long i

Lesson 7:   **i te   ight**

_1. **Mike had a fight at night.**

_2. **Ike had a tight bite.**

_3. **Spike had a light that was quite bright.**

_4. **The kite was on a flight.**

Lesson 8:   *Long i*

i n e	**i nd**
f <u>i n e</u>	f <u>i nd</u>
m <u>i n e</u>	bl <u>i nd</u>
n <u>i n e</u> ⑨	gr <u>i nd</u>
sh <u>i n e</u>	k <u>i nd</u>
w <u>i n e</u>	m <u>i nd</u>

Long i

Lesson 8:   **i n e   i nd**

_1. **Did he find the fine wine?**

_2. **Mike was kind.**

_3. **He did not hide the wine.**

_4. **The wine is mine!**

_5. **Do you mind?**

Lesson 9:   *Long i*

i r e   **i d e**

f **i r e**   h **i d e**

h **i r e**   r **i d e**

t **i r e**   s **i d e**

w **i r e**   t **i d e**

          w **i d e**

Long i

Lesson 9:   **i r e   i d e**

_1. **A wire is in the wide tire.**

_2. **Hide the fire on the side.**

_3. **Hire a ride by wire.**

Lesson 10: **i e**   *Long i*

l **i e**   t **i e**

p **i e**

Lesson 10: **i e**   *Long i*

_1. **Did he lie about my tie?**

_2. **The pie is mine.**

REVIEW: Lesson 6 - 10: *long i*

_1. **Find a fine wire for the tire.**

_2. **Light the fire on the side.**

REVIEW: Lesson 6 - 10: *long i*

_3. **Mice like ice.**

_4. **I like a bite of pie and wine.**

_5. **Hide the rice from light.**

192

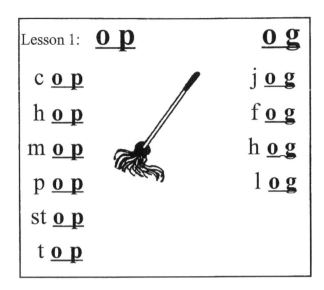

Lesson 1: **o p**   **o g**

c **o p**   j **o g**

h **o p**   f **o g**

m **o p**   h **o g**

p **o p**   l **o g**

st **o p**

t **o p**

Lesson 1 & 2: **o p**   **o g**

                        o m   **o x**

_1. **Stop at the top of a log, Mom.**

_2. **Got a hot spot on a mop?**

_3. **Did the cop jog a lot?**

_4. **Tom saw a fox in fog.**

_5. **The hog saw lox in the box.**

Lesson 2: **o m**   **o x**

m **o m**   b **o x**

T **o m**   f **o x**

                        l **o x**

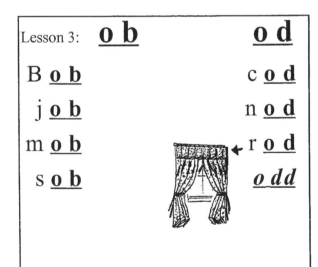

Lesson 3: **o b**   **o d**

B **o b**   c **o d**

j **o b**   n **o d**

m **o b**   r **o d**

s **o b**   *o dd*

Lesson 3: **o b**   **o d**

_1. **Bob did an odd job.**

_2. **Bob had a cod on the rod.**

_3. **Mom had a job for Bob.**

193   © Frederick J. Zorn, 2014

Lesson 4:   **o ck**   **o t**

d **o ck**   d **o t**

h **o ck**   g **o t**

l **o ck**   h **o t**

r **o ck**   l **o t**

s **o ck**   n **o t**

kn **o ck**   r **o t**

sh **o ck**   cl **o t**

st **o ck**   pl **o t**

sp **o t**

Lesson 4:   **o ck   o t**

_1. **Knock the pot on the spot.**

_2. **Did the clock shock a lot?**

_3. **The sock got hot on the rock.**

REVIEW: Lesson 1 - 4:

_1. **Knock a log on the job.**

_2. **Stop the fox on the spot.**

_3. **Mop the top of the rock, Bob.**

Lesson 5: **O**   *Long o*

g **o**   **O**h!

n **o**   s **o**

Lesson 5: **O**   *Long o*

_1. **Oh, no!**

_2. **So, go slow!**

Lesson 6:   *Long o*

oa	**ow**
b **oa** t	bl **ow**
c **oa** t	gr **ow**
fl **oa** t	kn **ow**
g **oa** t	l **ow**
m **oa** t	m **ow**
oa t	r **ow**
thr **oa** t	sh **ow**
	sl **ow**
	t **ow**
	thr **ow**

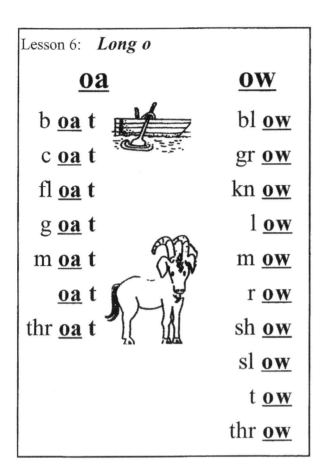

Lesson 6 :   **oa**   **ow**

_1. **Can a goat float in a boat?**

_2. **Go throw on a coat!**

_3. **I know he can float slow.**

_4. **Oh! Go slow. No!**

REVIEW: Lesson 5 - 6:   *Long O*

_1. **Oh! Did you show a goat?**

_2. **Row slow on a boat.**

_3. **Go show the coat.**

Lesson 7 - 10:   *Long o*
'e' at end makes the 'o' long

Lesson 7:   *Long o*   ('e' at end)

ote	**ope**
n **o te**	c **o pe**
t **o te**	h **o pe**
v **o te**	m **o pe**
qu **o te**	r **o pe**
wr **o te**	sl **o pe**

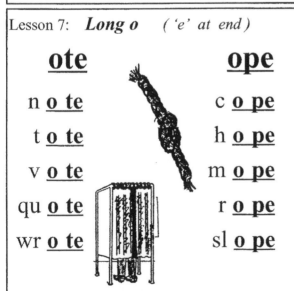

Lesson 7:   **ote**   **ope**

Long o   ('e' at end)

_1. **I woke and saw the rope**
    float by the boat.

_2. **I see smoke on the slope!**

_3. **Did you choke on smoke?**

_4. **He wrote a note of hope.**

Lesson 8   *Long o* (*'e' at end*)

o se   oke

h **o se**   ch **o ke**
n **o se**   p **o ke**
p **o se**   sm **o ke**
r **o se**   w **o ke**

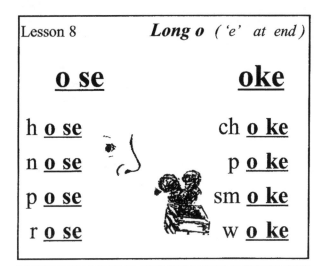

Lesson 9: **o ne**   *Long o* (*'e' at end*)

b **o ne**   st **o ne**
c **o ne**   z **o ne**
ph **o ne**

Lesson 10: **o de**   *Long o* (*'e' at end*)

b **o de**   m **o de**
c **o de**   r **o de**

Lesson 8 & 9:   *Long o* (*'e' at end*)
Lesson 8:   **o se   oke**
Lesson 9:   **o ne**

1. **Pose your nose on the phone.**
2. **Did you choke on smoke?**
3. **See the rose on the stone?**

Lesson 10: **o de** *Long o* (*'e'* at end)
1. **I rode by.**
2. **I know the code.**

REVIEW: Lesson 7 - 10   *Long O*

'e' at end makes the o long

1. **He rode with hope.**
2. **I know the phone code.**

REVIEW: Lesson 7 - 10   *Long O*
3. **I wrote a note on a stone.**
4. **Hope I cope when I vote.**
5. **I rode the whole slope.**
6. **Don't smoke!**

Weird o's			Lesson 11 & 12: *Long o*

Lesson 11: O O   *Long o*

oo k	**oo l**	**oo t**
b **oo k**	c **oo l**	b **oo t**
br **oo k**	f **oo l**	h **oo t**
c **oo k**	p **oo l**	r **oo t**
h **oo k**	t **oo l**	t **oo t**
l **oo k**	sch **oo l**	
t **oo k**	sp **oo l**	

Lesson 11: **O O -** *ook ool oot*

_1. **I took a cool boot to school.**

_2. **Look at the cool pool.**

_3. **Look in the pool for a**
      hook.

Lesson 12:   *Long o* (au sound)

ow	**own**	**ouse**
c **ow**	br **own**	bl **ouse**
h **ow**	cl **own**	h **ouse**
n **ow**	cr **own**	m **ouse**
pl **ow**	d **own**	sp **ouse**
	t **own**	

Lesson 12: ***ow own ouse*** (au sound)

_1. **Is a clown in a house now?**

_2. **How brown is the blouse?**

_3. **Did the spouse frown?**

197   © Frederick J. Zorn, 2014

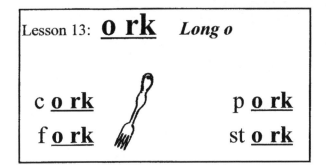

Lesson 13: **o rk**   *Long o*

c **o rk**   p **o rk**
f **o rk**   st **o rk**

Lesson 13: **o rk**   *Long o*
Lesson 14: **o y**   *Long o*

_1. **Look at the toy fork.**
_2. **A stork gave joy.**
_3. **A boy got a toy.**

Lesson 14: **o y**   *Long o*

b **o y**   s **o y**
j **o y**   t **o y**

REVIEW: Lesson 11 - 14   *Long O*

Weird Words: ***Oh, those O's!***

_1. **Know how the cow is now?**
_2. **Do you own a boot?**
_3. **Lock up the fork as a joke.**

REVIEW: Lesson 11 - 14   *Long O*

_4. **Cook a root at school.**
_5. **Tow the toy to town, now.**
_6. **I own one phone.**
_7. **Go downtown.**

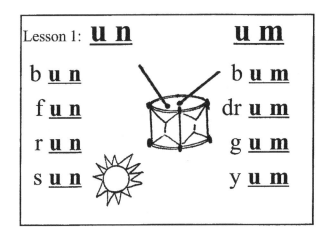

Lesson 1: **u n**   **u m**

b **u n**   b **u m**
f **u n**   dr **u m**
r **u n**   g **u m**
s **u n**   y **u m**

Lesson 1: **u n**   **u m**

_1. **I run in the sun.**
_2. **It's fun to drum.**
_3. **I had a bun and gum.**
_4. **The bun was fun.**
_5. **Gum? Yum!**

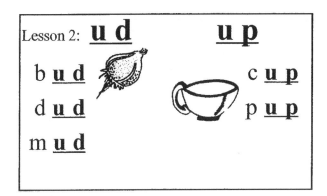

Lesson 2: **u d**   **u p**

b **u d**   c **u p**
d **u d**   p **u p**
m **u d**

Lesson 2: **u d**   **u p**

_1. **A bud was in a cup.**
_2. **The pup was in mud.**

Lesson 3: **u t**   **u s**

b **u t**   b **u s**
c **u t**   G **u s**
h **u t**   f **u ss**
n **u t**

Lesson 3: **u t**   **u s**

_1. **Gus cut up a nut in a hut.**
_2. ***Put*** **a pup on the bus.**
_3. **What a fuss on the bus!**

199

Lesson 4: **u b**   **u g**

c **u b**   b **u g**
p **u b**   d **u g**
r **u b**   h **u g**
s **u b**   j **u g**
t **u b**   l **u g**
                                   m **u g**
                                   r **u g**
                                   t **u g**
                                   pl **u g**

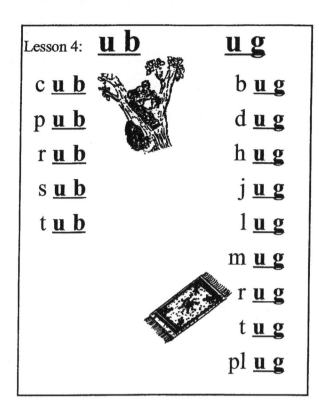

Lesson 5: **u ck**

b **u ck**   tr **u ck**
d **u ck**   str **u ck**
l **u ck**

Lesson 6: **ue**

Long u for words that end in e

bl **ue**   gl **ue**
cl **ue**   tr **ue**

Lesson 4: **u b**   **u g**

_1. **Gus had a mug in a tub.**
_2. **Lug a jug for a hug.**
_3. **Rub the plug in the rug!**

Lesson 5: **u ck**

_1. **Is a duck in the truck?**
_2. **What luck!**

REVIEW: Lesson 1 - 5:

_1. **It was us on the bus, Gus!**
_2. **Did a pup move a cup up?**
_3. **A cut bud is a dud in mud.**
_4. **It's fun to run in the sun.**

Lesson 6: **ue**

Long u for words that end in e

_1. **Is the glue blue?**
_2. **True!**

Review:

_1. Was the map in the mud?

_2. Len fed Kim the ham.

_3. Pop saw a cup in the lot.

_4. Find the ring in the den.

_5. Mom fit the mop in the tub.

_6. Peg had a pet at the vet.

_7. Ted is ten, tan and tall.

_8. Ken had fun with the top.

_9. Win a can with a big lid.

_10. The kid hid a red wig.

_11. Zip up the bag at the lake!

_12. There was mud in the jug.

_13. The boat was in the sun.

_14. Put the mum in a big cup.

_15. Did he see us run to a bus?

_16. The fox hid in the fog.

_17. I like gum for fun. Yum!

_18. I hope my coat has no spot.

_19. Was a bug in the lake?

_20. Tim hurt his rib at the pond.

_21. Hit the cork with a fork.

_22. Start the car in the dark.

_23. I hope they vote.

_24. Did Dad chat on a phone?

_25. The wall has a big crack.

_26. I saw ice melt on the ship.

_27. Ken had a friend with a key.

_28. The king had a big shock.

_29. How odd! A cod in a box.

_30. Dad had a pad for an ad.

_31. You go so slow!

_32. Did you read a cook book?

_33. Make a big tool for school.

_34. Hook the boot at the foot.

_35. A brown cow is in town.

_36. Sam ate sweet jam.

_37. Drink by the sink.

_38. There was a log on the lot.

_39. Did the vet have a pen?

_40. Glad to brag about a flag.

_41. A sack was on a big stack.

_42. The hay is for the May play.

_43. Did the clown poke a rug?

_44. Hide the pie in the bin.

_45. The hat was so flat.

_46. Dad had a nap in a cab.

_47. Tom is on a log with a goat.

_48. Get Mom to grind the pill.

_49. The light was quite bright.

_50. This is my best vest yet.

_51. Sell the fine wine now.

ABR: YOU CAN READ!

Adult Basic Reader Program

ABR Sight & Sound Guide to Word Recognition

Section 2: **Words**

Practical Literacy Units

◇ Key words and concepts needed to develop practical literacy skills.

◇ Key words in context units to expand a basic reading vocabulary.

◇ Key words in context to expand reading skills and academic concepts.

◇ Background knowledge to expand concepts and provide context.

by

Frederick J. Zorn, Ed.D.

Principal, Teacher, Adjunct Professor, Literacy Tutor

ABR: Tips for Tutors: Practical Literacy Units

- An extensive variety of important and familiar words in context units -

Tutor: Practical Literacy Units:

  _Expand a basic reading sight vocabulary.

  _Relate many already familiar words to words in print.

  _Cover a wide range of topics and concepts.

  _Help to build ability to read.

  _Help bridge education gaps.

Learner: _Will have exposure to a wide variety of words.

  _Will gain experience with a wide variety of topics.

Note: *Different type styles and formats are used for variety and interest.*

Tutor: _Select one unit per session. (20-40 minutes)

  _State topic. Give general overview.

  _Use each lesson to share and expand topic learning.

Note: *Concept development is an important supplement to word building.*

Tutor: _Read key words together. Point to each word.

  _Pronounce distinctly.

  _Relate illustrations (if any) to key words.

  _Find and use related visuals, books and supplements.

Learner: _Read and repeat words, phrases and sentences.

  _Share knowledge; ask questions.

  _Do exercises.

Goal: Exposure to new words in topic contexts.

  _Mastery of all words in a section is not key; exposure is.

  _Learn as many new words as possible and ENJOY.

~ Enjoy learning new words and concepts ~

Section 2: Words:
Practical Literacy Units
Table of Contents

The Body

Bones (skeleton): Shape body

_1. arm (upper, lower)
_2. finger
_3. foot
_4. hand
_5. jaw (chin)
_6. leg (upper, lower)
_7. rib (rib cage)
_8. skull
_9. spine (backbone)
_10. toe

Joints:

_1. ankle
_2. elbow
_3. hip
_4. knee
_5. ligament: Connects bones; holds joints together.
_6. shoulder
_7. wrist

Breathing:

_1. nose: Takes in air.
_2. lungs: Take in oxygen; give off carbon dioxide.
_3. windpipe (trachea): Takes air to the lungs.

Circulation: Moves blood

_1. artery (arteries): Takes fresh blood from the heart to the body.
_2. blood (blood vessels)
_3. heart
_4. vein: Takes used blood to the heart.

Digestion: Breaks up food

_1. esophagus: Food tube; from throat to stomach.
_2. gall bladder
_3. intestine - small, large
_4. liver
_5. mouth
_6. pancreas
_7. stomach
_8. throat: From mouth to esophagus.

Head, Neck:

__1. face
__2. hair
__3. teeth
__4. vocal cord

Muscles: Help us move

__1. muscle (600+)
__2. tendon: Attaches muscle to bones.

Nerves: Send messages

__1. brain
__2. spinal cord

Sense Organs:

__1. ear   - hearing
__2. eye   - sight
__3. nose   - smell
__4. skin   - touch
__5. tongue   - taste

Waste System:

__1. bladder: Collects, eliminates liquid wastes.
__2. kidney: Sends liquid to bladder.
__3. large intestine: Sends out solid waste.
__4. lung: Gives off carbon dioxide waste.

Other:

__1. abdomen: *stomach, intestines*
__2. chest: *heart, lungs*
__3. gland: Gives off needed chemicals in the body.
__4. reproductive organs

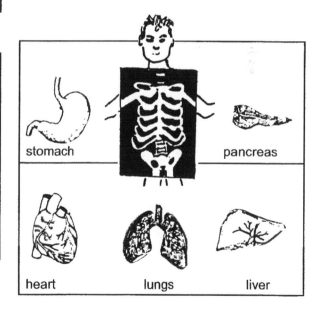

stomach   pancreas

heart   lungs   liver

Note: See Page 288 for additional Digestive System information.

Calendar Words:
Month - Season - Day - Time

Months (In Calendar Order)

1st	–	January	– 31 days
2nd	–	February	– 28 days**
3rd	–	March	– 31 days
4th	–	April	– 30 days*
5th	–	May	– 31 days
6th	–	June	– 30 days *
7th	–	July	– 31 days
8th	–	August	– 31 days
9th	–	September	– 30 days *
10th	–	October	– 31 days
11th	–	November	– 30 days *
12th	–	December	– 31 days

Months (In Alphabet Order)

__ April
__ August
__ December
__ February
__ January
__ July
__ June
__ March
__ May
__ November
__ October
__ September

*30 days has September,
April, June & November;
all the rest have 31,
except ** February, 28. (29 in a leap year)*

208

Day (In Calendar Order)

1 day / night = 24 hours (one full turn of the Earth)

_ Monday

_ Tuesday

_ Wednesday

_ Thursday

_ Friday

_ Saturday

_ Sunday

There are seven days in a week.

Day (In Alphabet Order)

1 day / night = 24 hours (one full turn of the Earth)

_ Friday

_ Monday

_ Saturday

_ Sunday

_ Thursday

_ Tuesday

_ Wednesday

4 Seasons*

_Summer	begins	June 21st
_Fall	begins	September 21st
_Winter	begins	December 21st
_Spring	begins	March 21st

*In The Northern Hemisphere

Parts of a Day

_ **morning**	– Daytime; before noon
_ **noon**	– 12 o'clock, day; Sun is overhead
_ **afternoon**	– Daytime, after Noon
_ **night**	– Earth turned away from the Sun
_ **midnight**	– 12 o' clock, night

_A.M. (a.m.)	= Midnight to Noon
_P.M. (p.m.)	= Noon to Midnight

National Observances

In Calendar Order

_1. **Martin Luther King's B' Day** – 3rd Monday in January (Day of Service)

_2. **Lincoln's Birthday** – February 12th

_3. **Washington's B'Day** – February 22nd

_4. **Presidents' Day** – 3rd Monday in February (Combines Lincoln's & Washington's B' Days)

_5. **Armed Forces Day** – 3rd Saturday in May

_6. **Memorial Day** – Last Monday in May

_7. **Flag Day** – June 14th

_8. **Independence Day** – July 4th (Date, Declaration of Independence signed)

_9. **Labor Day** – 1st Monday in September

_10. **Columbus Day** – 2nd Monday in October

_11. **Election Day** – Tuesday following the 1st Monday in November

_12. **Veterans Day** – November 11th (Originally, Armistice Day)

_13. **Thanksgiving** – 4th Thursday in November

United States: National Observances - In Calendar Order

_1. **Martin Luther King's B' Day** - January 15th * (Day of Service).
  □ Dr. Martin Luther King, Jr.
  □ An important Civil Rights leader.
  □ Used peaceful methods to fight injustice.
  □ August 28, 1963: Gave the *"I Have a Dream"* Speech (Lincoln Memorial).
  □ April 4, 1968, he was assassinated in Memphis, Tennessee.

_2. **Presidents' Day** - February 21st* -- Combines birthdays of:
  □ Abraham Lincoln - February 12th,
  □ George Washington - February 22nd.

_3. **Memorial Day** - May 30th *
  □ Honors War Dead of all American wars.
  □ Originally called Decoration Day when the graves of the Civil War dead were decorated with flags and flowers.

_4. **Flag Day** - June 14th
  □ Birthday of the United States flag.
  □ Date in 1777 when the Second Continental Congress proposed a U. S. flag: 13 red & white stripes (for the 13 Colonies) and a blue field with 13 white stars (for the 13 States).

_5. **Independence Day** - July 4th
  □ 1776: United States declared independence from Britain.
  □ Declaration of Independence was adopted and signed by the 13 Colonies.

_6. **Labor Day** - 1st Monday in September.
  □ Honors the labor movement and U.S. workers.

_7. **Columbus Day** - 2nd Monday in October.
  □ Honors explorer, Christopher Columbus.
  □ He discovered the American Continent (October 12, 1492).

_8. **Election Day** - 1st Tuesday after the 1st Monday in November.

_9. **Veterans Day** - November 11th
  □ Honors all veterans.
  □ Originally called Armistice Day.
  □ After World War I, Americans stopped for two minutes of silence at 11 a.m. on November 11, 1919 to honor those who died in World War I.
  □ Today, we honor all Veterans (former members of the Armed Forces), both living and dead, who served our country in all our wars.

_10. **Thanksgiving** - November 23rd**
  □ Celebrates the first harvest of the Pilgrims who settled at Plymouth Massachusetts.

  Note: *Observed Monday
           **Observed Thursday

Clothing: Things We Wear

To cover the chest:

_1. blouse

_2. jacket -

_3. shirt

_4. sweater -

_5. vest -

_6. undershirt (T, Athletic)

To cover the feet:

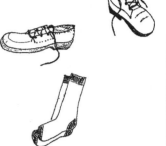

_1. boot -

_2. sandal

_3. shoe -

_4. slipper

_6. sneaker

_7. sock -

To cover the legs:

_1. jeans -

_2. pants (slacks, trousers)

_3. shorts

_4. skirt

To add to our clothes:

_1. belt -

_2. glove

_3. tie

To cover the chest & legs:

_1. coat (overcoat, raincoat)

_2. dress

_3. suit -

_4. pajama

Jewelry: Decorative metal or gems

_1. bracelet -

_2. earring (s)

_3. necklace

_4. pin

_5. ring -

_6. tie pin

_7. watch -

To cover the head:

_1. cap -

_2. hat

_3. hood

_4. scarf

- weird words -

□ boot	_ foot
□ shoe	_ hoe
□ watch	_catch

Patterns: Designs on cloth

1. Plaid:

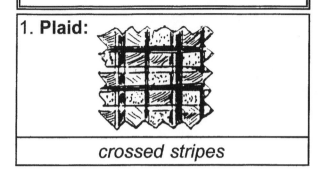

crossed stripes

2. Polka dots:

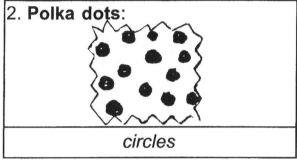

circles

3. Stripes:

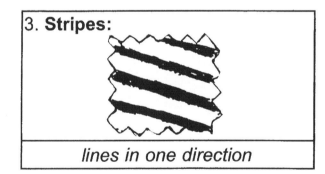

lines in one direction

4. Check:

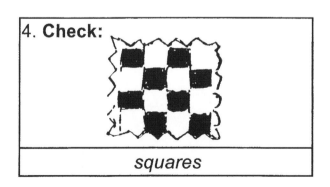

squares

Skills & *Drills*:

singular		plural
_belt	-	_belt<u>s</u>
_shoe	-	_shoe<u>s</u>
_tie	-	_tie<u>s</u>
_dress	-	_dress<u>es</u>
_watch	-	_watch<u>es</u>

weird words

_cap	-	_cape
_clothes	-	_close
_plaid	-	_said
_shirt	-	_skirt
_sweater	-	_sweeter
_vest	-	_west
_wear	-	_where

Things That Fasten

_buckle	_snap
_button	_strap
_clip	_velcro
_hook	_zipper
_laces	

Tongue twisters

- Close the clothes closet.
- Show the shoes.
- Short shirt.
- A better sweater.
- Blouse in the house.

a.

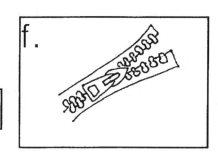

Clothing

Match:

_1. **coat**

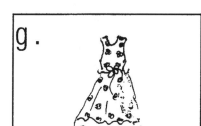

b.

_2. **dress**

_3. **hat**

g.

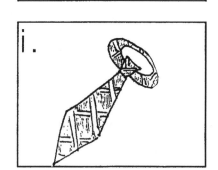

_4. **pin**

c.

_5. **shirt**

_6. **shorts**

h.

_7. **skirt**

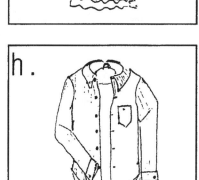

_8. **sneaker**

i.

_9. **tie**

d.

_10. **zipper**

Answers:
1 - c   2 - g   3 - b
4 - d   5 - h   6 - e   7 - j
8 - a   9 - i   10 - f

e.

j.

rainbow

Colors

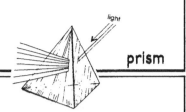
light
prism

Color:
- ☐ Sunlight is called 'white' light.
- ☐ It has all the colors of the rainbow.
- ☐ A prism is a pyramid shaped glass.
- ☐ When white light (sunlight) hits a prism, the light spreads out into all the colors of the rainbow.

- Red
- Orange
- Yellow
- Green
- Blue
- Indigo (dark violet / blue)
- Violet (light purple)

- ☐ A good way to remember the order is *R O Y G B I V.*

Name something that is:

red_____   orange_____

yellow_____   green_____

blue_____   purple_____

Mix paint:				
_1. **yellow**	+	**blue**	=	_____
_2. **yellow**	+	**green**	=	_____
_3. **red**	+	**white**	=	_____
_4. **red**	+	**yellow**	=	_____
_5. **black**	+	**white**	=	_____
_6. **blue**	+	**red**	=	_____

Answers: 1. green; 2. blue; 3. pink; 4. orange; 5. gray; 6. purple.

Compound Words

Two words together as one

_1. **afternoon**	after + noon
_2. **airplane**	air + plane
_3. **airport**	air + port
_4. **backbone**	back + bone
_5. **bedroom**	bed + room

_11. **cupcake**	cup + cake
_12. **doorknob**	door + knob
_13. **eggshell**	egg + shell
_14. **eyelash**	eye + lash
_15. **fireplace**	fire + place

_6. **birthday**	birth + day
_7. **breakfast**	break + fast
_8. **butterfly**	butter + fly
_9. **cookbook**	cook + book
_10. **cowboy**	cow + boy

_16. **flagpole**	flag + pole
_17. **flashlight**	flash + light
_18. **football**	foot + ball
_19. **goldfish**	gold + fish
_20. **grandmother**	grand + mother

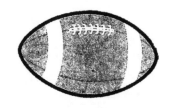

_21.	**hamburger**	ham + burger
_22.	**handshake**	hand + shake
_23.	**homework**	home + work
_24.	**horseshoe**	horse + shoe
_25.	**lifeguard**	life + guard

_36.	**pocketbook**	pocket + book
_37.	**popcorn**	pop + corn
_38.	**rainbow**	rain + bow
_39.	**rowboat**	row + boat
_40.	**sidewalk**	side + walk

_26.	**lunchroom**	lunch + room
_27.	**mailbox**	mail + box
_28.	**moonlight**	moon + light
_29.	**motorcycle**	motor + cycle
_30.	**newspaper**	news + paper

_40.	**skateboard**	skate + board
_42.	**something**	some + thing
_43.	**starfish**	star + fish
_44.	**strawberry**	straw + berry
_45.	**sunset**	sun + set

_31.	**nightgown**	night + gown
_32.	**notebook**	note + book
_33.	**oatmeal**	oat + meal
_34.	**pancake**	pan + cake
_35.	**playground**	play + ground

_46.	**toothpaste**	tooth + paste
_47.	**upstairs**	up + stairs
_48.	**wheelbarrow**	wheel + barrow
_49.	**workbook**	work + book
_50.	**wristwatch**	wrist + watch

Containers: Packaging

_1.	**bag:**	chips, flour
_2.	**bar:**	soap, candy
_3.	**book:**	stamps
_4.	**bottle:**	ketchup
_5.	**bowl:**	cereal

_16.	**package:**	hot dogs
_17.	**pitcher:**	lemonade
_18.	**pump:**	soap, lotion
_19.	**roll:**	toilet tissue
_20.	**six-pack:**	beer

_6.	**box:**	crackers, cereal
_7.	**can:**	soup, tuna
_8.	**carton:**	milk, eggs
_9.	*container:*	yogurt
_10.	**cup:**	coffee

_21.	**stick:**	butter, gum
_22.	**tub:**	margarine
_23.	**tube:**	toothpaste

_11.	**envelope:**	letter
_12.	**glass:**	milk
_13.	**jar:**	peanut butter
_14.	**loaf:**	bread
_15.	**pack:**	gum

_a.

_b.

_c.

_d.

_e.
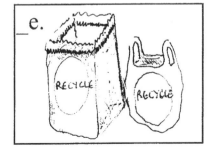

Containers:

Match: Picture & Name

__1. **bag**

__2. **bowl**

__3. **bottle**

__4. **box**

__5. **can**

__6. **carton**

__7. **cup**

__8. **jar**

__9. **pitcher**

__10. **tub**

Answers: 1 -e   2 -i
3 -g   4 -b   5 -h   6 -f
7 -d   8 -a   9 -c   10 -j

_f.
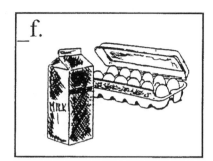

_g.

_h.
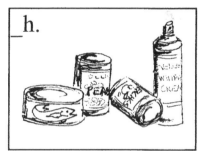

_i.
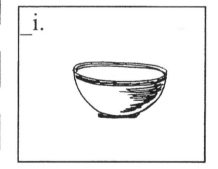

_j.

Contraction
A short way of writing two words as one.
In a contraction, an apostrophe (') goes in where the letters come out.

One Letter Missing:
Note: The letter not used in the contraction is underlined.

_1.	aren't	=	are	n<u>o</u>t
_2.	doesn't	=	does	n<u>o</u>t
_3.	don't	=	do	n<u>o</u>t
_4.	haven't	=	have	n<u>o</u>t
_5.	I'm	=	I	<u>a</u>m
_6.	it's	=	it	<u>i</u>s
_7.	we're	=	we	<u>a</u>re
_8.	you're	=	you	<u>a</u>re

Let's Read:

_1. **We're** going to the store.

_2. **I'm** here.

_3. I **haven't** eaten yet.

_4. **You're** early for your party.

_5. **Don't** go out yet!

_6. It **doesn't** look like rain.

_7. **It's** good to read.

_8. **Aren't** you ready yet?

220

Two or More Letters Missing:

To form a contraction, an apostrophe is used in place of the letters that come out.
Note: The letters not used in the contraction are underlined.

_1.	can't	=	can <u>no</u>t
_2.	I'd	=	I <u>woul</u>d
_3.	I've	=	I <u>ha</u>ve
_4.	they've	=	they <u>ha</u>ve
_5.	we've	=	we <u>ha</u>ve
_6.	you've	=	you <u>ha</u>ve
_7.	you'll	=	you <u>wi</u>ll

Let's Read:

_1. **I <u>can't</u> hear you.**   (can not)

_2. **<u>We've</u> been invited.** (we have)

_3. **<u>I've</u> eaten already.**   (I have)

_4. **<u>I'd</u> rather not go.**   (I would)

_5. **<u>You'll</u> be late.**   (you will)

_6. **<u>They've</u> been here.**   (they have)

apostrophe

Punctuation mark used is an apostrophe. (')

The **apostrophe** looks like a comma,

but it is placed at the top of the word.

It replaces the missing letters in the longer form of the word.

221

North

Northwest   Northeast

West   *   East

Southwest   Southeast

South

Direction:

left - center - right

Directions / Opposites:

_1. **above** **below**	**over** **under**

_6. narrow	thin
w i d e	**thick**

_2. **horizontal**	**vertical**

_7. short	l - o - n - g
small	**large**
light	**dark**

_3. *before - after - - next*

_8. full	empty
on	off
open	closed

_4. up	top	high
down	bottom	low

_9. in	out

_5. side	back front	side

_10.

intersect

Family: Related by birth or marriage

_1.	mother	- Your female parent
_2.	father	- Your male parent
_3.	sister	- Female child of your mother and father
_4.	brother	- Male child of your mother and father
_5.	daughter	- Your female child
_6.	son	- Your male child
_7.	aunt	- Sister / sister-in-law of your mother or father
_8.	uncle	- Brother / brother-in-law of your mother or father
_9.	niece	- Female child of your brother or sister
_10.	nephew	- Male child of your brother or sister
_11.	grandmother	- Mother of your mother or father
_12.	grandfather	- Father of your mother or father
_13.	granddaughter	- Female child of your son or daughter
_14.	grandson	- Male child of your son or daughter
_15.	sister-in-law	- Brother's wife. Spouse's sister. Spouse's brother's wife. *
_16.	brother-in-law	- Sister's husband. Spouse's brother. Spouse's sister's husband.

Spouse: Husband or Wife

_17.	cousin	- Male or female child of your aunt or uncle

Figure It Out!

_1. Your *maternal grandmother* has *3 daughters.*
How many maternal aunts do you have? _____

_2. Your *father's brother* has 3 children; your *father's sister* has 2;
How many *cousins* do you have on your *father's* side? _____

_3. Your *maternal grandmother* has 3 children;
your *paternal grandmother* has 2 children.
How many *aunts and uncles* do you have? _____

_4. Your *mother* has 3 sisters.
How many *sister-in-laws* does your father have on your *mother's*
side? _____

Answers: #1 -2 (1 is your mother);   #2 -5;   #3 -3 (1 is your mother, 1 is your father;   #4 -3

MATCH: Who Am I?   (There can be more than one answer.)

_1. Your aunt's child?   _ a. mother

_2. Your maternal grandmother's daughter? _ b. aunt

_3. Your uncle's wife?   _ c. grandfather

_4. Your mother's husband?   _ d. father

_5. Your cousin's mother?   _ e. niece

_6. Your brother-in-law's wife?   _ f. sister

_7. Your sister's son?   _ g. cousin

_8. Your father's father?   _ h. nephew

_9. Your sibling's daughter?   _ i. sister-in-law

Answers: 1 -g;   2 -a ,b;   3 -b;   4 -d;   5 -b;   6 -f, i;   7 -h;   8 -c;   9 -e.

Exercise: Write / Research:

_1. Tell 3 things about a favorite relative. _____

_2. Do you know your family history? Country:_____ State:____ City:_____
Note: *Sibling means brother or sister.*

Fruits & Nuts

Fruits are the fleshy part of plants that holds seeds. Nuts are dry fruits.

Fruits: *Have seeds*

_1. apple

_2. avocado -

_3. banana

_4. blueberry -

_13. mango -

_14. nectarine

_15. papaya -

_16. peach -

_17. pear

_5. cantaloupe

_6. cherry

_7. coconut -

_8. grapes

_18. pineapple

_19. raspberry -

_20. strawberry

_21. watermelon

_9. grapefruit -

_10. honeydew -

_11. lemon

_12. lime

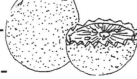
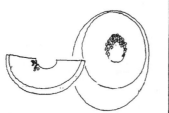

Nuts: *Dry fruits; hard shell*

_1. almond

_2. Brazil nut

_3. cashew

_4. peanut

_5. pecan

_6. pistachio

_7. walnut

226

© Frederick J. Zorn, 2014

a.

b.

c.

d.

e.

Fruits

Match: Picture & Name

__1. **apple**

__2. **banana**

__3. **cantaloupe**

__4. **cherry**

__5. **grapes**

__6. **lemon**

__7. **pear**

__8. **pineapple**

__9. **strawberry**

__10. **watermelon**

Answers: 1 -e   2 -i
3 -g   4 -f   5 -h   6 -c
7 -b   8 -d   9 -j   10 -a

f.

g.

h.

i.

j.

Fruits: Grouped by Type

Core: Seeds in the core.
_1. apple
_2. pear

Hard pit: Protects a seed inside.
_1. avocado
_2. cherry
_3. peach
Also: apricot, mango, plum, nectarine

Citrus: Thick peel, seeds.
_1. grapefruit
_2. lemon
Also: orange, lime

Grow in bunches; have seeds.
_1. grapes
Types: red, green, purple

Berries: Small, lots of tiny seeds.
_1. blueberry
_2. raspberry
_3. strawberry
Also: blackberry, cranberry

Melon: Thick cover; many seeds.
_1. cantaloupe
_2. watermelon
Also: honeydew

Tropical fruits: No seeds inside.
_1. banana
_2. coconut
_3. pineapple

~ Building Words ~

syllables
1 / 2 / 3 / 4

almond	**al** / mond
apple	**ap** / ple
avocado	av / o / **ca** / do
banana	ba / **nan** / a
cantaloupe	**can** / ta / loupe
cashew	**cash** / ew
cherry	**cher** / ry
coconut	**co** / co / nut
lemon	**lem** / on
mango	**man** / go
nectarine	nec / tar / **ine**
papaya	pa / **pa** / ya
pecan	pe / **can**
pistachio	pis / **tach** / i / o
raspberry	**rasp** / ber / ry
walnut	**wal** / nut

Note: Underlined syllable is accented.

*

Compound Words:

□ black	+ berry	=	blackberry
□ blue	+ berry	=	blueberry
□ grape	+ fruit	=	grapefruit
□ honey	+ dew	=	honeydew
□ pine	+ apple	=	pineapple
□ straw	+ berry	=	strawberry
□ water	+ melon	=	watermelon

Nuts

Match: Picture & Name

a.

__1. **almond**

__2. **Brazil nut**

b.

__3. **cashew**

__4. **peanut**

c.

__5. **pecan**

__6. **pistachio**

d.

__7. **walnut**

e.

f.

g.

Answers: 1 -e   2 -c
3 -g   4 -a   5 -b   6 -d
7 -f

© Frederick J. Zorn, 2014

Geometric Shapes: The outline of an object

circle
cir / cle

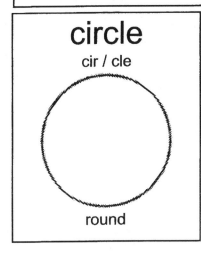

round

oval
o / val

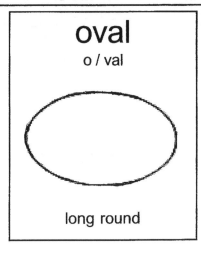

long round

sphere
(s-fear)

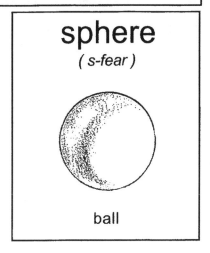

ball

triangle
tri / an / gle

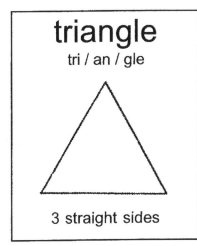

3 straight sides

right triangle

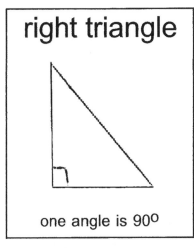

one angle is 90°

pyramid
pyr / a / mid

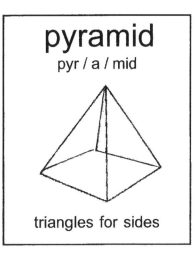

triangles for sides

square

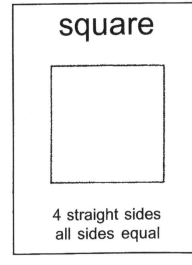

4 straight sides
all sides equal

rectangle
rec / tan / gle

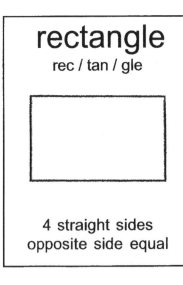

4 straight sides
opposite side equal

cube

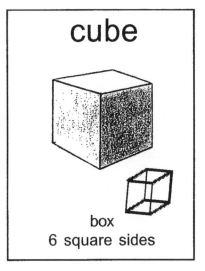

box
6 square sides

pentagon

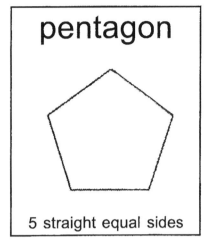

5 straight equal sides

hexagon

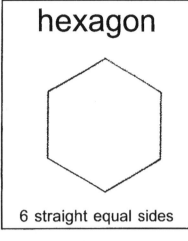

6 straight equal sides

octagon

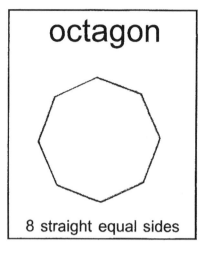

8 straight equal sides

parallelogram

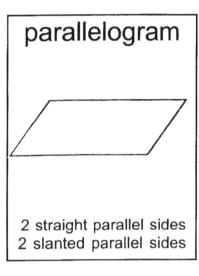

2 straight parallel sides
2 slanted parallel sides

trapezoid

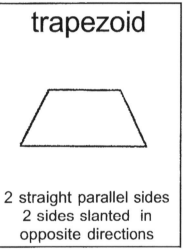

2 straight parallel sides
2 sides slanted in
opposite directions

parallel lines

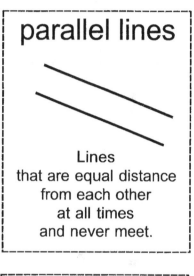

Lines
that are equal distance
from each other
at all times
and never meet.

cylinder

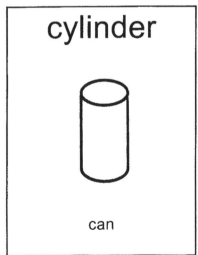

can

cone

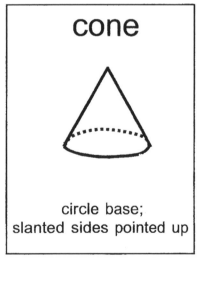

circle base;
slanted sides pointed up

angle

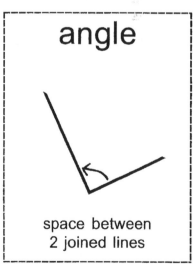

space between
2 joined lines

Greeting Card Words

Card Titles / Special Occasions:

_1. Across the Miles
_2. A Gift For You
_3. Best Wishes
_4. Best Wishes for a Speedy Recovery
_5. Congratulations

_6. For The New Baby
_7. Get Well Soon
_8. Goodbye
_9. Good Luck
_10. Good Luck In Your New Job

_11. Happy Anniversary
_12. Happy Birthday
_13. Happy Retirement
_14. Hope You're Feeling Better
_15. In Your New Home

_16. Thank You
_17. Thinking of You
_18. To Cheer You
_19. To My Valentine
_20. To The Graduate

_21. With Deepest Sympathy

Holidays:

_1. Chinese New Year
_2. Christmas
_3. Easter
_4. Father's Day
_5. Halloween
_6. Hanukkah (Chanukah)
_7. Kwanzaa
_8. Mother's Day
_9. New Year (January 1)
_10. Passover
_11. Rosh HaShanah
_12. Season's Greetings
_13. St. Patrick's Day
_14. Valentine's Day

Titles:

☐ Mr.   *Mister*
☐ Mrs.   *Misses*
☐ Ms.   *Miz*
☐ Miss   *Miss*
☐ Dr.   *Doctor* (medical or academic)
☐ Mr. & Mrs.
☐ . . . and Family

Salutations:

☐ Dear _____,

☐ To: _____

Closings:

☐ Best Wishes,

☐ Sincerely,

☐ Sincerely yours,

Envelope Address:

☐ Name

☐ Address

☐ City, State

☐ Zip Code

Good Wishes:

☐ Best Wishes

☐ Congratulations

☐ Goodbye

☐ Good Luck

☐ Happy . . .

☐ Thank You

☐ Thinking of You

Special Occasions:

☐ Anniversary

☐ Bar Mitzvah

☐ Birth

☐ Birthday

☐ Confirmation

☐ Graduation

☐ New Home

☐ New Job

☐ Promotion

☐ Retirement

☐ Sympathy

Relatives:

_mother	_father
_sister	_brother
_daughter	_son
_aunt	_uncle
_niece	_nephew
_grandmother	_grandfather
_granddaughter	_grandson
_sister-in-law	_brother-in-law
_cousin	

Homonyms:

Words that sound alike but have different meanings

_ad	_add
_ant	_aunt
_ate	_eight

_bear	_bare
_be	_bee
_beat	_beet
_berry	_bury
_blue	_blew
_buy _ by	_bye

_cell	_sell
_cent	_sent
_cents	_sense

_dear	_deer
_dew _do	_ due

_flea	_flee
_flew	_flu
_flour	_flower
_for	_four

_heal	_heel
_hear	_here
_heard	_herd
_"hi"	_high
_him	_hymn
_hoarse	_horse
_hole	_whole

_in	_inn

_made	_maid
_mail	_male
_meat	_meet
_morning	_mourning

_new	_knew
_night	_knight
_not	_knot
_no	_know

_one	_won
_our	_hour

_pail	_pale
_pain	_pane
_pair	_pear
_peace	_piece
_plane	_plain
_poor _pour	_pore

_right	_rite
_road _rode	_rowed

_sail	_sale
_sea	_see
_sew	_so
_son	_sun
_stair	_stare

_their	_there	_they're
_threw		_through
_to	_too	_two
_toe		_tow

_waist	_waste
_wait	_weight
_wear	_where
_weak	_week
_which	_witch

Homonyms: *Circle the correct word*

_1. If I'm late, please __ for me.
wait, weight

_2. I saw a __ in the park.
dear, deer

_3. Mary is a __ in a motel.
made, maid

_4. The dress is nice but so __.
plain, plane

_5. Did you __ that shirt today?
buy, by, bye

_6. Was the dress on __?
sail, sale

_7. Please don't __ the food.
waist, waste

_8. I can't __ you.
hear, here

_9. So, __ are you going?
wear, where

_10. I need to __ a letter today.
mail, male

_11. I know __ book to read.
which, witch

_12. I bought a __ car?
knew, new

_13. I'll eat __ for dinner.
meat, meet

_14. I __ two magazines.
read, red

_15. Please __ the juice!
poor, pour, pore

_16. We are going __ the store.
to, too, two

_17. I just made __ cakes.
for, four

_18. Turn ____ at the light.
right, write

Job Application   Date _____

Name: Last:_____   First:_____

Middle:_____

Date of Birth:_____ Social Security Number:____

Address:_____ Telephone: (   )_____

City_____ State_____ Zip_____

Position Applying For: _____

Education: High School:_____ Did you Graduate?____

Other:_____

Work Experience:

Employer:_____ Position:_____ Date:____

Have you ever been convicted of a crime? ___Yes   ___No

In emergency notify:_____Phone_____

Applicant's Signature_____ Date:_____

Job Application Terms: Alphabetical order

_1.	**Address:**	Place where you live and can be contacted
_2.	**Age:**	How old you are
_3.	**Applicant's:**	*of the applicant*
_4.	**City:**	Where you live
_5.	**Convicted of a crime:**	Convicted by a court

_6.	**Date:**	Month, Day, Year of the application
_7.	**Date of Birth:**	Date you were born (month, day, year)
_8.	**Education:**	Grade completed, graduate, school
_9.	**Employer:**	Person or company you work for
_10.	**Graduate:**	Have a high school or college diploma

_11.	**High school:**	Grades 9 -12
_12.	**In emergency notify:**	Person who can help you
_13.	**Name:**	Use First, Middle, Last (No nicknames)
_14.	**Other:**	Other than what is already listed
_15.	**Position:**	Job you hold or held

_16.	**Position applying for:**	Job you are here for
_17.	**Signature:**	Sign your name
_18.	**Social Security Number:**	The number on your card
_19.	**State:**	Place where you live
_20.	**Telephone:**	Where you can be reached or message left
_21.	**Work experience:**	Places you worked; positions held; dates
_22.	**Zip Code:**	Where you live

Jobs / Occupations

_1. **actor**

_2. **architect**

_3. **artist** -

_4. **athlete** -

_5. **auto mechanic** -

_6. **baker** -

_7. **banker**

_8. **barber** -

_9. **beautician**

_10. **bricklayer**

_11. **butcher**

_12. **carpenter** -

_13. **cashier**

_14. **chef** -

_15. **clergy**

_16. **computer analyst**

_17. **construction worker**

_18. **dentist** -

_19. **doctor** (physician) -

_20. **electrician**

_21. **factory worker**

_22. **farmer**

_23. **fire fighter** -

_24. **florist** -

_25. **housekeeper**

_26. **landscaper** -

_27. **lawyer**

_28. **letter carrier**

_29. **librarian** -

_30. **model**

_31. **nurse** -

_32. **optician** -

_33. **painter** -

_34. **photographer** -

_35. **plumber** -

_36. **police person** -

_37. **pharmacist** -

_38. **repairperson**

_39. **salesperson** -

_40. **secretary**

_41. **security guard**

_42. **teacher**

_43. **trucker**

_44. **veterinarian** -

_45. **waiter** -

List Others:

Mail: Letter, Envelope

U.S. MAIL

Letter: Parts of a letter

_1. *Letter Head* (if any)

_2. **sender's street address**

_3. **sender's city, state, zip code**

_4. **date**

_5. **greeting** *(Dear ____)* ,

_6. **body of letter** _____ . _____ .
_____ . _____ . _____ . _____ .
_____ . _____ . _____ . _____
_____ . _____ . _____ .

_7. **closing** *(Sincerely)* ,

_8. **sender's signature** _____

Envelope: Parts of an envelope

FROM: _1. **sender's return address**   _2. *stamp*
_____ (____)

TO:

_3. **name** _____

_4. **street address** _____

_5. **city, state, (zip code)** _____

32¢
U.S. POSTAL SERVICES

Menu
A list of food in a restaurant

Juice

_orange   _tomato
_grapefruit

Soup

_chicken   _pea
_clam chowder   _tomato
_vegetable

Salad

_lettuce
_tomato
_onion
_garlic
_hot peppers
_sweet peppers

Sandwiches (See Entree list)

_hoagies
_sandwich
_club sandwich (3 slices of bread)
_pita pocket

Dressings

_Russian   _Italian
_Vinegar & Oil
_Thousand Island

Entree

_chicken salad
_corned beef
_flounder
_ham
_hamburger
_pizza
_roast beef
_tuna fish
_turkey

Cheese

_American   _Provolone
_Cheddar   _Swiss
_Cottage cheese

ABR: YOU CAN READ! Words: PRACTICAL LITERACY UNITS

Potatoes

_French fries
_mashed potatoes
_baked potato
_sweet potato
_home fries

Vegetables

_beets
_broccoli
_cabbage
_carrots
_coleslaw
_string beans

Eggs

_omelet
_any style (scrambled, poached, soft boiled)

Bread

_rye, white, whole grain
_bagel
_roll
_English muffin
_toast

Desserts

_applesauce
_cake
_ice cream (vanilla, chocolate, strawberry)
_fruit salad
_pie
_pudding (rice, bread, tapioca)
_jello

Breakfast Menu

_cold cereal
_hot cereal
_pancakes
_waffles
_fruit (banana, peaches, blueberries)

Beverage

_coffee
_hot chocolate
_juice
_milk
_tea

WRITE IN ORDER

© Frederick J. Zorn, 2014

Numbers

Numeral		Name		Roman Numerals
0	-	zero		-
1	-	one	-	I
2	-	two	-	II
3	-	three	-	III
4	-	four	-	IV
5	-	five	-	V
6	-	six	-	VI
7	-	seven	-	VII
8	-	eight	-	VIII
9	-	nine	-	IX
10	-	ten	-	X
11	-	eleven	-	XI
12	-	twelve	-	XII
13	-	thirteen	-	XIII
14	-	fourteen	-	XIV
15	-	fifteen	-	XV
16	-	sixteen	-	XVI
17	-	seventeen	-	XVII
18	-	eighteen	-	XVIII
19	-	nineteen	-	XIX

20	- twenty	- XX	70	- seventy	- LXX
30	- thirty	- XX	80	- eighty	- LXXX
40	- forty	- XL	90	- ninety	- XC
50	- fifty	- L	100	- one hundred	- C
60	- sixty	- LX	1000	- one thousand	- M

Whole Numbers with Zeros: Note spacing of numbers

_one	=	1
_ten	=	10
_one hundred	=	100
_one thousand	=	1,000
_one million	=	1,000,000
_one billion	=	1,000,000,000
_one trillion	=	1,000,000,000, 000

Number Order Words:

_first	- 1st	_eleventh	- 11th
_second	- 2nd	_twelfth	- 12th
_third	- 3rd	_thirteenth	- 13th
_fourth	- 4th	_fourteenth	- 14th
_fifth	- 5th	_fifteenth	- 15th
_sixth	- 6th	_sixteenth	- 16th
_seventh	- 7th	_seventeenth	- 17th
_eighth	- 8th	_eighteenth	- 18th
_ninth	- 9th	_nineteenth	- 19th
_tenth	- 10th	_twentieth	- 20th

_thirtieth	- 30th	_seventieth	- 70th
_fortieth	- 40th	_eightieth	- 80th
_fiftieth	- 50th	_ninetieth	- 90th
_sixtieth	- 60th	_one hundredth	- 100th

Learning Concept: **Multiple numbers:** *x = multiplied by*

single = 1 x;   *double* = 2 x;   *triple* = 3 x;   *quadruple* = 4 x

Numbers: **Decimals**

.1	=	one tenth	=	*one out of ten*
.01	=	one hundredth	=	*one out of a hundred*
.001	=	one thousandth	=	*one out of a thousand*

Numbers: **Fractions**

1	=	one	=	*one whole*
3/4	=	three quarters	=	*three parts out of four*
1/2	=	one half	=	*one part out of two*
1/4	=	one quarter	=	*one part out of four*
1/8	=	one eighth	=	*one part out of eight*
1/16	=	one sixteenth	=	*one part out of sixteen*

Numbers: **Percent** % (per 100 parts)

1	=	100%	=	*100/100*	*one whole*
3/4	=	75%	=	*75/100*	*75 parts out of 100*
1/2	=	50%	=	*50/100*	*50 parts out of 100*
1/4	=	25%	=	*25/100*	*25 parts out of 100*
1/10	=	10%	=	*10/100*	*10 parts out of 100*
1/100	=	1%	=	*1/100*	*one part out of 100*

Roman Numerals

Symbols Used

$$I \quad = \quad 1$$

$$V \quad = \quad 5$$

$$X \quad = \quad 10$$

$$L \quad = \quad 50$$

$$C \quad = \quad 100$$

$$D \quad = \quad 500$$

$$M \quad = \quad 1000$$

$$\overline{V} \quad = \quad 5000$$

(A bar over a letter means multiplication by 1000)

Grammar: **Prepositions**

Words that start a phrase that explains a noun (or pronoun).
A prepositional phrase adds information to the main thought of a sentence.

_1. **about**

_2. **above**

_3. **across**

_4. **after**

_5. **against**

_6. **along**

_7. **among**

_8. **around**

_9. **at**

_10. **before**

_11. **behind**

_12. **below**

_13. **beneath**

_14. **beside**

_15. **between**

_16. **beyond**

_17. **by**

_18. **down**

_19. **during**

_20. **except**

_21. **for**

_22. **from**

_23. **in**

_24. **into**

_25. **near**

_26. **of**

_27. **off**

_28. **on**

_29. **over**

_30. **past**

_31. **since**

_32. **through**

_33. **throughout**

_34. **to**

_35. **toward**

_36. **under**

_37. **until**

_38. **up**

_39. **upon**

_40. **with**

_41. **within**

_42. **without**

Let's Read: **Preposition Phrases**

_1. across the street
_2. above the clouds
_3. after the game
_4. around the corner
_5. at the store
_6. before dinner
_7. by the water
_8. behind the fence
_9. below the belt
_10. between the lines

_11. by the way
_12. down the street
_13. for dinner
_14. from now on
_15. in the way
_16. near me
_17. off the wall
_18. on the floor
_19. over the rainbow
_20. past the light

_21. since he called
_22. through the door
_23. to the house

_24. under the bridge
_25. until it stops
_26. up the river
_27. with meals
_28. without strings

Let's Read: **Sentences with Preposition Phrases**.
(Underline the preposition phrase in each.)

_1. I ate a cookie before dinner.
_2. Don't go near the water.
_3. Take it with meals.
_4. John lives down the street.
_5. We ate after the game.

_6. The cat is in the car.
_7. Do you live near by?
_8. Put the box on the floor.
_9. Since he called, I will go.
_10. You go under the bridge.

_11. She waited until it stopped.
_12. We flew above the clouds.
_13. It's on a table near a wall.
_14. Do we have fish for dinner?
_15. Go to the party in the school.

Signs: Give information and direction in words and symbols.

_1. **Adults Only**
_2. **Ask Attendant for Key**
_3. **Beware of Dog**
_4. **Bus Stop**
_5. **Caution**
_6. **Curve**
_7. **Danger**
_8. **Detour**
_9. **Do Not Block Driveway**
_10. **Do Not Enter -**

_11. **Do Not Pass**
_12. **Elevator**
_13. **Emergency Exit**
_14. **End** (of) **Construction**
_15. **Entrance**
_16. **Exit**
_17. **Fire Extinguisher**
_18. **First Aid** (basic medical help)
_19. **For Rent**
_20. **For Sale**

_21. **Help Wanted**
_22. **Hospital -**
_23. **In - Out**
_24. **Information**
_25. **Keep Left**

_26. **Keep Out**
_27. **Ladies** (Women)
_28. **Lane Ends**
_29. **Loading Zone**
_30. **Lost and Found**
_31. **Mechanic On Duty**
_32. **Men** (Gentlemen)
_33. **Merge**
_34. **Miles Per Hour (mph)**
_35. **No Left Turn**

_36. **No Littering**
_37. **No Loitering**
_38. **No Smoking**
_39. **No Trespassing**
_40. **No "U" Turn -**
_41. **No Parking**
_42. **No Passing Zone**
_43. **No Turn On Red**
_44. **One Way -**
_45. **Open**

_46. **Out of Order**
_47. **Playground**
_48. **Police Station**
_49. **Post Office**
_50. **Private Property**

_51. **Railroad Crossing**
_52. **Reduce Speed**
_53. **Right Turn Only**
_54. **Road Closed**
_55. **Roadwork Ahead**
_56. **School Zone**
_57. **Slippery When Wet**
_58. **Slow**
_59. **Speed Limit -**
_60. **Stop -**

_61. **Wait For Green**
_62. **Walk**
_63. **Wet Paint**
_64. **Wrong Way**
_65. **Yield -**

Street Signs:

_1. **Avenue**
_2. **Boulevard**
_3. **Lane**
_4. **Plaza**
_5. **Road**
_6. **Street**

Highway Signs:

_1. **Expressway**
_2. **Highway**
_3. **Interstate -**
_4. **Route**
_5. **Toll Plaza**
_6. **Turnpike**

Business

_1. **Auto Dealership**
_2. **Bakery**
_3. **Bank**
_4. **Car Wash**
_5. **Check Cashing**
_6. **Dry Cleaning**
_7. **Flowers**
_8. **Furniture**
_9. **Gas Station**
_10. **Hair Salon**

_11. **Hotel**
_12. **Insurance**
_13. **Jewelry**
_14. **Laundromat**
_15. **Lottery**
_16. **Mall**
_17. **Museum**
_18. **Parking**
_19. **Pet Shop**
_20. **Pharmacy**

_21. **Real Estate**
_22. **Restaurant -**
_23. **Restroom -**
_24. **Stadium**
_25. **Theater**
_26. **Travel**
_27. **Video**
_28. **Zoo**

Syllables: Breaking words into sound parts
A sound part is a letter or letters said together.

Some words have:

1	sound part	Ex:	<u>cat</u>
2	sound parts	Ex.	<u>mam</u> / <u>mal</u>
3	sound parts	Ex:	<u>el</u> / <u>e</u> / <u>phant</u>
4 or 5	sound parts	Ex:	<u>hip</u> / <u>po</u> / <u>pot</u> / <u>a</u> / <u>mus</u>

Breaking Words Into Syllables:

<u>Consonant - vowel - consonant:</u> Can be one sound. Do Not Break:

Ex: _ <u>bat</u>   _ <u>cat</u>   _ <u>rat</u>   _ <u>man</u>

       _ <u>fox</u>   _ <u>dog</u>   _ <u>pig</u>   _ <u>cow</u>

<u>Vowel - consonant - vowel:</u> Can be one sound. Do <u>not</u> break.

Ex: _ <u>ape</u>

<u>Consonants blends</u> count as one letter. Do <u>not</u> break: (Ex: bl, nk, ph, sk, wh)

Ex: _ <u>wh</u>ale   _ wo<u>lf</u>   _ sk<u>u</u>nk   _ hor<u>se</u>

       _ el / e /<u>ph</u>ant   _ <u>ant</u>   _ bu<u>ll</u>

Break between <u>any two consonants</u>.
Break between <u>double consonants</u>.

Ex: _ wa<u>l</u> / <u>r</u>us   _ zeb / ra

 _ do<u>l</u> / <u>ph</u>in   _ mon / key

 _ chi<u>p</u> / mu<u>nk</u>   _ po<u>r</u> / <u>c</u>u / pine

 _ ka<u>n</u> / ga / roo   _ a<u>r</u> / <u>m</u>a / di<u>l</u> / <u>l</u>o

 _ hi<u>p</u> / <u>p</u>o / pot / a / mus

 _ ma<u>m</u> / <u>m</u>al   _ do<u>n</u> / <u>k</u>ey

 _ ra<u>b</u> / <u>b</u>it   _ ra<u>c</u> / <u>c</u>oon

 _ gri<u>z</u> / <u>z</u>ly   _ squi<u>r</u> / <u>r</u>el

Some <u>vowels blend</u> as one letter. Do <u>not</u> break.

Ex: _ g<u>oa</u>t   _ s<u>ea</u>l   _ b<u>ea</u>r

 _ d<u>ee</u>r   _ m<u>oo</u>se   _ sh<u>ee</u>p

Most large words break between a <u>consonant</u> and <u>vowel</u>.

Ex: _ p<u>o</u> / <u>l</u>ar   _ ti / ger

 _ bi / son   _ c<u>a</u> / <u>m</u>el

 _ b<u>ea</u> / <u>v</u>er   _ leo / pard

 _ gi / <u>r</u>affe   _ lla / ma

 _ hy / e / na   _ rh<u>i</u> / <u>n</u>o<u>c</u> / <u>er</u> / <u>o</u>s

---

Some words break between <u>two vowels</u>.

Ex: _ l<u>i</u> / <u>o</u>n

Syllables: **Dinosaurs**
Break the names into syllables by drawing slash lines.

_1. Break off the suffix - *saurus.*

_2. Break between any <u>two consonants</u>. **(Am / mo) (Sal / ta) (Al / ber / to)**

_3. Do <u>not</u> break <u>consonant blenders</u>. **(Ul / <u>tr</u>a) (<u>Ch</u>in / de) (<u>St</u>e / go)**

_4. Break between any <u>two vowels</u>. **(Pl<u>i / o</u>)**

_5. Do not break <u>vowel blenders</u>. **(S<u>au</u> / rus)**

_6. Break between a <u>vowel</u> and a <u>consonant.</u> **(Ba / ro) (Ca / ma / ra)**

Example: **U l t r a s a u r u s**

_1. U l t r a / **<u>s a u r u s</u>**

_2. U <u>l</u> / <u>t</u> r a / s a u r u s

_3. U l / <u>t r</u> a / s a u r u s

_4.-5. U l / t r a / s <u>a u</u> r u s

_6. U l / t r <u>a</u> / s a <u>u</u> / <u>r</u> u s

Exercise: **Dinosaurs**
Draw slash lines to break each dinosaur name into syllables. Pronounce.

_1. Ultrasaurus   Ul / tra / sau / rus

_2. Chindesaurus   Chin / de / sau / rus

_3. Ammosaurus   Am / mo / sau / rus

_4. Barosaurus   Ba / ro / sau / rus

_5. Saltasaurus   Sal / ta / sau / rus

_6. Albertosaurus   Al / ber / to / sau / rus

_7. Camarasaurus   Ca / ma / ra / sau / rus

_8. Stegosaurus   Ste / go / sau / rus

_9. Tyrannosaurus Rex Ty / ran / no / sau / rus / Rex

_10. Plateosaurus   Pla / te / o / sau / rus

_11. Anchisaurus   An / chi / sau / rus

_12. Dilophosaurus   Di / lo / pho / sau / rus

_13. Heterodontosaurus He / te / ro / don / to / sau / rus

_14. Pliosaurus   Pli / o / sau / rus

_15. Alamosaurus   Al / a / mo / sau / rus

_16. Scutellosaurus   Scu / tel / lo / sau / rus

_17. Elaphrosaurus   El / a / phro / sau / rus

symbols

Things used to represent words or actions.

+ plus, addition	**%** per cent; per hundred (50%)
- minus, subtraction	**#** number (# 12)
X times, multiplication	**@** at (@ $3)
÷ divide, division	**&** and

Symbols: Things used to represent words or actions

$ dollars ($5)	**<** less than; 5 < 7
¢ cents (50¢)	**>** more than; 7 > 5
* *asterisk; notes at bottom of page	**TM** trademark; identifies a product
= equals	**©** Copyright; identifies writing ownership
o degrees; temperature; 75°	

Time

Time Words: alphabet order

- _ century
- _ day
- _ decade
- _ half hour
- _ hour
- _ leap year
- _ minute
- _ millennium
- _ month
- _ season
- _ second
- _ week
- _ year

Time Words: context order

- _ morning
- _ noon
- _ afternoon
- _ night
- _ midnight

- _ o'clock
- _ quarter after
- _ quarter of

- _ sun
- _ moon
- _ revolution (Earth orbits the Sun)
- _ rotation (Earth turns on its axis)

Time

second – minute – hour

☐ **60 seconds = 1 minute**

☐ **60 minutes = 1 hour**

☐ **24 hours = 1 day**

= 1 calendar day = Day & night

= 1 turn *(rotation)* of Earth on its axis*

= From midnight to midnight

*axis: Imaginary line from N-S Pole through Earth's center about which Earth turns *(rotates)*.

day – week – month – year

☐ **7 days = 1 week**

☐ **52 weeks = 1 year**

☐ **12 months = 1 year**

- Approximately 4 weeks = 1 month
- 29 1/2 days = 1 Moon trip around Earth

☐ **365 1/4 days = 1 year**

- One Earth trip around the Sun

☐ **366 days = 1 leap year**

- Add February 29th every 4th year.

Parts of one day:

☐ **morning** - Sunrise to noon.

☐ **noon** - 12 o'clock in the day; Sun is directly above.

☐ **afternoon** - Daytime, after Noon.

☐ **night** - Sunset to sunrise.

☐ **midnight** - 12 o'clock at night; Sun is away from us.

decade – century – millennium

☐ **decade = 10 years**

☐ **century = 100 years**

1st Century	=	1	to	99
20th Century	=	1900	to	1999
21st Century	=	2000	to	2999

Note: 1st Century is not the beginning of time.

☐ **millennium = 1000 years**

noon – midnight

☐ **noon** (12 o'clock) - Sun is directly over.

☐ **midnight** (12 o'clock) - Sun is directly over the Earth's other side.

clock

◇ **o'clock** = *of the clock*

☐ **clock** - Measures time in hours, minutes and sometimes seconds.

• **Digital:** Displays numbers.

• **Mechanical:** 2 hands on a round face.
 - <u>short</u> hand points to the <u>hour</u>.
 - <u>long</u> hand points to the <u>minute</u>.

Reading a Mechanical Clock:

# on the clock:	1	2	3	4	5	6
Minutes:	5	10	15	20	25	30

# on the clock:	7	8	9	10	11	12
Minutes:	35	40	45	50	55	60

Vegetables & Grains

Plants eaten with the main meal.
Can be roots, bulbs, tubers, stems, leaves, buds, fruits, seeds, fungus, grains.

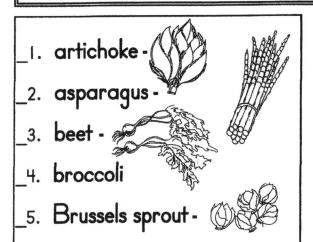

_1. artichoke -
_2. asparagus -
_3. beet -
_4. broccoli
_5. Brussels sprout -

_16. mushroom
_17. onion
_18. pepper -
_19. potato
_20. pumpkin -

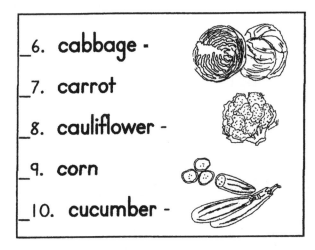

_6. cabbage -
_7. carrot
_8. cauliflower -
_9. corn
_10. cucumber -

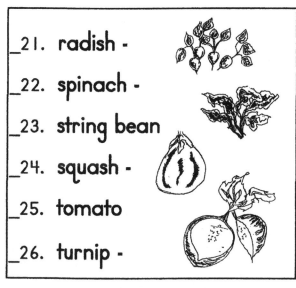

_21. radish -
_22. spinach -
_23. string bean
_24. squash -
_25. tomato
_26. turnip -

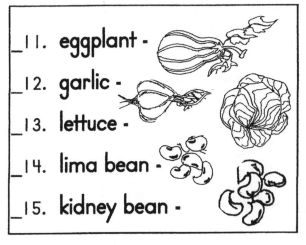

_11. eggplant -
_12. garlic -
_13. lettuce -
_14. lima bean -
_15. kidney bean -

Grains: Small hard seeds of grass plants.

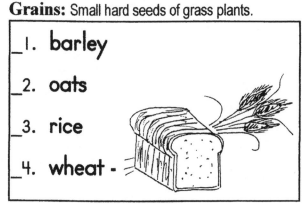

_1. barley
_2. oats
_3. rice
_4. wheat -

258

_a.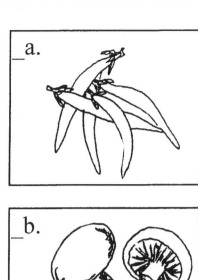

Vegetables:

Match: Picture & Name

_1. **broccoli**

_f.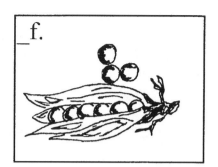

_2. **corn**

_b.

_3. **carrot**

_g.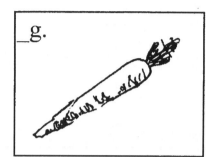

_4. **mushroom**

_5. **onion**

_h.

_c.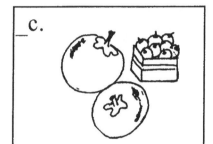

_6. **peas**

_7. **potato**

_i.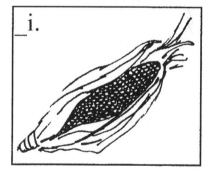

_d.

_8. **string bean**

_9. **tomato**

_10. **wheat**

Answers: 1 -e   2 - i
3 -g   4 -b   5 -h   6 -f
7-d   8 -a   9 -c   10 -j

_e.

_j.

Vegetables/Grains: Grouped

Roots: Grow underground
_1. beet   _3. radish
_2. carrot   _4. turnip

Bulbs: Underground buds; send down roots
_1. garlic   _2. onion

Tubers: Underground stems
_1. potato

Stems: Hold the leaves
_1. asparagus (shoots)
_2. celery (stalks)

Leaves:
_1. cabbage   _3. spinach
_2. lettuce
Also: escarole

Buds: Flowers
_1. broccoli   _3. cauliflower
_2. Brussels sprouts
Also: artichoke

Fruit: Has seeds (Used as a vegetable)
_1. cucumber   _4. pumpkin
_2. eggplant   _5. squash
_3. peppers   _6. tomato

Grain: Small hard seed of grasses
_1. corn   _3. wheat
_2. rice
Also: oats, rye, millet

Seeds: Beans
_1. kidney bean   _3. pea (in pods)
_2. lima bean   _4. string bean

Fungus: Feed on living matter in soil
_1. mushroom

~ Building Words ~

syllables	1	2	3	4

artichoke	**ar** / ti / choke
asparagus	as / **par** / a / gus
broccoli	**broc** / co / li
Brussels	**Brus** / sels
cabbage	**cab** / bage
carrot	**car** / rot
cauliflower	**cau** / li / flow / er
cucumber	**cu** / cum / ber
garlic	**gar** / lic
kidney	**kid** / ney
lettuce	**let** / tuce
lima	**li** / ma
mushroom	**mush** / room
onion	**on** / ion
pepper	**pep** / per
radish	**ra** / dish
spinach	**spin** / ach
tomato	to / **ma** / to
turnip	**tur** / nip
zucchini	**zuc** / **chi** / ni (squash)

Note: Underlined syllable is accented.

Vote

Voting is our most important right as citizens.

Key Words:

_1. **absentee ballot:**   If away, we can cast one before the election.

_2. **ballot:**   The official list of candidates. (Those running for office)

_3. **candidate:**   A person running for office in an election.

_4. **district:**   The local area where we vote.

_5. **elect** (ion):   We vote to choose government representatives.

_6. **Party:**   Major Political Parties: *Democrat & Republican.*

_7. **legal age:**   The legal voting age in the United States is 18.

_8. **polls:**   'Polling place;' where we are registered to vote.

_9. **primary:**   Election to choose candidates to run in the General

Election. Each Party has its own candidates.

_10. **register:**   We must sign up to vote before the election.

_11. **secret:**   We vote by a secret ballot. (By paper or voting machine)

_12. **vote:**   The way we choose our government officials.

Voter Registration: Application Sample

_1a. _New Registration _Name Change _Address Change _Change of Party

_1b. Date of Registration_____ Year_____ Party Affiliation_____

_2. Last Name_____First Name_____Middle Name / Initial_____

_3a. Address of Residence:_____City_____State_____

_3b. Municipality where you live: (city, borough, township)

_3c. County where you live:

_4. Mailing address (if different from residence)

_5. Date of Birth: _____/_____/_____ (month / day / year)

_6. Previous Registration (If applicable):

Name_____ Address_____Year___

_7. In which party do you wish to register? __Republican __Democratic

__No affiliation __Other (please state)_____

You must register with a party if you want to take part in that party's primary.

8. I HEREBY DECLARE THAT:

a. On the date of the next election, I will:

___Be a United States citizen for at least one month.

___Be at least 18 years of age.

___Have resided in this state and election district for at least 30 days.

b. I have not been confined in a penal institution for a conviction of a

felony within the last five years; and

c. I am legally qualified to vote.

AND I HEREBY AFFIRM THAT the information provided is true.

I understand this registration is the equivalent of an affidavit;

if the registration has a materially false statement, I will be

subject to penalties for perjury.

9. Place signature with full name (or mark) below.

X _____

10. Print Your Name:_____ Date: __/__/__

11. Name of person assisting in completing this application: (if any)

Name:_____

Address:_____Telephone Number_____

Note: Photo I.D. and/or official Birth Certificate may be required to register and to vote.

Building Words: **Word Enders**

Noun: Add *-s*

(Single)	(Plural)
_1. apple	apple**s**
_2. arrow	arrow**s**
_3. bed	bed**s**
_4. boy	boy**s**
_5. cat	cat**s**

(Single)	(Plural)
_6. clock	clock**s**
_7. egg	egg**s**
_8. flower	flower**s**
_9. girl	girl**s**
_10. hat	hat**s**

(Single)	(Plural)
_11. key	key**s**
_12. map	map**s**
_13. net	net**s**
_14. onion	onion**s**
_15. pig	pig**s**
_16. ring	ring**s**
_17. tie	tie**s**
_18. zipper	zipper**s**

Noun: Add *-es*

(Single)	(Plural)
_1. ax	ax**es**
_2. box	box**es**
_3. dish	dish**es**
_4. dress	dress**es**
_5. inch	inch**es**
_6. kiss	kiss**es**
_7. watch	watch**es**
_8. wish	wish**es**

Noun: Change *-y to -i*
Then add *-es*

(Single)	(Plural)
_1. bab**y**	bab**ies**
_2. fl**y**	fl**ies**
_3. lad**y**	lad**ies**
_4. sk**y**	sk**ies**

Note: **Single** = one
Plural = more than one

Building Words: **Word Enders**

Noun: Add *-er*

_1.	the cook	cook**er**
_2.	the dress	dress**er**
_3.	the help	help**er**
_4.	the pack	pack**er**
_5.	the paint	paint**er**
_6.	the plant	plant**er**
_7.	the print	print**er**
_8.	the talk	talk**er**

Noun: Add *-ful*

_1.	care	care**ful**
_2.	help	help**ful**
_3.	thought	thought**ful**
_4.	use (n.)	use**ful**

Noun: Add *-less*

_1.	care	care**less**
_2.	help	help**less**
_3.	thought	thought**less**
_4.	use (n.)	use**less**

Adjective: Add *-er*

_1.	cold	cold**er**
_2.	warm	warm**er**
_3.	new	new**er**
_4.	old	old**er**
_5.	soft	soft**er**
_6.	hard	hard**er**
_7.	light	light**er**
_8.	dark	dark**er**

Adjective: Add *-est*

_1.	cold	cold**est**
_2.	warm	warm**est**
_3.	new	new**est**
_4.	old	old**est**
_5.	soft	soft**est**
_6.	hard	hard**est**
_7.	light	light**est**
_8.	dark	dark**est**

Building Words: Word Enders

Verb: Add -ed *(Past Tense)*

(Present)	(Past)
_1. ask	ask**ed**
_2. brush	brush**ed**
_3. cook	cook**ed**
_4. dress	dress**ed**
_5. fix	fix**ed**

(Present)	(Past)
_6. look	look**ed**
_7. mix	mix**ed**
_8. pack	pack**ed**
_9. pull	pull**ed**
_10. smell	smell**ed**

(Present)	(Past)
_11. stay	stay**ed**
_12. stuff	stuff**ed**
_13. talk	talk**ed**
_14. wait	wait**ed**
_15. walk	walk**ed**

Note: **Present** = *now*
Past = *before now*

Verb: Add -d *(Past Tense)*

(Present)	(Past)
_1. care	care**d**
_2. change	change**d**
_3. decide	decide**d**
_4. smile	smile**d**
_5. tie	tie**d**

Verb: Change -y to -i
Then add -ed

(Present)	(Past)
_1. carr**y**	carr**ied**
_2. fr**y**	fr**ied**
_3. marr**y**	marr**ied**
_4. tr**y**	tr**ied**
_5. worr**y**	worr**ied**

Irregular Verbs: *Words change, not just endings*

(Present)	(Past)	(Present)	(Past)
_1. br**ea**k	br**o**ke	_11. ma**k**e	ma**d**e
_2. c**o**me	c**a**me	_12. r**i**de	r**o**de
_3. d**o**	d**i**d	_13. r**u**n	r**a**n
_4. dr**i**nk	dr**a**nk	_14. sa**y**	sa**id**
_5. dr**i**ve	dr**o**ve	_15. s**ee**	s**aw**
_6. **eat**	**ate**	_16. s**i**t	s**a**t
_7. g**e**t	g**o**t	_17. **take**	**took**
_8. g**i**ve	g**a**ve	_18. thi**nk**	tho**ught**
_9. **go**	**went**	_19. w**ea**r	w**o**re
_10. kn**o**w	kn**e**w	_20. wr**i**te	wr**o**te

Building Words: **Word Enders** / *-ion, -tion, - ian*

Verb to Noun: Add *-ion*

(Verb)   (Noun)

	(Verb)	(Noun)
_1.	act	act**ion**
_2.	attract	attract**ion**
_3.	collect	collect**ion**
_4.	connect	connect**ion**
_5.	construct	construct**ion**

	(Verb)	(Noun)
_6.	correct	correct**ion**
_7.	digest	diges**tion**
_8.	direct	direct**ion**
_9.	elect	elect**ion**
_10.	inspect	inspect**ion**

_11.	instruct	instruct**ion**
_12.	interrupt	interrupt**ion**
_13.	intersect	intersect**ion**
_14.	invent	invent**ion**
_15.	react	react**ion**
_16.	subtract	subtract**ion**

Note: *-ion, -tion, - ian* = *shun*

Verb to Noun: Drop - *e* Add - *ion*

	(Verb)	(Noun)
_1.	donat**e**	donat**ion**
_2.	educat**e**	educat**ion**
_3.	frustrat**e**	frustrat**ion**
_4.	illustrat**e**	illustrat**ion**
_5.	imitat**e**	imitat**ion**
_6.	locat**e**	locat**ion**
_7.	operat**e**	operat**ion**

Verb to Noun: Drop -*e* Add - *ation*

	(Verb)	(Noun)
_1.	combin**e**	combin**ation**
_2.	appreciat**e**	appreci**ation**
_3.	medicat**e**	medic**ation**
_4.	imagin**e**	imagin**ation**
_5.	invit**e**	invit**ation**
_6.	prepar**e**	prepar**ation**
_7.	perspir**e**	perspir**ation**

Verb to Noun: Add *-ian*

_1.	magic	magic**ian**
_2.	music	music**ian**

Functional Sight Words: Chart

Directions

___right
___left
___center
___up
___down
___above
___back
___bottom
___front
___over
___side
___top
___under
___after
___around
___before
___middle
___next
___curve
___intersect
___north
___south
___east
___west

Order

___first
___second
___third
___fourth
___fifth
___sixth
___seventh
___eighth

Colors

___red
___orange
___yellow
___green
___blue
___violet
___white
___black
___brown
___gray
___purple
___pink
___rose
___lavender
___light
___dark

Shapes

___circle
___triangle
___square
___rectangle
___parallelogram
___trapezoid
___pentagon
___hexagon
___octagon
___sphere
___pyramid
___cube
___prism
___cylinder
___solid
___flat

Time

___day
___night
___morning
___twilight
___midnight
___late
___early
___fast
___slow
___second
___minute
___hour
___half-hour
___day
___week
___month
___year
___leap year
___century

Abbreviations

___lb.   (pound)
___oz.   (ounce)
___pt.   (pint)
___qt.   (quart)
___gal.   (gallon)
___tbs.   (tablespoon)
___tsp.   (teaspoon)
___in.   (inch)
___ft.   (foot, feet)
___yd.   (yard)
___mi.   (mile)
___g   (gram)

Measures

___pound   (lb)
___ounce   (oz)
___ton   (t, tn)
___pint   (pt)
___quart   (qt)
___gallon   (gal)
___tablespoon   (tbs)
___teaspoon   (tsp)
___inch   (in)
___foot   (ft)
___yard   (yd)
___mile   (mi)
___gram   (g)
___kilogram   (kg)
___millimeter   (mm)
___centimeter   (cm)
___meter   (m)
___milliliter   (ml)
___liter   (l)
___half
___whole

Sizes

___big
___little
___wide
___narrow
___long
___short
___small
___medium
___large
___extra large

Numbers

___zero
___one
___two
___three
___four
___five
___six
___seven
___eight
___nine
___ten
___eleven
___twelve
___thirteen
___fourteen
___fifteen
___sixteen
___seventeen
___eighteen
___nineteen
___twenty
___thirty
___forty
___fifty
___sixty
___seventy
___eighty
___ninety
___hundred
___thousand
___million
___billion
___trillion

Months

___January
___February
___March
___April
___May
___June
___July
___August
___September
___October
___November
___December

Days

___Monday
___Tuesday
___Wednesday
___Thursday
___Friday
___Saturday
___Sunday

Math Terms

___add
___subtract
___multiply
___divide
___fraction
___decimal
___square root
___per cent
___algebra
___geometry
___number
___numeral

Symbols

1. $+$ (plus)
2. $-$ (minus)
3. X (multiply)
4. $\div$ (divide)
5. $\%$ (per cent)
6. $\#$ (number)
7. $@$ (at)
8. $\&$ (and)
9. $\$$ (dollar)
10. $\cent$ (cent)
11. $*$ (asterisk)
12. TM (trademark)
13. $©$ (copyright)
14. o (degree)
15. π (pi)
16. $=$ (equal)
17. $\neq$ (unequal)
18. $<$ (less than)
19. $>$ (more than)

(Note #18, 19: Small end points to smaller number. Big end to larger number. *Ex: 10 >5;* 10 is greater than 5. Ex: 5 < 10; *5 is less than 10.*)

Punctuation Marks

___period
___exclamation point
___question mark
___comma
___semicolon
___colon
___parenthesis
___quotation mark
___apostrophe

Application Terms

___Name
___Address
___Telephone
___Age
___Date of Birth
___City
___State
___Zip Code
___Previous Job Experience
___Signature
___References
___Emergency Contact

Words Of Praise

Note: You already do this, right?

_1. A-Ok!

_2. Awesome!

_3. Beautiful!

_4. Correct!

_5. Creative!

_6. Do Your Best!

_7. Excellent!

_8. Exceptional!

_9. Fantastic!

_10. Good!

_11. Good For You!

_12. Good Job!

_13. Great!

_14. How Nice!

_15. I'm Proud of You!

_16. I Knew You Could Do It!

_17. Looking Good!

_18. Nice!

_19. Nice Work!

_20. Nothing Can Stop You Now!

_21. Now You've Got It!

_22. Outstanding!

_23. Perfect!

_24. Phenomenal!

_25. Sensational!

_26. Super!

_27. Terrific!

_28. Way to Go!

_29. Wonderful!

_30. WOW!

P.S. Remember, a *smile* is worth a 1000 words

_31. You're Important!

_32. You Made My Day!

_33. You're A Winner!

_34. You're Special!

Prefix (before)	Words: Root Words	Suffix (end)

Add prefix and / or suffix to root word to make a new word.

Prefixes:
- bi -
- dis -
- ex -
- im -
- in -
- mis -
- non -
- pre -
- re -
- un -

Root Words:
1. change
2. cycle
3. feel
4. friend
5. health
6. kind
7. like
8. obey
9. pay
10. play
11. polite
12. sense
13. take
14. turn
15. thought

Suffixes:
- able
- d
- ed
- ful
- ing
- less
- ly
- ment
- ness
- s
- y

Answers: Ex:

_ bicycle   _ misspell
_ dislike   _ nonsense
_ exchange   _ prepay
_ impolite   _ recycle, return
_ intake   _ unkind

Answers: Ex:

_ payable   _ kindly, friendly
_ cycled, played   _ payment
_ playful   _ politeness
_ feeling   _ turns, senses
_ thoughtless   _ healthy
_ thoughtfulness   _ healthfully

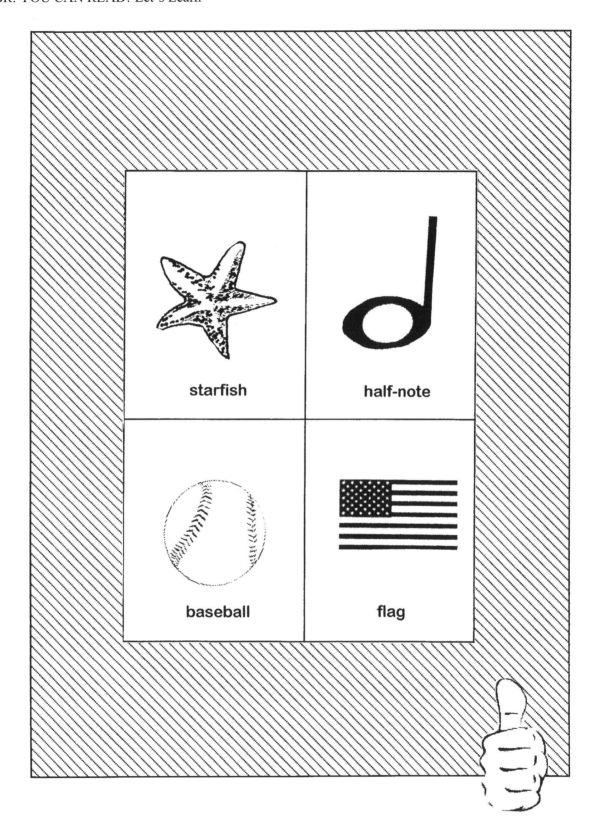

starfish

half-note

baseball

flag

ABR: YOU CAN READ!

Adult Beginning Reader Program

Section 3: **Let's Learn**

by

Frederick J. Zorn, Ed.D.

Principal, Teacher, Adjunct Professor, Literacy Tutor

ABR Tips for Tutors: Let's Learn
Topics that go beyond basic vocabulary and concept understanding.

Tutor: _Let's Learn topics are important to know.
Learner: _Will see many new words in print.
              _Will become familiar with many important concepts.

Tutor: _Select any topic.
              _Use one topic per session, 20-30 minutes.
              _Use after basic letter & word units have been done.
              _Introduce the topic in general terms.
              _Note key words. Use picture cues.
Learner: _Share knowledge as the topic is covered.

Tutor: _Read key words together. Repetition is important.
Learner: _Read sentences and other information; tutor assists.
              _Discuss as go along. Ask questions.
Tutor: _Use supplements as desired: Stories, pictures, puzzles.

Note: Let's Learn / Civics: (Pp. 335 - 358)
     _Topics about the United States are grouped together.

Goal: _Build reading skills and help fill in academic learning gaps.
           _Gain exposure to new words and concepts.
           _Mastery of all words and concepts is not necessary.
           _Enjoy new learnings.

~ Enjoy learning new concepts and words. ~

ABR: YOU CAN READ!

Adult Beginning Reader Program

ABR Sight & Sound Guide to Expanding Word Recognition

Section 3: **Let's Learn**

Beyond Basics: Expanded Vocabulary & Concepts

Food, Geography, Health/Wellness, Music, Grammar, Punctuation, Science, Sports & others

◇ To expand vocabulary in content areas.

◇ To build academic concepts and words to expand knowledge.

◇ To bridge general education gaps.

◇ To provide background knowledge to expand concepts and give context.

by

Frederick J. Zorn, Ed.D.

Principal, Teacher, Adjunct Professor, Literacy Tutor

Section 3: Let's Learn

Beyond Basics: Vocabulary & Concepts

Table of Contents

Birds: Animals with a backbone, wings, beak; lay eggs

___1. blue jay

___2. cardinal

___3. chicken – *hen, rooster*

___4. crow

___5. dove

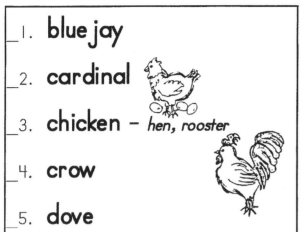

___16. peacock

___17. pelican –

___18. penguin

___19. pheasant –

___20. pigeon –

___6. duck –

___7. eagle

___8. flamingo

___9. goose –

___10. gull (seagull)

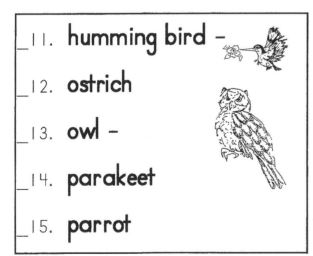

___21. quail –

___22. robin

___23. stork –

___24. sparrow –

___25. swan

___11. humming bird –

___12. ostrich

___13. owl –

___14. parakeet

___15. parrot

___26. toucan

___27. turkey –

___28. woodpecker –

Note: Pictures are not to scale.

Let's Read: # What is a bird?

_1. **A bird is an animal with a backbone**.

☐ Backbone animals are called vertebrates.

☐ Bones give an animal shape.

_2. **Birds have feathers.**

☐ Different birds have different color feathers.

_3. **Birds have wings.**

☐ Most birds use their wings to fly.

☐ Not all birds can fly.

☐ Different birds have different kinds of wings.

_4. **Birds have beaks**.

☐ A beak is hard and is used to get food.

☐ Different birds have different kinds of beaks.

_5. **Birds lay eggs in nests.**

☐ The baby bird hatches from the egg.

☐ Different birds lay different kinds of eggs.

☐ Different birds build different kinds of nests.

_6. **Birds live in all parts of the world.**

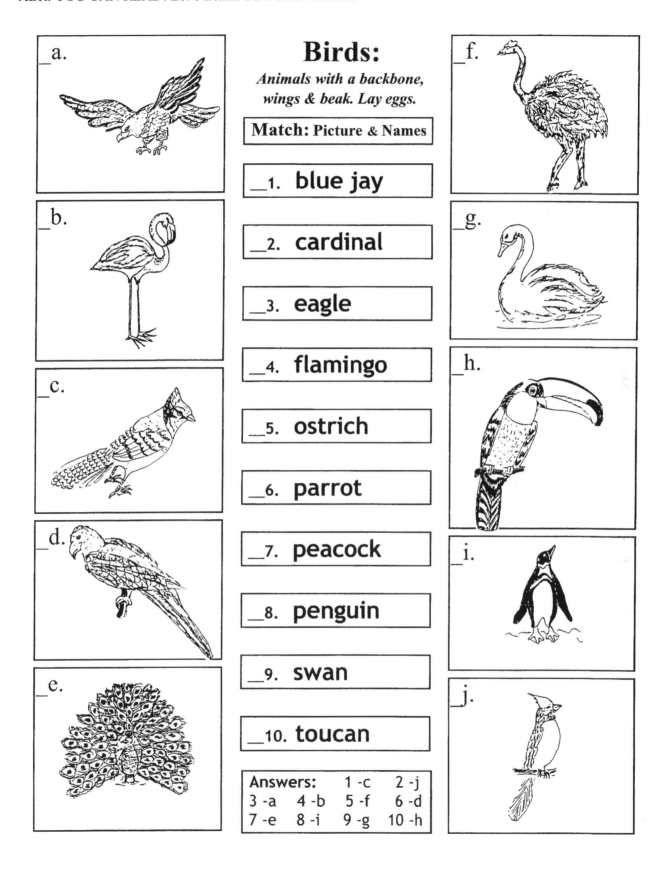

Birds:

Animals with a backbone, wings & beak. Lay eggs.

Match: Picture & Names

___1. **blue jay**

___2. **cardinal**

___3. **eagle**

___4. **flamingo**

___5. **ostrich**

___6. **parrot**

___7. **peacock**

___8. **penguin**

___9. **swan**

___10. **toucan**

Answers:	1 -c	2 -j
3 -a	4 -b	5 -f	6 -d
7 -e	8 -i	9 -g	10 -h

Buildings, Furniture, Furnishings

Types of Homes:
_1. **apartment**
_2. **condo** (condominium)
_3. **duplex**
_4. **house**
_5. **single**
_6. **twin**

Rooms in Buildings:
_1. **bathroom**
_2. **bedroom**
_3. **den**
_4. **dining room**
_5. **kitchen**
_6. **living room**

Appliances:
_1. **dishwasher**
_2. **microwave**
_3. **refrigerator**
_4. **stove**

Plumbing:
_1. **bathtub**
_2. **shower**
_3. **sink**
_4. **toilet**

Parts of Buildings:
_1. **ceiling**
_2. **closet**
_3. **door**
_4. **floor**
_5. **outlet**
_6. **roof**
_7. **shelf**
_8. **stairs**
_9. **wall**
_10. **window**

Furnishings:
_1. **curtains**
_2. **drapes**
_3. **lamp**
_4. **linens**
_5. **mirror**
_6. **ornament**
_7. **picture**
_8. **rug**

Furniture:
_1. **bed**
_2. **bookcase**
_3. **cabinet**
_4. **chair**
_5. **china closet**
_6. **desk**
_7. **dresser**
_8. **sofa**
_9. **table**

Hardware:
_1. **faucet**
_2. **hinge**
_3. **light fixture**
_4. **lock & key**
_5. **shower head**

Electrical:
_1. **clock**
_2. **computer**
_3. **radio**
_4. **telephone**
_5. **television**

Buildings:

Match: Picture & Name

__1. **bed**

__2. **chair**

__3. **desk**

__4. **lamp**

__5. **refrigerator**

__6. **rug**

__7. **shower**

__8. **sink**

__9. **stove**

__10. **toilet**

Answers: 1 -d   2 -i
3 -g   4 -h   5 -e   6 -f
7 -b   8 -a   9 -c   10 -j

check: A way to pay bills

(a) **101**

(c) <u>3-33</u>
333

(b) Date_____ 20_____

Pay to the Order of (d) _____ $_____ (e) _____

_____ (f) _____ Dollars

NATIONAL READING BANK

Memo:_____ (h)_____   (g)_____

0333''' 0033: ''' 333333 3''' 0030

(a) **101**

(c) <u>3-33</u>
333

(b) Date *August 20,* 20*13*

(d) Pay to the Order of *Better Reading* _____ (e)$*50* *50/100*

(f) *Fifty Dollars and 50/100* _____ Dollars

NATIONAL READING BANK   SAMPLE

(h) Memo: For *Reading Book*   (g) *I Can Read*

0333''' 0033: '''333333 3''' 0030

Parts:
- a. Check number: — Number in your checkbook in number order.
- b. Date: — Date you write the check.
- c. Bank ID number: — Identifies the bank when you deposit the check.
- d. Pay to the Order of: — Who you are giving the check to.
- e. Amount of check: — Write in numbers. (Ex: $25, $12); coin part in numbers /100
- f. Amount in words: — Must be the same amount as (e). Dollar part in words; Coin part as a fraction over /100.
- g. Signature Line: — Sign the same way the bank has it on file.
- h. Memo line: — What check is for.

Checks:

_1. **Checks** are used to pay for things.

_2. **Banks** pay out from your Savings or Checking Accounts.

_3. The amount of the check is written in both **numbers and words**.

_4. The check **amount** must be the same in both number and word forms.

_5. Make sure to **sign** the check.

_6. When cashing a check, **endorse** it (write your name) on the line on the back.

_7. Use the same **name** to endorse the check that is on the front.

_8. Keep a **record** of your checks and balance in the book the bank sends.

_9. Check your **balance** (total) each month to know how much is in the bank.

Writing Numbers: #1 - 19

1 = one	6 = six	11 = eleven	16 = sixteen
2 = two	7 = seven	12 = twelve	17 = seventeen
3 = three	8 = eight	13 = thirteen	18 = eighteen
4 = four	9 = nine	14 = fourteen	19 = nineteen
5 = five	10 = ten	15 = fifteen	

Writing Numbers:

#20 - 90 (by tens)		#100 - 900 (by 100's)	
20 = twenty	60 = sixty	100 = one hundred	600 = six hundred
30 = thirty	70 = seventy	200 = two hundred	700 = seven hundred
40 = forty	80 = eighty	300 = three hundred	800 = eight hundred
50 = fifty	90 = ninety	400 = four hundred	900 = nine hundred
		500 = five hundred	

Practice: Write out: Ex: $ 27 = *Twenty seven dollars.*

$235 = *Two hundred and thirty five dollars.*

_1. $76   = _____ _____ *dollars.*

_2. $777   = _____ _____ *and* _____ _____ *dollars*

_3. $12   = _____ *dollars*

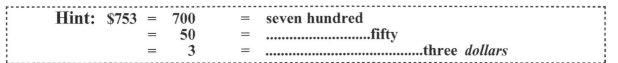

Hint: $753 = 700 = **seven hundred**
=   50 = ...**fifty**
=   3 = ...**three** *dollars*

Science: **Chemistry**
The study of the basic substances that make up all matter.

_1. **Everything is made up of matter.**

- □ **element:**   - All matter is made up of just 100+ elements.
- □ **atom:**   - The smallest form of an element.
  - Atoms have an inside (nucleus) and an outside (orbit).
  - The nucleus has protons (+); the orbit has electrons (-).
- □ **symbol:**   - Letters used to identify an element.

Element name	Symbol	Element name	Symbol
Aluminum	Al	Iron	Fe
Calcium	Ca	Nitrogen	N
Carbon	C	Oxygen	O
Chlorine	Cl	Potassium	K
Copper	Cu	Sodium	Na
Helium	He	Sulfur	S
Hydrogen	H	Zinc	Zn

- □ **Periodic Chart:**   - An organized chart of all the 100+ elements:

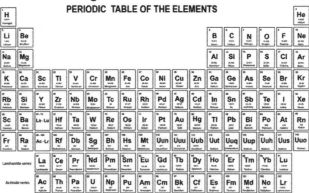

PERIODIC TABLE OF THE ELEMENTS

_2. **Elements can combine to make compounds.**

- □ **compound:**   - New substance formed when elements combine. (Ex: H_2O)

- □ **molecule:**   - The smallest form of a compound. (Made up of atoms.)

- □ **formula:**   - Shows the number of atoms of each element in one molecule of the compound:

- □ H_2O (water)   = 2 *H* atoms,   1 *O* atom

- □ NaCl   (Sodium Chloride / salt)   = 1 *Na* atom,   1 *Cl* atom

- □ $C_6H_{12}O_6$ (Glucose)   = 6 *C* atoms,   12 *H* atoms,   6 *O* atoms

- □ H_2SO_4 (Sulfuric Acid)   = 2 *H* atoms,   1 *S* atom,   4 *O* atoms

- □ CO_2 (Carbon Dioxide)   = 1 *C* atom,   2 *O* atoms

Citizenship: **Citizen:** Requirements & Privileges

To be a citizen, you must:

_1. Be born in the United States

or

_2. Be the child of a United States Citizen

or

_3. Go through the Naturalization process

A citizen can:

_1. Vote (if qualified).

_2. Live anywhere in the United States.

_3. Have a federal government job.

_4. Travel with a United States passport.

_5. Petition for close relatives to come live in the U. S.

_6. Have all the rights in the 𝕮𝖔𝖓𝖘𝖙𝖎𝖙𝖚𝖙𝖎𝖔𝖓.

_7. Run for elected office (if qualified).

Food: What happens to food in the body?
Food is broken up (digested) for the body to use.

Organs of the Digestive System:

_1. mouth

_2. esophagus

_3. stomach

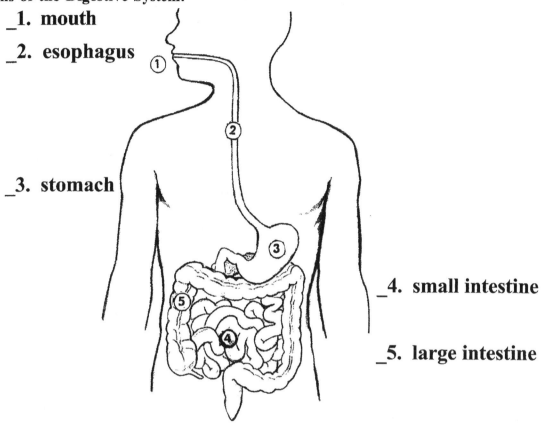

_4. small intestine

_5. large intestine

The Digestive System:

_1. In the **mouth**, we bite, chew and wet the food we eat.

_2. We then swallow the food pieces down the **esophagus**.

_3. Food goes to the **stomach** where it is partially digested (broken down).

_4. Digested food then goes to the **small intestine** for more digestion.

_5. Here, the food **nutrients** are then sent into the **blood** to all body parts.

_6. The body needs these **nutrients** to live.

_7. Unused food goes to the **large intestine**.

_8. There, unneeded waste is sent out of the **body**.

Food: Eat food that gives the body what it needs.

Food Groups: Eat from all food groups.

☐ **Protein:** Ex: **Meat, chicken, turkey, fish, beans, peas, nuts, eggs**

☐ **Grains:** Ex: **Breads, pasta, cereals, rice, oats, corn**
Note: Whole-grains have an outer coat (bran).

☐ **Vegetables:** Ex: **Broccoli, carrots, lettuce, cabbage, potatoes, cauliflower, spinach.**
Pod vegetables: Ex: **Beans, peas, soy products**

☐ **Fruits:** Ex: **Apples, bananas, peaches, pears, oranges**

☐ **Dairy:** Ex: **Milk, cheese, yogurt**

Vitamins: Needed by the body for growth and nutrition.
Must come from foods since they cannot be made in the body.

☐ **Vitamin A**   - Ex: Milk, eggs, yellow vegetables, fruits
☐ **Vitamin B**   - Ex: Egg yolk, liver, meat, vegetables
☐ **Vitamin C**   - Ex: Oranges, green leafy vegetables
☐ **Vitamin D**   - Ex: Milk, fish; sunshine
☐ **Vitamin E**   - Ex: Grains, fruits, vegetables
☐ **Vitamin K**   - Ex: Green vegetables

Weight & Calories: More calories than needed becomes body fat.
☐ Adults need 1500 -3000 calories of nutritious food a day.

Geography: **Continents, Oceans**

Continents: 7 Major Land Masses

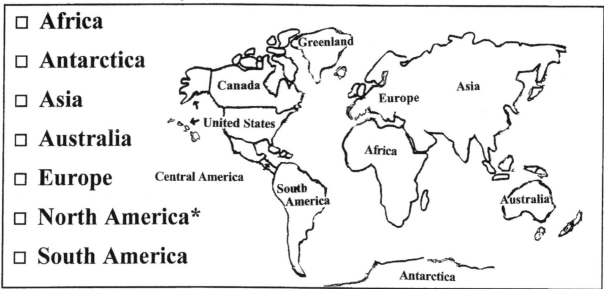

- ☐ **Africa**
- ☐ **Antarctica**
- ☐ **Asia**
- ☐ **Australia**
- ☐ **Europe**
- ☐ **North America***
- ☐ **South America**

*North America: Includes U.S., Canada, Mexico, Central America and usually Greenland.

Oceans: 5 Major Salt Water Bodies

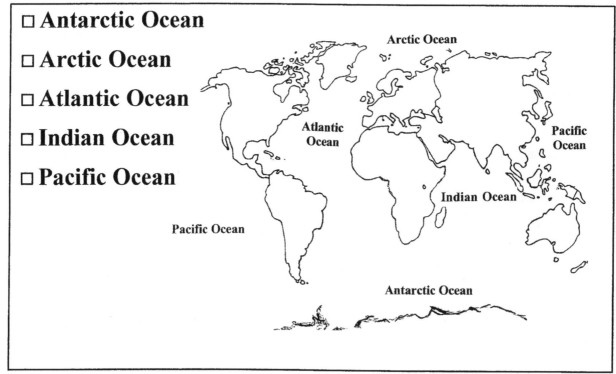

- ☐ **Antarctic Ocean**
- ☐ **Arctic Ocean**
- ☐ **Atlantic Ocean**
- ☐ **Indian Ocean**
- ☐ **Pacific Ocean**

Geography: **The United States**

_1. **Continental U.S.:**   _3000 miles E/W; 1500 miles N/S (approximate)
   _**Boundaries**:   _Atlantic Ocean *(E)*; Pacific Ocean *(W)*;
                                 _Canada *(N)*, Mexico / Gulf of Mexico *(S)*

☐ **Mountain Ranges:** _Appalachian, Rocky, Sierra Nevada, Cascade
☐ **Great Plains:**   _Between the Appalachian & Rocky Mountains
☐ **Continental Divide:**   _Formed by the highest of the Rockies
                                    _Rivers *E*, flow *E*; rivers *W* flow *W*

☐ **Major Rivers:**   _Mississippi, Missouri, Ohio, Colorado, Rio Grande
☐ **Lakes: Great Lakes:** *(N)*   _Superior, Michigan, Huron, Erie, Ontario
        Great Salt Lake *(W)*
☐ **Deserts:** *(SW)*   _Mojave, Gila, Painted Desert

_2. **Alaska**   _NW of Canada; Mt. McKinley; Yukon River
_3. **Hawaii**   _Island chain in the Pacific Ocean; 8 main islands

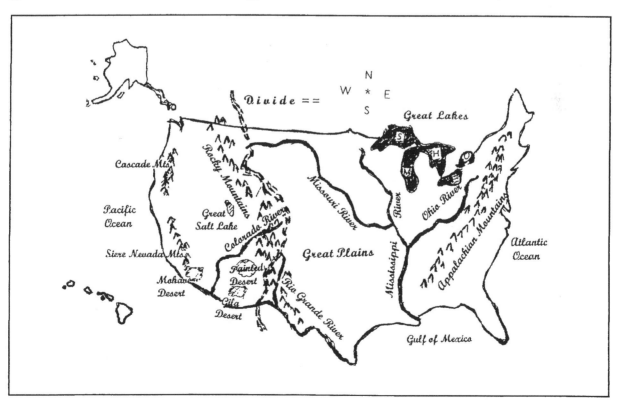

291

Grooming: Things we use to make us look better.

Grooming: Teeth, Mouth

_1. dental floss
_2. mouthwash
_3. toothbrush
_4. toothpaste
_5. tooth whitener

Grooming: Hair

_1. comb
_2. conditioner
_3. hairbrush
_4. hair color
_5. hair dryer
_6. hair gel
_7. hair spray
_8. mousse
_9. shampoo

Grooming: Shaving

_1. after shave
_2. electric razor
_3. razor
_4. razor blade
_5. shaving cream, gel

Grooming: Perspiration / Odor

_1. antiperspirant
_2. body powder
_3. cologne
_4. deodorant
_5. perfume
_6. soap

Grooming: Cosmetics

_1. blush
_2. concealer
_3. foundation
_4. lip liner
_5. lipstick

_6. eyebrow pencil
_7. eyelash brush
_8. eye liner
_9. eye shadow
_10. mascara

Grooming: Skin Care

_1. cream
_2. lotion

Grooming: **Eye Care**

_1. contact lenses
_2. contact lens solution
_3. eye drops
_4. eye wash

Grooming: **Bath Care**

_1. bath oil
_2. bubble bath
_3. soap
_4. water

_5. bath pillow
_6. shower cap
_7. towel
_8. washcloth

Grooming: **Nail Care**

_1. cuticle stick
_2. emery board
_3. nail file
_4. nail polish
_5. scissors

Grooming: **Tools**

_1. cotton balls
_2. mirror
_3. scale
_4. tissues
_5. tweezers

Laundry: **Clean Clothes**

_1. bleach
_2. detergent
_3. fabric softener
_4. stain remover

_5. hanger
_6. iron
_7. washer and dryer

Grooming: **Places**

_1. barber
_2. cosmetics counter
_3. dry cleaner
_4. hairdresser, beauty salon
_5. laundromat
_6. pharmacy

Health / Wellness: Check Up
The doctor examines you to find out how you are.

Symptoms: Sign of something wrong.

_1. **anxiety**   - mood swings

_2. **appetite**   - loss of

_3. **breathing**   - short of breath

_4. **color**   - flushed, pale

_5. **constipation**

_6. **cough**

_7. **cut, bruise**

_8. **diarrhea**

_9. **dizziness**

_10. **fever**

_11. **headache**

_12. **infection**

_13. **itch**

_14. **lump**

_15. **memory**   - loss of

_16. **joints**   - sore

_17. **movement**   - limited, uncontrolled

_18. **nose**   - stuffy

_19. **numbness**

_20. **pain**

_21. **rash**

_22. **speech**   - slurred

_23. **swelling**

_24. **temperature**   - high or low

_25. **throat**   - sore

_26. **vision**   - blurred

What the doctor checks:

_1. **blood**   (blood test)

_2. **blood pressure**   (pressure gauge)

_3. **body fluids**   (urinalysis)

_4. **body temperature** (thermometer)

_5. **bones**   (x-ray)

_6. **eyes, ears, nose, throat**

_7. **heart health**   (electrocardiogram)

_8. **heart rate**   (stethoscope)

_9. **lungs**

_10. **organs**

_11. **weight**   (scale)

Health / Wellness: **Doctors and their Specialties**

	Specialty	Specialist: Pronunciation (syllables)
_1.	**allergy**	- **al** ler gist
_2.	**birth**	- ob ste **tri** cian
_3.	**blood**	- he ma **tol** o gist
_4.	**bones**	- or tho **pe** dist
_5.	**cancer**	- on **col** o gist
_6.	**children's doctor**	- pe di a **tri** cian
_7.	**ear-nose-throat**	- o to rhi no lar yn **gol** o gist
_8.	**emotions**	- psy **chi** a trist
_9.	**eye health**	- oph thal **mol** o gist
_10.	**eye vision**	- op **tom** e trist
_11.	**feet**	- po **di** a trist
_12.	**general practice**	- **pri** mary care
_13.	**glands**	- en do cri **nol** o gist
_14.	**heart**	- car di **ol** o gist
_15.	**inside organs**	- in **tern** ist
_16.	**liquid waste system**	- u **rol** o gist
_17.	**nerves**	- neu **rol** o gist
_18.	**skin**	- der ma **tol** o gist
_19.	**solid waste system**	- proc **tol** o gist
_20.	**stomach, intestines**	- gas tro en ter **ol** o gist
_21.	**surgery**	- **sur** geon
_22.	**teeth / gums**	- **den** tist / - per i o **don** tist
_23.	**women's doctor**	- gy ne **col** o gist
_24.	**x-rays**	- ra di **ol** o gist

Note: M.D. = Doctor of Medicine   D.D.S. = Doctor of Dental Surgery
        Ph.D. = Doctor of Philosophy (academic studies)

Ice Cream: Flavors

Ice Cream Flavors: Fruits

_1. Dutch __Apple__
_2. __Banana__
_3. __Banana__ Fudge
_4. __Banana__ Split
_5. __Blueberry__ Cheesecake

_6. __Cherry__ Cheesecake
_7. __Cherry__ Vanilla
_8. Chocolate Covered __Cherry__
_9. __Coconut__ Almond Fudge
_10. __Orange__ Creamy

_11. __Peach__
_12. Rum __Raisin__
_13. Black __Raspberry__
_14. Chocolate __Raspberry__ Truffle
_15. White Chocolate __Raspberry__

_16. __Strawberry__
_17. __Strawberry__ Cheesecake

Ice Cream Flavors: Nuts

_1. Butter __Almond__
_2. Chocolate __Almond__
_3. Chocolate __Peanut__ Butter
_4. __Peanut__ Butter, PB Cup

_5. Butter __Pecan__
_6. __Pistachio__
_7. Chocolate __Walnut__
_8. Maple __Walnut__

Ice Cream Flavors: Chocolate

_1. __Chocolate__
_2. Dark __Chocolate__
_3. Death by __Chocolate__
_4. __Chocolate__ Chip
_5. __Chocolate__ __Chocolate__ Chip
_6. Mint __Chocolate__ Chip
_7. Mocha __Chocolate__ Chip
_8. __Chocolate__ Turtle
_9. Double __Chocolate__ Fudge
_10. __Chocolate__ Marshmallow

Ice Cream Flavors: Vanilla

_1. __Vanilla__
_2. __Vanilla__ Bean
_3. __Vanilla__ Fudge
_4. __Vanilla__ Peanut Butter
_5. French __Vanilla__

Ice Cream: Natural Flavorings:

_1. __Cinnamon__
_2. __Cinnamon__ Swirl
_3. __Coffee__

Ice Cream Flavors: Candy, Cake

_1. __Butterscotch__
_2. __Pralines__ & Cream
_3. __Rocky Road__
_4. __Cookie Dough__

Ice Cream Natural Ingredients: **Fruits**

_1. apple
_2. banana
_3. blueberry
_4. cherry (black)
_5. coconut
_6. grapefruit (pink)
_7. lemon
_8. lime
_9. orange
_10. peach
_11. pineapple
_12. raisin
_13. raspberry (red, black)
_14. strawberry
_15. watermelon

Ice Cream Natural Ingredients: **Basics**

_1. cream & milk
_2. egg (yolks)
_3. sugar

Ice Cream Natural Ingredients: **Nuts**

_1. almond
_2. macadamia nut
_3. peanut
_4. pecan
_5. pistachio nut
_6. walnut

Ice Cream Ingredients: **Natural Flavors**

_1. chocolate: Ground, roast Cacao seeds.
_2. cinnamon: Dried inner Laurel bark.
_3. coffee: Roast, ground beans.
_4. licorice: Black extract from the dried root of a pea family plant.
_5. maple: Boiled down maple tree sap.
_6. mint: Mint plant leaves.
_7. peppermint: Oil from a mint plant.
_8. teaberry: Wintergreen leaf oil.
_9. vanilla: Orchid family pod or bean.

Ice Cream Ingredients: **Prepared Flavors**

_1. butter pecan: Butter roast pecans
_2. chocolate chip: Small pieces of dark chocolate.
_3. mocha: Coffee & chocolate flavor
_4. peanut butter: Paste made by grinding roasted peanuts.
_5. Rocky Road: Chocolate ice cream, nuts & marshmallows

Ice Cream Ingredients: **Candy**

_1. butterscotch: Melt brown sugar, butter.
_2. caramel: Heat sugar & milk.
_3. fudge: Butter, milk, sugar, flavoring.
_4. marshmallow: Sugar, starch, corn syrup, gelatin; w/powdered sugar.
_5. praline: Pecans, almonds or other nuts browned in boiling sugar.

Mammals: Have backbones, give milk, grow the baby inside their body.

Mammals: **Primates:**

Man, ape, monkey *(tail)*.

_1. **baboon** (monkey)

_2. **chimpanzee** (ape)

_3. **gorilla** (ape) -

_4. **orangutan** (ape)

Mammals: **Bears**

_1. **black bear** -

_2. **grizzly bear** -

_3. **panda**

_4. **polar bear** -

Mammals: **Canines** (sharp teeth)

_1. **dog**

_2. **fox** -

_3. **hyena** -

_4. **wolf** -

Mammals: **Armor, Pouch, Toothless or Flying**

_1. **armadillo** (armor) -

_2. **anteater** (no teeth)

_3. **bat** (flying)

_4. **kangaroo** (pouch)

_5. **opossum** (pouch) -

Mammals: **Felines** (cat like)

_1. **cat**

_2. **leopard** -

_3. **lion** -

_4. **panther**

_5. **raccoon** -

_6. **skunk** -

_7. **tiger** -

Mammals: **Rodents**

_1. **beaver** -

_2. **chipmunk**

_3. **mouse**

_4. **porcupine** (quills) -

_5. **rabbit** (long ears) -

_6. **rat**

_7. **squirrel**

298

Mammals: **Hoof** (hooves)

Mammals: **Water** (breathe air)

_1. **buffalo** -

_2. **bull**

_3. **cow**

_4. **camel** -

_5. **deer**

_6. **donkey**

_7. **elephant** -

_8. **goat**

_9. **giraffe** -

_10. **hippopotamus** -

_11. **horse** -

_12. **llama** -

_13. **moose** -

_14. **pig, hog** -

_15. **rhinoceros** -

_16. **sheep** -

_17. **zebra** -

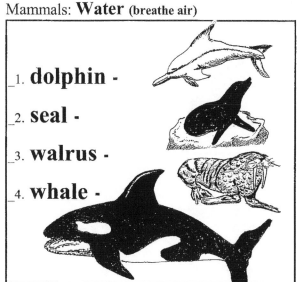

_1. **dolphin** -

_2. **seal** -

_3. **walrus** -

_4. **whale** -

Mammal Babies

_1. **calf** (cow) -
(elephant, seal, whale, hippo)

_2. **cub** (bear) -
(fox lion tiger)

_3. **fawn** (deer) -

_4. **foal** (horse) -
(mule, zebra)

_5. **kid** (goat) -

_6. **kitten** (cat) -

_7. **lamb** (sheep) -

_8. **puppy** (dog) -

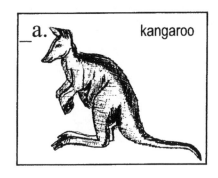

a. kangaroo

b. monkey

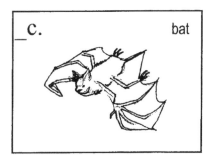

c. bat

d. cat

e. wolf

Mammals:

Match: Picture & Group

__1. **bear**

__2. **can fly**

__3. **canine**

__4. **feline**

__5. **hoof**

__6. **live in water**

__7. **no teeth**

__8. **pouch**

__9. **primate**

__10. **rodent**

Answers: 1 -h   2 -c
3 -e   4 -d   5 -i   6 -f
7 -g   8 -a   9 -b   10 -j

f. dolphin

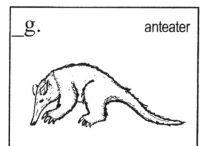

g. anteater

h. polar bear

i. donkey

j. rat

Measurement

Length: How long or wide or high something is.

- ☐   12   inches   (in)   =   1 foot   (ft)
- ☐   3   feet   (ft)   =   1 yard   (yd)
- ☐ 5280   feet   (ft)   =   1 mile   (mi)

Metric: **2.54 centimeters (cm)   =   1 inch   (in)**

Weight: How heavy something is.

- ☐   16   ounces (oz)   =   1 pound (lb)
- ☐ 2000   pounds (lb)   =   1 ton   (t, tn)

Metric: **454 grams (g)   =   1 pound (lb)**

Volume: How much space something takes up.

- ☐ 2   pints   (pt)   =   1 quart   (qt)
- ☐ 4   quarts (qt)   =   1 gallon (gal)

Temperature: How much heat something has.

F = Fahrenheit Scale      C = Centigrade Scale

- ☐ **Freezing Point** (of water)   = 32° F   = 0° C
- ☐ **Boiling Point** (of water)   = 212° F   = 100° C
- ☐ **Normal Body Temperature**   = 98.6° F

U. S. Money: Coins & Bills

Coins: Metal Money (copper & zinc) is printed by the United States Mint.
Bills: Paper Money is printed by the United States Treasury.

1¢ Penny
Abraham Lincoln
16th President

5¢ Nickel
Thomas Jefferson
3rd President

10¢ Dime
Franklin Roosevelt
32nd President

25¢ Quarter
George Washington
1st President

50¢ Half-dollar
John F. Kennedy
35th President

$1 One dollar
George Washington
1st President

$5 Five dollars
Abraham Lincoln
16th President

$10 Ten dollars
Alexander Hamilton
1st Secretary of the Treasury.
Established Bank of the U.S.

$20 Twenty dollars
Andrew Jackson
7th President

$50 Fifty dollars
Ulysses S. Grant
18th President

$100 One hundred dollars
Benjamin Franklin
Member of Continental Congress

a.

Circle; longest note

Music Symbols:

Help read, write & play music

Match: Symbol & name

e.

1/2 tone above a note

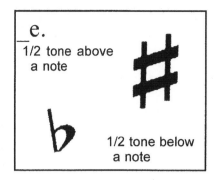

1/2 tone below a note

1. whole note

b.

Notes shown: F A C E
Full: E F G A B C D E

2. half note

3. quarter note

f.

Symbol on a staff to show notes below Middle C.

c.

Dark circle with line.

4. eighth note

5. staff

6. G-Clef (Treble Clef)

g.

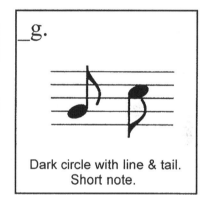

Dark circle with line & tail. Short note.

d.

Symbol on a staff to show notes above Middle C.

7. Bass Clef

8. sharp & flat

Answers: 1 -a   2 -h
3 -c   4 -g   5 -b   6 -d
7 -f   8 -e

h.

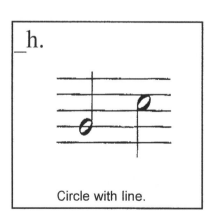

Circle with line.

Music: **Musical Instrument Families**

Brass: *Wind.* Made of brass. Press valves. Long, loud, with bell shaped ends.

☐ **French horn** -

☐ **trombone** -

☐ **trumpet** -

☐ **tuba** -

Woodwinds: *Wind.* Blow air, cover holes. Mouthpiece or thin reed that vibrates.

☐ **bassoon** -

☐ **clarinet**

☐ **flute** -

☐ **oboe** -

☐ **piccolo** -

☐ **saxophone**

Percussion: Makes sound when hit or shaken; keeps rhythm.

☐ **cymbal**

☐ **drum:** bass, snare -

☐ **gong** -

☐ **piano**

☐ **tambourine** -

☐ **triangle** -

☐ **xylophone**

Strings: Made of wood. Hollow inside. Strings vibrate with bow & when plucked.

☐ **violin** (smallest)

☐ **viola** -

☐ **cello** -

☐ **bass / double bass** -

☐ **banjo** -

☐ **guitar**

☐ **harp**

☐ **mandolin** -

☐ **ukulele** -

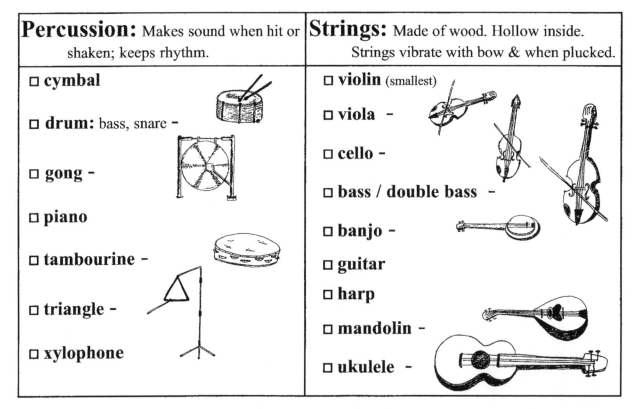

☐ **Pitch:** How high or low a note sounds. Its number of sound wave vibrations / second.
- **Higher** pitch: **Shorter** string, **shorter** air column, **tighter** string -- *More vibrations.*
- **Lower** pitch: **Longer** string, **longer** air column, **looser** string. -- *Fewer vibrations.*

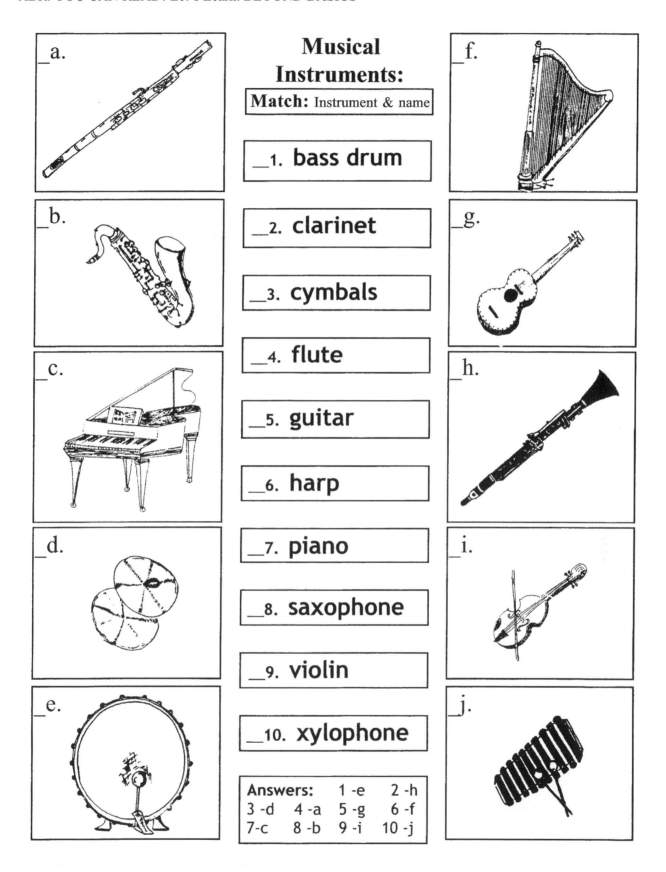

Musical Instruments:

Match: Instrument & name

__1. **bass drum**

__2. **clarinet**

__3. **cymbals**

__4. **flute**

__5. **guitar**

__6. **harp**

__7. **piano**

__8. **saxophone**

__9. **violin**

__10. **xylophone**

Answers: 1 -e 2 -h
3 -d 4 -a 5 -g 6 -f
7 -c 8 -b 9 -i 10 -j

Grammar: Parts of Speech
Each word in a sentence has a job to do.

Key Words: Parts of Speech:

_1. **noun**	_4. **verb**	_7. **conjunction**
_2. **pronoun**	_5. **adverb**	_8. **article**
_3. **adjective**	_6. **preposition**	_9. **interjection**

Parts of Speech: What each word in a sentence tells or does.

_1. **noun** — *Who or what is being talked about.* (Specific)

_2. **pronoun** — *Who or what is being talked about.* (General)

_3. **adjective** — *Describes who or what is being talked about.*

_4. **verb** — *The action that is taking place.*

_5. **adverb** — *Describes the action that takes place.*

_6. **preposition** — *Word or phrase that explains another word.*

_7. **conjunction** — *Connects words or groups of words.*

_8. **article** — *Introduces a noun.* (Specific or General)

_9. **interjection** — *Expresses strong feeling.*

_1. **Noun:** *A person, place or thing.*

Examples: **John**   **city**   **boat**

All nouns are underlined.

_1. <u>Mary</u> had a big <u>hat.</u>

_2. The <u>bird</u> built a <u>nest</u> in a <u>tree</u>.

_3. <u>Tom</u> and <u>Dave</u> went to the <u>game</u> in a <u>car</u>.

_2. **Pronoun:** *Used instead of a noun.*

Examples:	**I**	**you**	**he**	**she**	**it**
	we	**you**	**they**		
	me	**him**	**her**	**them**	

All pronouns are underlined.

_1. <u>He</u> lost the watch <u>I</u> gave <u>him.</u>

_2. Did <u>you</u> make <u>her</u> a sandwich?

_3. <u>They</u> built a big nest from the leaves <u>we</u> left <u>them</u>.

_3. **Adjective:** *Describes a noun.* (Which one? What kind? How many?)

Examples: **happy** person   **red** bird   **four** pencils.

All adjectives are underlined.

_1. The shirt was <u>red</u>, <u>green</u> and <u>blue.</u>

_2. I like your <u>new</u> hat.

_3. I ate <u>hot</u> rolls and <u>mashed</u> potatoes.

_4. The <u>new</u> team won <u>three</u> games.

     © Frederick J. Zorn, 2014

_4. **Verb:** *Shows action.* (What someone *does*, *did* or *will do*.)

Examples: John **works**   Mary **jumped**   cat **will eat**

Examples: All verbs are underlined.

_1. Betty <u>lost</u> a ring.

_2. My dog <u>is</u> big.

_3. The bell <u>rang</u>.

_4. <u>Did</u> you <u>walk</u> the dog?

_5. **Adverb:** *Describes a verb.* *(how, when, where)*

Examples: ran **quickly**   ate **yesterday**   dropped **here**

Examples: All adverbs are underlined.

_1. The children sat <u>quietly.</u>

_2. Mary talked <u>softly</u> to her friend.

_3. The ball bounced <u>high</u>.

_6. **Preposition:** *Starts a phrase that adds information or description about a noun/pronoun or verb in the sentence.* *(Acts like an adjective or adverb.)*

(who, when, where, how)

Examples: **at** the table   **from** the store   **to** her friend

---

Examples: All prepositions are underlined.   *(The prepositional phrase is:)*

_1. The children sat <u>at</u> the table.   *(at the table)*

_2. Mary talked <u>to</u> her friend.   *(to her friend)*

_3. I walked home <u>from</u> the store.   *(from the store)*

_7. **Conjunction:** *Connects words.* (Ex: *and, but, or*)

Examples: John **and** Mary   The cat ate, **but** I didn't.

Examples: All conjunctions are underlined.

_1. Betty lost a ring, <u>but</u> I found it.

_2. My dog is big <u>and</u> friendly.

_3. Did you walk the dog <u>or</u> go home?

_8. **Article:** *Introduces a noun.* (*the, a, an*)

Note: Use "an" before a vowel.

Examples: <u>the</u> boy   <u>a</u> ring   <u>an</u> apple

Examples: All articles are underlined.

_1. Betty lost <u>a</u> ring.

_2. <u>The</u> dog is big.

_3. I ate <u>an</u> olive.

_9. **Interjection:** *Expresses strong feeling.*

Examples: <u>Wow!</u>   <u>Oh!</u>   <u>Ouch!</u>   <u>Oops!</u>

Examples: All interjections are underlined.

_1. <u>Oh my</u>! Betty lost a ring.

_2. That dog is big. <u>Wow!</u>

_3. <u>Oops!</u> I rang the bell by mistake.

Parts of Speech: **Exercises:**

☐ **Underline all nouns:** *A noun is a person, place, or thing.*

_1. **Washington is where the President lives.**

_2. **Bill ate meat, potatoes, and ice cream at dinner.**

_3. **The teacher read a story from a book at the library.**

> *Answers: 1 - Washington, President   2 - Bill, meat, potatoes, ice cream, dinner*
> *3 - teacher, story, book, library*

☐ **Underline all pronouns:** *A pronoun substitutes for a noun.*

_1. **I think she is Mary's sister.**

_2. **He took the clothes to the cleaners for us.**

_3. **Do they look alike?**

> *Answers: 1 - I, she   2 - he, us   3 - they*

☐ **Underline all adjectives:** *An adjective describes a noun.*

_1. **I ate a big dinner.**

_2. **Did you see that big dog with the sharp teeth?**

_3. **I read a large book at the new library.**

> *Answers: 1 - big   2 - big, sharp   3 - large, new*

☐ **Underline all verbs:** *A verb is a word that shows action.*

_1. **Mary met friends after school.**   _3. **The team won the big game.**

_2. **I walked home, ran up the stairs, and ate dinner.**

> Answers: *1 - met   2 - walked, ran, ate   3 - won*

☐ **Underline all adverbs:** *An adverb is a word that describes the action.*

_1. **Dave smiled broadly.**   _3. **He stood tall in line.**

_2. **They quickly walked home.**

> Answers: *1 - broadly   2 - quickly   3 - tall*

Health / Wellness: **Prescription**

_1. A prescription is a note written by a doctor to a pharmacist.
_2. It tells what medicine to get and directions for taking it.
_3. A pharmacist is a specialist in knowing about medicines.
_4. A pharmacy is a place where medicines are prepared and sold.
_5. A pharmacist uses the note from the doctor to fill the prescription for you.

---

sample

Dr. G. E. Twell
98.6 Fahrenheit Degrees Road
Good Health, PA 19000
Tel: 123 - 456-7890

PRESCRIPTION

Date: _____

Patient's Name: _____
Patient's Address: _____
Patient's Tel. No: _____

Name of medication

dosage

directions

_____
Doctor's Signature

Number of Refills: ____ (*X times*)

Label Information

☐ **Name of the medicine:**   **Brand and/or generic** (no brand) **name.**

☐ **Dose:**   **How much medicine to give and when.**

☐ **Ingredients:**   **What is in it.**

☐ **Directions:**   **When, how, and how much to take.**

Prescription: Key Terms
Instructions from a doctor to a pharmacist for a medicine for a patient.

Definitions:

_1.	**brand name**	- Commercial name
_2.	**date**	- Of prescription
_3.	**directions**	- When & how to take it
_4.	**doctor**	- Who gave the medicine
_5.	**dose**	- How much & when to take

_6.	**expiration date**	- Not to use after
_7.	**generic name**	- Not a brand name
_8.	**ingredients**	- Chemicals in it
_9.	**label**	- Has directions on it
_10.	**medicine**	- You take it to get better

_11.	**O.T.C.**	- Over The Counter; no prescription needed
_12.	**patient**	- Who the medicine is for
_13.	**pharmacist**	- Prepares medicine
_14.	**symptoms**	- Signs of sickness
_15.	**teaspoonful**	- Small spoon

Types of Medications:

_1.	**antacid**	- Stops excess stomach acid
_2.	**antibiotic**	- Kills bacteria
_3.	**anti-inflammatory**	- Stops swelling
_4.	**antiseptic**	- Kills germs
_5.	**decongestant**	- Stops stuffed nose
_6.	**laxative**	- Stops constipation
_7.	**vitamin**	- Helps nutrition

Medicines: Different forms

☐ **capsule:**

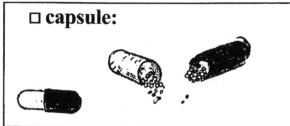

☐ **cream, ointment:**

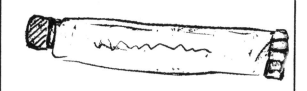

☐ **drops, liquid:**

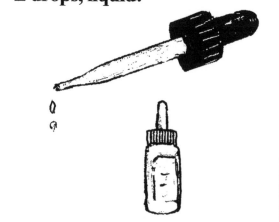

☐ **tablet, pill:**

Prescription: **Labels**
Note: Important medication information to know.

_1. **By Prescription only.**

_2. **Do not refill.**

_3. **Do not take if symptoms persist.**

_4. **Do not take on an empty stomach.**

_5. **Do not give to children under age ___.**

_6. **Do not use after _____ (date).**

_7. **For external use only.**

_8. **Give 10 drops.**

_9. **Keep in refrigerator.**

_10. **Keep out of reach of children.**

_11. **May cause drowsiness.**

_12. **Not to exceed . . . (your limit).**

_13. **1 teaspoonful every 2 hours.**

_14. **One capsule once a day.**

_15. **Shake well before using.**

_16. **Take as needed.**

_17. **Take with food or milk.**

_18. **Take 1 hour before meals.**

_19. **Take 1 tablet every 4 hours.**

_20. **Use only under supervision of your doctor.**

Punctuation

1. period
Stop. The end.

○

□ *Today is my birthday.*
□ *He is Mr. T. Green.*

2. question mark
Ends a question

?
○

□ *May we eat the cake now?*

3. exclamation point
Excited stop

□ *Wow! That's great!*

4. comma
Pause

,

□ *Mary, Sara, and Matt came to a party.*
□ *March 9, 2004*

5. semicolon
Longer pause

○
,

□ *He did not save his money; he spent it.*

6. colon
Things are to follow

○
○

□ *It had 3 colors: red, blue, and green.*

7. quotation marks

What someone is saying

66   99

☐ *Mike said,* *"Please pass the butter."*

8. apostrophe

Goes in where letters are left out
Shows ownership or possession

'

☐ *you're*   (you are)
☐ *can't*   (can not)
☐ *Matt's balloon*   (balloon of Matt)

Punctuation Answers:
1. -- store.
2. -- oranges, potatoes, -- carrots.
3. "How -- cost," --asked?
4. Wow!
5. I'm -- home. -- alone.
6. -- today?
7. --food: tuna, potatoes, slaw.
8. -- dessert, -- pie (home made).
9. "If you're coming, let's go."

9. parentheses (2)

An extra bit of information

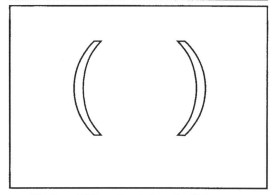

☐ *Today (Monday) is a holiday.*

Punctuate:

_1. I went to the store

_2. I bought oranges potatoes
     and carrots

_3. How much did it cost I asked

_4. Wow

_5. I m going home I will eat
     lunch alone

_6. Is the restaurant open today

_7. They have nice food tuna
     potatoes cole slaw

_8. For dessert they have
     apple pie home made

_9. If you re coming let s go

Sea Animals: Soft body with no backbone.

Two-shells:
☐ Hard shells joined in back.
☐ Protect the soft body inside.
☐ Shells open at the front.
☐ Moves by a foot that comes out.

Soft Body with Legs:
☐ Soft body.
☐ Legs that reach out.

_clam

_mussel

_oyster

_scallop

_snail

_octopus

8 legs

_squid

10 legs

Legs that bend:
☐ Soft body. Hard shell cover.

Starfish: (It is not a fish)
☐ Hard one-piece cover.
☐ 5 or more arms like the points of a star.
☐ Has a mouth in the center.

_crab

5 pair of legs that bend.

_lobster

5 pair of legs.
One pair has large claws.

_shrimp

Small.

Soft Body:
- □ Look like plants.
- □ Soft body.
- □ No shell or cover.

_coral
Live in large groups.
Form coral reefs.
Has hard outside.

_sponge
Live in large groups.
Open space inside.
Can hold water.

_jellyfish
Clear soft body.
Has tentacles (arms).

_sea anemone
Looks like a pretty plant.
Has tentacles and sticks to rocks.

Skills & Drills: Sea animals

Tongue Twister

"She sells seashells by the seashore.

prefix: **octo = 8**

octo pus　　=　*8 legs*

Key Words: **Sea animals**

_1.	clam	_9.	sea anemone
_2.	coral	_10.	scallop
_3.	crab	_11.	shrimp
_4.	jellyfish	_12.	slug
_5.	lobster	_13.	snail
_6.	mussel	_14.	sponge
_7.	octopus	_15.	squid
_8.	oyster	_16.	starfish

Syllables: Breaking words apart

_1.	cor	al		
_2.	lob	ster		
_3.	mus	sel		
_4.	oc	to	pus	
_5.	oys	ter		
_6.	scal	lop		
_7.	ten	ta	cle	
_8.	a	nem	o	ne

Explain These Sayings:
- _1. **You're a crab.**
- _2. **Move at a snail's pace.**
- _3. **Red as a lobster.**
- _4. **He's a shrimp.**
- _5. **Clam up!**
- _6. **Claw your way to the top.**
- _7. **Don't go into your shell!**
- _8. **Learns like a sponge.**
- _9. **Scalloped potatoes** (edge).
- _10. **Spineless!**
- _11. **Acts like a jellyfish.**
- _12. **A coral reef.**

Rhymes:
- □ A selfish *shellfish*.
- □ See the *sea animals*.
- □ Do *mussels* have muscles?

a.

b.

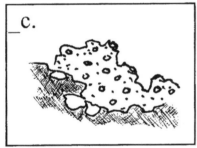

c.

d.

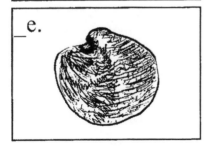

e.

Sea Animals:
Soft Body & No Backbone

Match: Picture & name

__1. **clam**
2 joined hard shells

__2. **crab**
5 pair of legs that bend

__3. **jellyfish**
No shell, clear, has tentacles

__4. **octopus**
8 legs that reach out

__5. **oyster**
2 joined hard shells

__6. **lobster**
5 pair of legs, one w/ claws

__7. **scallop**
Fan shape shells with ridges

__8. **snail**
1 hard shell. Moves slowly

__9. **sponge**
Soft. Holds water

__10. **starfish**
Hard cover, 5 points. Not a fish

Answers: 1 -e   2 -i
3 -g   4 -b   5 -h   6 -f
7 -d   8 -a   9 -c   10 -j

f.

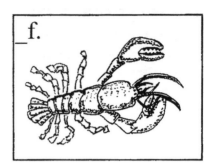

g.

h.

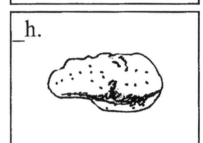

i.

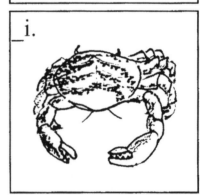

j.

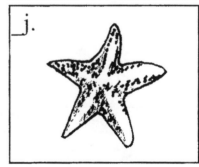

Solar System: The Sun and 9 planets

_1. Planets moving around a sun make up a solar system.

_2. A sun is a star.

_3. A star gives off heat and light.

_4. Our Solar System has a sun and 9 planets.

_5. The Sun is the center of our Solar System.

_6. Our Sun gives off heat and light to the planets.

_7. Each planet moves around the Sun in its own path (orbit).

_8. Earth is one of the 9 planets moving around the Sun.

_9. The 9 planets in order of distance from the Sun are:

Planet	Facts	Pronunciation
_1. **Mercury**	- Closest planet to the Sun	(**Mer** cu ry)
_2. **Venus**	- Second planet from the Sun	(**Ve** nus)
_3. **Earth**	- Our planet, 3rd from the Sun	(**Earth**)
_4. **Mars**	- 4th planet from the Sun	(**Mars**)
_5. **Jupiter**	- The largest planet	(**Ju** pi ter)
_6. **Saturn**	- Has rings around it	(**Sat** urn)
_7. **Uranus**		(**U** ran us)
_8. **Neptune**		(**Nep** tune)
_9. **Pluto**	- Farthest from the Sun	(**Plu** to)

- and that's our Solar System.

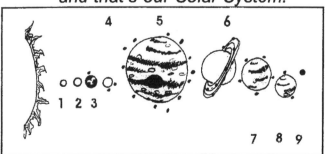

Grammar: **Sentence:** Subject and Predicate
A group of words that make a complete thought

Key Words: Grammar

_sentence	
_subject	**_predicate**

_1. *Sentence:*   A group of words that makes a complete thought.

_2. *Subject:*   The person or thing a sentence is about.

_3. *Predicate:*   What the subject is doing in a sentence.

Sentence:

_1. A <u>sentence</u> is used when we read, write and speak.

_2. A <u>sentence</u> gives us a complete thought.

_3. A complete thought has who or what the <u>sentence</u> is about <u>and</u> what they are doing.

_4. The <u>subject</u> of a <u>sentence</u> is *who or what the <u>sentence</u> is about.*

_5. A <u>subject</u> has a <u>noun</u> or a <u>pronoun</u>.

_6. The <u>predicate</u> is *what the <u>subject</u> is doing.*

_7. A <u>predicate</u> has a <u>verb</u>.

A sentence has two parts: Subject and Predicate

> ***Subject:*** The name of the person, place or thing the sentence is about.
> Subjects have nouns or pronouns.
>
> Examples: The **<u>house</u>** was big.   **<u>Mary</u>** made a hat.

All simple subjects are underlined.

1. The <u>desk</u> is in the room

2. The <u>man</u> rode a bike.

3. <u>It</u> tastes good.

> ***Predicate:*** The action the subject does, did or will do.
> Predicates have verbs.
>
> Examples: The house **<u>was</u>** big.   The bird **<u>built</u>** a nest.

All simple predicates are underlined.

1. He <u>bought</u> a big house.

2. Mary <u>made</u> a hat with flowers on it.

3. The bird <u>built</u> a nest in a large oak tree.

4. Tom and Dave <u>went</u> to the game.

Exercise: *Underline* the simple subject. *Double underline* the simple predicate.

1. The man rode a blue bike to the park by the lake.

2. Mary wore a big hat with red and white flowers on it.

3. I bought three bags of groceries.

Answers: 1 - man; rode.   2 - Mary; wore.   3 - I; bought

Sports: Games Played for Entertainment or Competition

Key Words: **Sports Games**

_1. Baseball -
_2. Basketball
_3. Bowling
_4. Football
_5. Golf
_6. Ice Hockey
_7. Soccer
_8. Table Tennis (Ping-Pong)
_9. Tennis
_10. Volleyball

Key Words: **Places:**

_1. alley (lane)	_11. gutter
_2. backboard	_12. hole
_3. base	_13. line
_4. basket	_14. mound
_5. court	_15. net
_6. diamond	_16. plate
_7. fairway	_17. rink
_8. fence	_18. table
_9. field	_19. tee
_10. goal	_20. zone

Key Words: **Things used:**

_1. ball	_6. paddle
_2. bat	_7. pin
_3. club	_8. puck
_4. glove	_9. racket
_5. hand	_10. stick

Key Words: **Actions**

_1. block	_10. pitch
_2. catch	_11. roll
_3. dribble	_12. serve
_4. drive	_13. shoot
_5. fumble	_14. slide
_6. hit	_15. swing
_7. jump	_16. tackle
_8. kick	_17. throw
_9. pass	_18. volley

Key Words: **Scoring**

_1. Down	_7. Safe
_2. Foul	_8. Spare
_3. Out	_9. Strike
_4. Penalty	_10. Stroke
_5. Point	_11. Walk
_6. Run	

Weird Words

one	-	zone
foot	-	boot
pong	-	song
putt	-	put

Balls: In Sports

Match: Picture & name

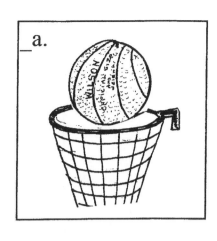

__1. **baseball**

__2. **basketball**

__3. **bowling ball**

__4. **football**

__5. **golf ball**

__6. ping-pong ball

__7. **soccer ball**

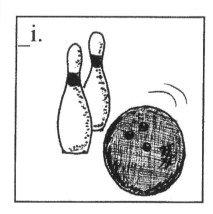

__8. **tennis ball**

__9. **volleyball**

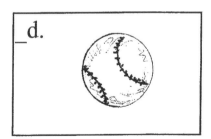

Answers: 1 -d   2 -a
3 -i   4 -b   5 -h   6 -g
7 -c   8 -e   9 -f

Table Setting: The correct way

Key Words:

_1. plate:

Dinner (Center)	**Salad**	**Bread & Butter** (upper Left)

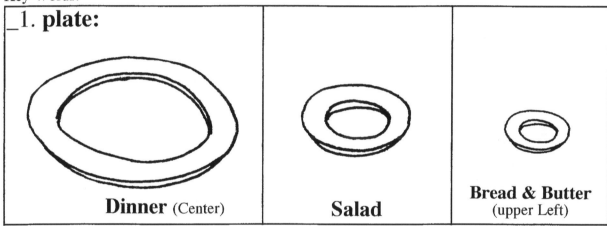

_2. Silverware

Fork (on Left)	**Spoon** (on Right)	**Knife** (on Right)
Salad (outside) / **Dinner** (next to plate)	**Soup** / **teaspoon**	(next to plate, cutting edge in)

_3. **Beverage:**		
Glass	**Cup & Saucer**	**Wine glass**

$\underline{F}or$ $\underline{P}eople$ $\underline{K}nowing$ $\underline{S}etups$

It really is a breeze.

$\underline{F}orks$ - $\underline{P}late$ - $\underline{K}nife$ - $\underline{S}poons$

~ and you'll set up with ease.

To Do:
- Serve from the left.
- Cut as you eat, not all at once.
- Silverware: Place by use from the outside in.
    - *Left:*   Forks
    - *Right:*   Knife, Spoons
- Dinner Plate: *Center*
- Salad Plate: *Left of forks*
- Bread Plate: *Above the forks with butter knife across*
- Glasses, Cup & Saucer: *Upper Right*

Napkin: *Choices*
- Folded, Left of the forks
- Folded, Center top of the dinner plate
- Under the forks
- Rolled in a napkin ring

Teeth

Teeth: Cut, chew and grind food:

☐ We bite and chew our food.

☐ Teeth cut and grind food.

☐ This makes food small enough to swallow.

☐ Adults have 32 teeth (16 in each jaw, upper and lower).

Teeth: 4 different kinds

☐ Each kind of tooth has its own job and location in the mouth.

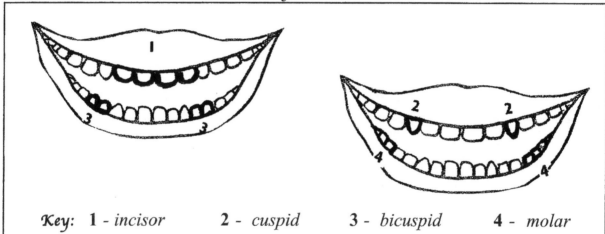

Key: **1** - *incisor*   **2** - *cuspid*   **3** - *bicuspid*   **4** - *molar*

Kind	Description	Number / mouth	Number / jaw
_1. **incisor:**	_Flat front tooth *Cuts food*	8	4
_2. **cuspid:**	_Sharp one-pointed tooth *Canine or eye tooth*	4	2
_3. **bicuspid:**	_Two-pointed tooth *Premolars*	8	4
_4. **molar:**	_First, second, third molar *3rd molar is called the Wisdom Tooth*	12	6

Tooth: Three Main Parts:

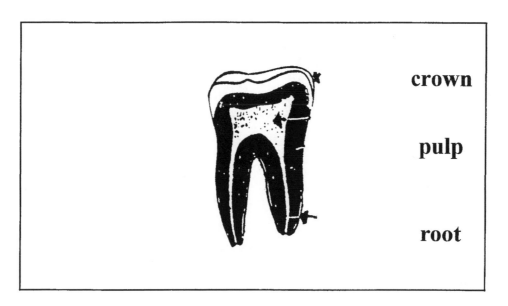

The three main parts of a tooth are:

☐ **crown**:   _Top outside; hard enamel.   *- Protects the inside.*

☐ **pulp**:   _Soft inside of tooth.   *- Has nerves, blood vessels.*

☐ **root**:   _Bottom of tooth; long.   *- Goes into the gum.*

Questions:

_1. Adults have _____ teeth in their mouth.

_2. The top part of a tooth is called the _____ .

_3. Teeth are held in the gum by the _____ .

_4. Incisor means to _____ . *(Hint: incision)*

_5. The third molar is sometimes called the _____ tooth.

Answers: *#1 - 32;   #2 - crown;   #3- root;   #4- cut;   #5 - wisdom.*

Tools: **6 simple machines:** Help us do work

Key Words:

_1. incline   _3. pulley   _5. wedge

_2. lever   _4. screw   _6. wheel & axle

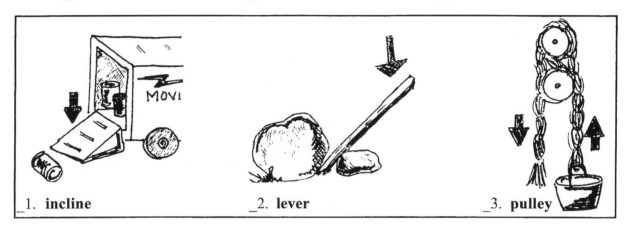

_1. **incline**   _2. **lever**   _3. **pulley**

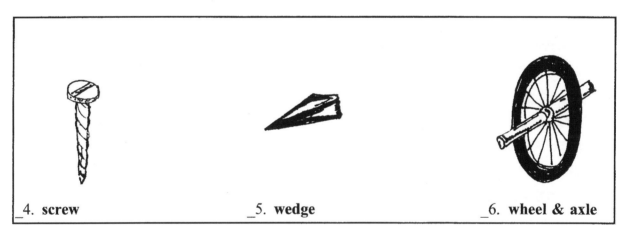

_4. **screw**   _5. **wedge**   _6. **wheel & axle**

Let's Read:

_1. There are 6 simple machines.

_2. A simple machine helps us do *'work.'*

_3. Other machines are made up of one or more of these 6 simple machines.

_4. Machines help us do some things easier.

_5. Machines help us do some things we could not do without them.

_6. *'Work'* (W) in science is the amount of force (F) it takes to move an object over a certain distance (d). *The formula is:* $W = F \times d$

Tools: Help us make or do things

_1. **drill** - Makes holes.

_2. **file** - Smoothes out wood or metal.

_3. **hammer** - Hits nails into wood.

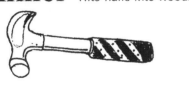

_4. **nail** - Pointed, holds wood together.

_5. **pliers** - Pull out nails.

_6. **saw** - Cuts wood.

_7. **scissors** - Cuts paper, cloth, or metal.

_8. **screw** - Has slants. (Holds wood together.)

_9. **screwdriver** - Forces screws into wood.

_10. **vise** - Holds wood or metal.

_11. **wrench** - Holds pipes.

The 50 United States

Numbers refer to the Alphabet Listing of States.

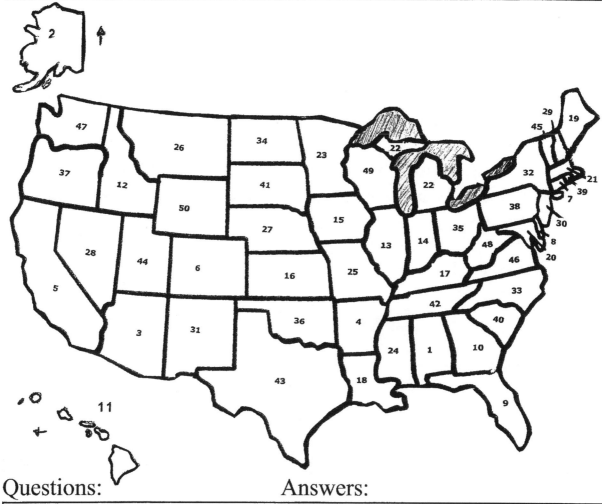

Questions:

Answers:

_ 1. Number of states? — 50

_ 2. 49th & 50th States? — Alaska (49th); Hawaii (50th)

_ 3. Admitted in ___ ? — 1959

_ 4. Continental U.S. is? — The 48 connected states

_ 5. It has __ Time Zones? — 4 (Eastern, Central, Mountain, Western)

_ 6. The capital of the U.S. is? — Washington, D.C. (District of Columbia)

_ 7. Is it part of a state? — No; it is its own Federal District

_ 8. There were __ original states? — 13 (Had been the 13 Colonies)

_ 9. State powers are? — All those not in the Constitution

_ 10. U.S. territories are? - Guam (W. Pacific); Puerto Rico, Virgin Islands (Caribbean)

50 United States: Alphabetical + U.S. Territories

_1. Alabama

_2. Alaska

_3. Arizona

_4. Arkansas

_5. California

_6. Colorado

_7. Connecticut

_8. Delaware

_9. Florida

_10. Georgia

_11. Hawaii

_12. Idaho

_13. Illinois

_14. Indiana

_15. Iowa

_16. Kansas

_17. Kentucky

_18. Louisiana

_19. Maine

_20. Maryland

_21. Massachusetts

_22. Michigan

_23. Minnesota

_24. Mississippi

_25. Missouri

_26. Montana

_27. Nebraska

_28. Nevada

_29. New Hampshire

_30. New Jersey

_31. New Mexico

_32. New York

_33. North Carolina

_34. North Dakota

_35. Ohio

_36. Oklahoma

_37. Oregon

_38. Pennsylvania

_39. Rhode Island

_40. South Carolina

_41. South Dakota

_42. Tennessee

_43. Texas

_44. Utah

_45. Vermont

_46. Virginia

_47. Washington

_48. West Virginia

_49. Wisconsin

_50. Wyoming

U.S. Territories

_ Guam

_ Puerto Rico

_ Virgin Islands

50 United States: State Capitals - Abbreviations (U.S. Postal Code)

States:	Abbreviations	State Capitals	States:	Abbreviations	State Capitals
1. **Alabama**	AL	Montgomery	31. **New Mexico**	NM	Santa Fe
2. **Alaska**	AK	Juneau	32. **New York**	NY	Albany
3. **Arizona**	AZ	Phoenix	33. **North Carolina**	NC	Raleigh
4. **Arkansas**	AR	Little Rock	34. **North Dakota**	ND	Bismarck
5. **California**	CA	Sacramento	35. **Ohio**	OH	Columbus
6. **Colorado**	CO	Denver	36. **Oklahoma**	OK	Oklahoma City
7. **Connecticut**	CT	Hartford	37. **Oregon**	OR	Salem
8. **Delaware**	DE	Dover	38. **Pennsylvania**	PA	Harrisburg
9. **Florida**	FL	Tallahassee	39. **Rhode Island**	RI	Providence
10. **Georgia**	GA	Atlanta	40. **South Carolina**	SC	Columbia
11. **Hawaii**	HI	Honolulu	41. **South Dakota**	SD	Pierre
12. **Idaho**	ID	Boise	42. **Tennessee**	TN	Nashville
13. **Illinois**	IL	Springfield	43. **Texas**	TX	Austin
14. **Indiana**	IN	Indianapolis	44. **Utah**	UT	Salt Lake City
15. **Iowa**	IA	Des Moines	45. **Vermont**	VT	Montpelier
16. **Kansas**	KS	Topeka	46. **Virginia**	VA	Richmond
17. **Kentucky**	KY	Frankfort	47. **Washington**	WA	Olympia
18. **Louisiana**	LA	Baton Rouge	48. **West Virginia**	WV	Charleston
19. **Maine**	ME	Augusta	49. **Wisconsin**	WI	Madison
20. **Maryland**	MD	Annapolis	50. **Wyoming**	WY	Cheyenne
21. **Massachusetts**	MA	Boston			
22. **Michigan**	MI	Lansing			
23. **Minnesota**	MN	St. Paul			
24. **Mississippi**	MS	Jackson			
25. **Missouri**	MO	Jefferson City			
26. **Montana**	MT	Helena			
27. **Nebraska**	NE	Lincoln			
28. **Nevada**	NV	Carson City			
29. **New Hampshire**	NH	Concord			
30. **New Jersey**	NJ	Trenton			

U.S. Territories:

- **Guam:** Pacific Ocean island, 3000 mi W of Hawaii; 1,500 mi E of the Philippines; 1,550 mi S of Japan.
- **Puerto Rico:** Caribbean Island, 1000 mi SE of Florida.
- **U.S. Virgin Islands:** Caribbean Sea & Atlantic Ocean, 40 mi E of Puerto Rico; 4 main islands: St. Thomas, St. John, St. Croix, Water Island + smaller islands. *(To the W are the British Virgin Islands.)*

Unusual Pronunciations: **Weird Words**

t<u>ough</u>
c<u>ough</u>
d<u>ough</u>

hicc<u>ough</u>
thor<u>ough</u>
thr<u>ough</u>

b<u>ear</u>d

h<u>ear</u>d

d<u>ead</u>

b<u>ead</u>

m<u>eat</u>
gr<u>eat</u>
thr<u>eat</u>

n<u>urse</u>

w<u>orse</u>

h<u>orse</u>

m<u>oth</u>
m<u>oth</u>er

b<u>oth</u>
b<u>oth</u>er

br<u>oth</u>
br<u>oth</u>er

h<u>ere</u>

th<u>ere</u>

d<u>ear</u>
f<u>ear</u>

b<u>ear</u>
p<u>ear</u>

d<u>ose</u>
r<u>ose</u>
l<u>ose</u>

w<u>art</u>

c<u>art</u>

l<u>augh</u>ter

d<u>augh</u>ter

<u>g</u>oose

<u>ch</u>oose

c<u>ork</u>

w<u>ork</u>

c<u>ard</u>

w<u>ard</u>

f<u>ont</u>

fr<u>ont</u>

word

sword

d<u>o</u>   t<u>o</u>

g<u>o</u>   s<u>o</u>

ABR: YOU CAN READ!

Adult Beginning Reader Program

Section 3: **Let's Learn**

Civics / Government

Government – History – Symbols – Documents

☐ To expand understanding of basic Civics concepts.

☐ Build vocabulary and reading skills.

by

Frederick J. Zorn, Ed.D.

Principal, Teacher, Adjunct Professor, Literacy Tutor

ABR Tips for Tutors: Civics
To expand reading vocabulary and concept understanding
of the United States and its government.

Tutor: _Explain: Civics topics are important to know.
Learner: _Will see many new words in print.
  _Will become familiar with important concepts.

Tutor: _Select one topic, 20-30 minute session.
  _Emphasize key words.
Learner: _Share knowledge.

Tutor: _Read key words together. Repetition is important.
Learner: _Read sentences and other information; tutor assists.
  _Discuss as go along. Ask questions.
Tutor: _Find supplements to relate: Stories, pictures.

Civics Topics: Note;
  _New citizens are expected to know facts about the U.S.
  _The U.S. Citizenship & Immigration Service (USCIS) uses a
  Civics Test. Some of the topics are included in this section.

Goal: _Exposure to new words and concepts.
  _Mastery of all words or concepts is not necessary.
  _Select lessons of interest and ENJOY.
  _ Remember, learning to read and understand new words is key.

~ Enjoy learning concepts and words about Civics. ~

Section 3: Let's Learn

Civics / Government

Table of Contents

United States Government: 3 Branches
Washington, D. C.

Executive Branch

Article 2, Constitution

President

Elected every 4 years.

Limit 2 terms

White House

Legislative Branch

Article 1, Constitution

Congress: 2 parts

☐ **House of Representatives**

☐ **Senate**

Capitol

☐ **House of Representatives**: 435 Congress persons   - 2 year terms
From each State. *Number based on State populations*
Entire House up for reelection every 2 years

☐ **Senate:**   100 senators   - 2 from each State   - 6 year term
1/3 elected every 2 years

Judicial Branch

Article 3, Constitution

Supreme Court

Highest Court in the United States
Interprets the **Constitution** and Laws
9 Supreme Court Justices
Life Time Appointments
Appointed by the President,
Confirmed by the Congress

Supreme Court

Note: All other powers not listed in the **Constitution** are given to the States.
Article 4, 6 - **Constitution**

Executive Branch: **President** - Article 2, Constitution
Head of the Executive Branch of the U. S. Government. Lives in the White House.

Questions	Answers
_1. *Term?*	-4 year term (2 term limit)
_2. *Elected when?*	-1st Tuesday in November, every 4 years
_3. *Vice President elected?*	-Along with the President
_4. *Qualifications for President?*	-Be at least 35 years old
	-Be a Natural-born citizen
	-Live in the U.S. for at least 14 years
_5. *Takes office?*	-At noon, January 20th, after the election
	-20th Amendment, Constitution
_6. *Ceremony called?*	-The Inauguration: takes Oath of Office
_7. *Who installs?*	-Chief Justice of the Supreme Court
_8. *President's Duties?*	-Heads the Executive Branch
	-Signs bills into law
	-Commander-in-Chief of the U.S. Military
_9. *Source?*	-Constitution, Article 2
_10. *Title?*	-"Mr. President"
_11. *Advisers?*	-The Cabinet

Oath of Office of the President: Constitution - Article 2, Section 1

"I do solemnly swear (or affirm) that I will
faithfully execute the office of President of the United States,
and will to the best of my ability,
preserve, protect and defend the Constitution of the United States."

Executive Branch: The Presidents of the United States

NP/F   1st:
George Washington
1789-1797
V.P. John Adams

F   2nd:
John Adams
1797-1801
V.P. Thomas Jefferson

R (DR)   3rd:
Thomas Jefferson
1801-1809
V.P. Aaron Burr,
George Clinton

R   4th:
James Madison
1809-1817
V.P. George Clinton,
Elbridge Gerry

R   5th:
James Monroe
1817-1825
V.P. Daniel D. Thompkins

To date, all were of the Revolution, Continental Congress, Declaration of Independence & Constitution generation.

R   6th:
John Quincy Adams
1825-1829
V.P. John C. Calhoun

R (D)   7th:
Andrew Jackson
1829-1837
V.P. John C. Calhoun,
Martin VanBuren

R   8th:
Martin VanBuren
1837-1841
V.P. Richard M. Johnson

W   9th:
William Henry Harrison
1841 (March to April)
V.P. John Tyler

W/NP   10th:
John Tyler
1841-1845
V.P. None

D   11th:
James K. Polk
1845-1849
V.P. George M. Dallas

W   12th:
Zachary Taylor
1849-1850
V.P. Millard Fillmore

W   13th:
Millard Fillmore
1850-1853
V.P. None

D   14th:
Franklin Pierce
1853-1857
V.P. William R. King

D   15th:
James Buchanan
1857-1861
V.P. John C. Breckinridge

R/U   16th:
Abraham Lincoln
1861-1865
V.P. Hannibal Hamlin,
Andrew Johnson

R   17th:
Andrew Johnson
1865-1869
V.P. None

R   18th:
Ulysses S. Grant
1869-1877
V.P. Schuyler Colfax,
Henry Wilson

R   19th:
Rutherford B. Hayes
1877-1881
V.P. William A. Wheeler

R   20th:
James A. Garfield
1881
V.P. Chester A. Arthur

R   21st:
Chester A. Arthur
1881-1885
V.P. None

D   22nd:
Grover Cleveland
1885-1889
V.P. Thomas A. Hendricks

R | 23rd:
Benjamin Harrison
1889-1893
V.P. Levi P. Morton

D | 24th:
Grover Cleveland
1893-1897
V.P. Adlai E. Stevenson

R | 25th:
William McKinley
1897-1901
V.P. Garret A. Hobart,
Theodore Roosevelt

R | 26th:
Theodore Roosevelt
1901-1909
V.P. Charles W. Fairbanks

R | 27th
William H. Taft
1909-1913
V.P. James S. Sherman

D | 28th:
Woodrow Wilson
1913-1921
V. P. Thomas R. Marshall

R | 29th:
Warren G. Harding
1921-1923
V.P. Calvin Coolidge

R | 30th:
Calvin Coolidge
1923 - 1929
V.P. Charles G. Dawes

R | 31st:
Herbert Hoover
1929-1933
V.P. Charles Curtis

D | 32nd:
Franklin D. Roosevelt
1933-1945
V.P. John N. Garner
Henry A. Wallace
Harry S Truman

D | 33rd:
Harry S Truman
1945-1953
V.P. Alben W. Barkley

R | 34th:
Dwight D. Eisenhower
1953-1961
V.P. Richard M. Nixon

D | 35th
John F. Kennedy
1961-1963
V.P. Lyndon B. Johnson

D | 36th:
Lyndon B. Johnson
1963-1969
V.P. Hubert H. Humphrey

R | 37th:
Richard M. Nixon
1969-1974
V.P. Spiro T. Agnew
Gerald R. Ford

R | 38th:
Gerald R. Ford
1974-1977
V.P. Nelson Rockefeller

D | 39th:
James E. Carter
1977-1981
V.P. Walter Mondale

R | 40th:
Ronald Reagan
1981-1989
V.P. George Bush

R | 41st:
George H. W. Bush
1989-1993
V.P. Daniel Quayle

D | 42nd:
William J. Clinton
1993-2001
V.P. Albert Gore

R | 43rd:
George W. Bush
2001 - 2009
V.P. Richard Cheney

D | 44th:
Barack Obama
2009 -
V.P. Joseph Biden

Political Party	
D	= Democrat
DR (R)	= Democratic-Republican
F	= Federalist
NP	= No Party
R	= Republican (Democratic)
R	= Republican (After 1854)
U	= Union (1864, Republican)
W	= Whig

Legislative Branch: Congress - Article 1, Constitution
Senate and House of Representatives
2 Part Lawmaking Branch of the National Government: Meets in the Capitol Building.

Questions	Answers
_1. *2 parts (Houses)?*	-Senate; House of Representatives
_2. *Function?*	-Makes Laws for the United States
_3. *Elected by?*	-The people in each State
_4. *Only Congress has the power to:*	-Declare war
_5. *Duties are from the:*	-Constitution: Article 1
_6. *Congress meets?*	-Capitol Building, Washington, D.C.

Congress: Senate

Questions	Answers
_1. *The Senate is?*	-One of the 2 parts of Congress
_2. *How many senators?*	-100, 2 from each State
_3. *Elected for a__ year term.*	-6 (No limit on reelection)
_4. *When elected?*	-1/3 elected every 2 years
_5. *The Senate meets?*	-Capitol Building, 2nd floor - North Wing
_6. *Qualifications:*	-Be 30+ years old
	-Be a citizen for at least 9 years
	-Live in the State that elects you
_7. *Who presides?*	-Vice-President of the U.S.
	-President Pro Tem of the Senate
_8. *President Pro Tem?*	-Usually, longest serving Majority Party Senator

Congress: House of Representatives

Questions	Answers
_1. *The House of Representatives is?*	-One of the 2 parts of Congress
_2. *There are __ congresspersons?*	-435
_3. *How many from each state?*	-From each State district by population
_4. *Elected for a _ year term?.*	-2 (No limit on reelection)
_5. *When elected?*	-Entire house, every 2 years
_6. *House meets where?*	-Capitol Building - South Wing
_7. *Qualifications:*	-Be 25+ years old
	-Be a citizen for at least 7 years
	-Live in the State that elects you
_8. *Title is:*	-Congressman, Congresswoman or Representative
_9. *Who presides?* (in charge?)	-The Speaker of the House
_10. *How chosen?*	-Candidate of the Majority Party
	-Elected by the House each new Congress

Glossary: Key Terms

_1. **candidate** (can di date)	-one running for office
_2. **Congress** (con gress)	-Legislative Branch of Government
_3. **elect** (ed) (e lect)	-choose by vote
_4. **majority** (ma jor i ty)	-the greater number
_5. **president** (pres i dent)	-elected person in charge
_6. **preside** (s) (pre side)	-be in charge
_7. **qualification** (s) (qual i fi ca tion)	-suitable qualities for a job
_8. **representative** (rep re sen ta tive)	-chosen to act or speak for others
_9. **senator** (sen a tor)	-member of the Senate
_10. **speaker** (speak er)	-head of the House of Representatives

---

Judicial Branch: **Supreme Court** - Article 3, Constitution
Highest Federal Court of the U. S. Government.

Questions:	Answers:
_1. *Judicial Branch is the?*	-Supreme Court
_2. *The Supreme Court is ?*	-The highest court in the U.S.
_3. *Meets where?*	-Supreme Court Building, Washington
_4. *What does it do?*	-Interprets the Constitution & laws
_5. *Made up of?*	-9 Supreme Court Justices
_6. *Who appoints them?*	-The President
	-Senate must approve
_7. *How long is an appointment?*	-Lifetime appointments
_8. *Head of the Supreme Court is?*	-The Chief Justice
_9. *How chosen?*	-The 9 Justices vote
_10. *What cases does it hear?*	-Cases on Constitution & Federal law
_11. *How does it get a case?*	-It goes through lower courts
	-Justices vote to accept a request
_12. *The Last Court of Appeal?*	-No other court has higher power
_13. *Supreme law of the land is?*	-The U.S. Constitution
_14. *"Is a law constitutional?"*	-Whether or not the law fits what
	the Constitution says or implies

United States: **The Beginnings, 1776**

Independence Hall

Philadelphia, Pennsylvania

☐ *Declaration of Independence* was signed here on July 4, 1776.
☐ The **Continental Congress** and **Constitutional Convention** met here.

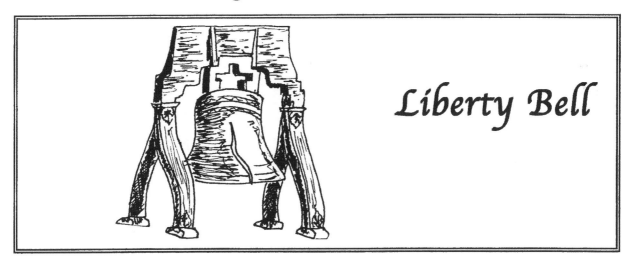

Liberty Bell

☐ The **Tower Bell** of Independence Hall rang, July 4, 1776, the date the *Declaration of Independence* was signed.
☐ Inscribed is: *"Proclaim Liberty throughout all the land unto all the inhabitants thereof."*

United States: **The 13 Colonies**

_1. **New Hampshire**

_2. **Massachusetts**

_3. **New York**

_4. **New Jersey**

_5. **Connecticut**

_6. **Rhode Island**

_7. **Pennsylvania**

_8. **Delaware**

_9. **Maryland**

_10. **Virginia**

_11. **North Carolina**

_12. **South Carolina**

_13. **Georgia**

Overview:

_1. *The Explorers were?* — From European countries; came by ship

_2. *They claimed land:* — Land they discovered in the New World

_3. *They claimed land for?* — Their European country

_4. *Britain gave away claimed land as:* — Land grants to form settlements

_5. *First settlements:* — Jamestown, VA, 1607; Plymouth, Mass., 1620 (The Pilgrims)

_6. *Settlements grew into larger colonies:* — The 13 British Crown Colonies

_7. *The 13 Colonies united & declared independence:* — July 4, 1776

_8. *Colonies became U.S. States when?* — They ratified the **Constitution**

Note: Claim (v): Declaring something as true.

50 United States: In Order of Statehood

1. Delaware	Dec. 7, 1787
2. Pennsylvania	Dec. 12, 1787
3. New Jersey	Dec. 18, 1787
4. Georgia	Jan. 2, 1788
5. Connecticut	Jan. 9, 1788
6. Massachusetts	Feb. 6, 1788
7. Maryland	April 28, 1788
8. S. Carolina	May 23, 1788
9. New Hampshire	June 21, 1788
10. Virginia	June 25, 1788
11. New York	July 26, 1788
12. N. Carolina	Nov. 21, 1789
13. Rhode Island	May 29, 1790

13 Colonies became States when they ratified the Constitution. (Note Dates.)

14. Vermont	March 4, 1791
15. Kentucky	June 1, 1792
16. Tennessee	June 1, 1796
17. Ohio	March 1, 1803
18. Louisiana	April 30, 1812

19. Indiana	Dec. 11, 1816
20. Mississippi	Dec. 10, 1817
21. Illinois	Dec. 3, 1818
22. Alabama	Dec. 14, 1819
23. Maine	March 15, 1820

24. Missouri	Aug. 10, 1821
25. Arkansas	June 15, 1836
26. Michigan	Jan. 26, 1837
27. Florida	March 3, 1845
28. Texas	Dec. 29, 1845

29. Iowa	Dec. 28, 1846
30. Wisconsin	May 29, 1848
31. California	Sept. 9, 1850
32. Minnesota	May 11, 1858
33. Oregon	Feb. 14, 1859

34. Kansas	Jan. 29, 1861
35. W. Virginia	June 19. 1863
36. Nevada	Oct. 31, 1864
37. Nebraska	March 1, 1867
38. Colorado	Aug. 1, 1876

39. N. Dakota	Nov. 2, 1889
40. S. Dakota	Nov. 2, 1889
41. Montana	Nov. 8, 1889
42. Washington	Nov. 11, 1889
43. Idaho	July 3, 1890

44. Wyoming	July 10, 1890
45. Utah	Jan. 4, 1896
46. Oklahoma	Nov. 16, 1907
47. New Mexico	Jan. 6, 1912
48. Arizona	Feb. 14, 1912

49. Alaska	Jan. 3, 1959
50. Hawaii	Aug. 21, 1959

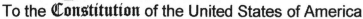

𝕻reamble (introduction)

To the 𝕮onstitution of the United States of America

_1. **We the People**

_2. **of the United States,**

_3. **in order to form a more perfect Union,**

_4. **establish Justice,**

_5. **insure domestic Tranquility,**

_6. **provide for the common defence,**

_7. **promote the general Welfare**

_8. **and secure the Blessings of Liberty**

_9. **to ourselves and our Posterity,**

_10. **do ordain and establish**

_11. **this Constitution**

_12. **for the United States of America.**

End of the Preamble to the 𝕮onstitution

Key Words & Glossary:

_1. **common** — for all of us

_2. **defence** — defense, protection

_3. **domestic** — at home

_4. **establish** — put in place

_5. **insure** — be sure we have

_6. **just** (justice) — fairness under law

_7. **liberty** — freedom

_8. **ordain** — to order

_9. **posterity** — those coming after

_10. **promote** — help make happen

_11. **secure** v. — make sure we keep

_12. **tranquil** (-ity) — peace

_13. **union** — country

_14. **welfare** — good

The Constitution

- The basis of individual freedoms and the United States Government -

Signed: September 17, 1787 - *Ratified: By June 21, 1788 - Adopted: July 2, 1788 - In effect: March 4, 1789

☐ Preamble: We the People . . .

☐ Articles 1 - 7: Key Points From The Original Constitution:

1. THE LEGISLATIVE BRANCH: Congress: 2 part system:

☐ **House of Representatives**: **- 2 year terms**
  435 Congress persons, by State population
☐ **Senate**: **- 6 year term**
  100 Senators, 2 from each state (1/3 elected every 2 years)

2. EXECUTIVE BRANCH: President / Vice-President

3. JUDICIAL BRANCH: Supreme Court; other courts
  Trial by Jury

4. STATES: Rights, Duties and relationships

5. AMENDMENTS: Amending the Constitution

6. SUPREME LAW OF THE LAND: Law carries to all States

7. RATIFYING THE CONSTITUTION: *
  9 of the 13 States needed to vote <u>for</u> the Constitution

End of The Original Constitution: Key Points

Constitution: Bill of Rights - Amendments: 1-10

_1. Freedom: **
- □ of Religion
- □ of Speech
- □ of The Press
- □ of Peaceful assembly
- □ to Ask the government to correct grievances

_2. Right to keep and bear arms: As necessary for a well regulated militia for security of a free state. *(arms = defense weapons)*

_3. No Quartering of Soldiers: In peacetime without consent. *(quartering = housing)*

_4. Freedom from Search: Without warrant & probable cause. *(without good legal reason)*

_5. Protection of Accused in Criminal Cases.
- □ Not be a witness against yourself.
- □ Not have life, liberty, or property taken without Due Process. *(of law)*
- □ Not have private property taken without just pay. *(just = fair)*
- □ Not be subject to the same offense twice. *(offense = criminal charge)*
- □ Grand Jury: 12 - 23 people. Decides if evidence warrants a trial. *(warrants = justifies)*

_6. Rights of Accused in Criminal Cases:
- □ Speedy and public trial.
- □ Impartial jury of the State & District where crime took place.
- □ Told the nature & cause of accusations.
- □ Be faced by the witnesses.
- □ Have process for getting defense witnesses.
- □ Have a defense lawyer.

_7. Trial by Jury in common law suits: Value of loss over $20.

_8. No excessive fines or bail; No cruel or unusual punishment.

_9. Other rights not expressed are kept by the people

_10. Powers not stated or prohibited are for the States and the People.

- End of Bill of Rights -

**Amendment 1, *The Right to:*
- □ *Worship as you choose.*
- □ *Say what you want.*
- □ *Print / publish your opinion.*
- □ *Meet in a group peacefully.*
- □ *Ask the government to change.*

The Flag: The symbol of the United States.

1790's: Betsy Ross Flag, 13 stars

1945, at Iwo Jima

1912: 48 star flag

Let's Read: The Flag:

1. The flag of the United States of America is **Red, White and Blue**:

   □ 13 Stripes - *7 Red, 6 White*   - For the original 13 States / Colonies.

   □ 50 Stars - White   - 1 for each State.

   □ Blue Field (background)   - For the 50 white stars.

2. The flag is also known as the ***Stars & Stripes***.

3. Stars were added for each new state. - 13 stripes remained the same.

   □ By 1912, there were 48 stars.   - 1912 - 1959

   □ July 4, 1960, 50 stars for 50 states.   - The new flag was raised at Ft. McHenry

   National Monument, Baltimore, Maryland after Alaska and Hawaii

   became new states on August 21, 1959.

◇ **Flag Day is June 14th.**   - The birthday of the Stars and Stripes.

On this date in 1777, the Second Continental Congress set the first official

United States Flag as 13 red and white strips and 13 while stars on a blue field.

The Pledge of Allegiance

First published in a magazine in 1892.
It became official by an Act of Congress on June 22, 1942.

_1.   I pledge allegiance

_2.   to the flag

_3.   of the United States of America

_4.   and to the Republic

_5.   for which it stands,

_6.   one Nation under God,

_7.   indivisible,

_8.   with Liberty and Justice

_9.   for all.

Glossary: The Pledge of Allegiance

_1. **allegiance**   - loyalty, duty of citizenship
_2. **pledge**   - promise, fairness in law
_3. **flag**   - the symbol of the country
_4. **indivisible**   - can't divide
_5. **justice**   - fairness in law
_6. **liberty**   - freedom; rights
_7. **Republic**   - nation; citizens have power through elected representatives
_8. **stand** (s)   - what it represents

Star-Spangled Banner by Francis Scott Key*

National Anthem of the United States.
Written in 1814; became official in 1931.

_1. **O! say, can you see, by the dawn's early light,**

_2. **What so proudly we hailed**

_3. **at the twilight's last gleaming,**

_4. **Whose broad stripes and bright stars,**

_5. **through the perilous fight**

_6. **O'er the ramparts we watched,**

_7. **were so gallantly streaming?**

Ft. McHenry Flag
15 stars, 15 stripes

_8. **And the rockets' red glare,**

_9. **the bombs bursting in air**

_10. **Gave proof through the night**

_11. **that our flag was still there.**

_12. **O! say, does that star-spangled banner yet wave**

_13. **O'er the land of the free**

_14. **and the home of the brave?**

Glossary: *Star-Spangled Banner*

_1.	*gallantly streaming*	- Proudly waving in the breeze
_2.	*oh say!*	- Please tell me!
_3.	*o'er the ramparts we watched*	- Seeing over the fort's defensive walls
_4.	*perilous fight*	- Dangerous battle
_5.	*so proudly we hailed*	- We saw with pride
_6.	*star-spangled banner*	- Flag with decorative stars
_7.	*twilight's last gleaming*	- Faint light just before dark
_8.	*yet wave*	- Flag still flying; the battle is not lost

◇ *Key was on a British ship. It was bombing American Fort McHenry in Baltimore Harbor.
◇ Americans at the Fort were protecting Baltimore from British attack. (War of 1812)

America: My Country 'Tis Of Thee

Words: Samuel F. Smith, 1831. (Music from God Save the King, 1744)

First performed at a children's gathering at Park Street Church, Boston, July 4, 1831

Verse 1:

_1. **My country 'tis of thee,**

_2. **Sweet land of liberty,**

_3. **Of thee I sing.**

_4. **Land where my fathers died!**

_5. **Land of the Pilgrim's pride!**

_6. **From every mountain side,**

_7. **Let freedom ring!**

Glossary: *America: My Country 'Tis Of Thee*

_1. **father** (s)   - People that came before & made our country possible
_2. **freedom**   - Right to act, speak, think freely
_3. **liberty**   - Freedom from oppressive government restrictions
_4. **mountain (side)**   - From all over
_5. **Pilgrim** (s)   - Came on the Mayflower
_6. **pride**   - Deep satisfaction from their achievement
_7. **thee**   - You
_8 **'tis**   - It is

America The Beautiful - Song

Words: Katherine Lee Bates, Poet; Written on Pike's Peak, 1893.
Music: Based on "*Materna*" by Samuel Augustus Ward

Verse 1:

_1. **O! beautiful for spacious skies,**

_2. **for amber waves of grain,**

_3. **For purple mountain majesties**

_4. **above the fruited plain.**

_5. **America! America! God shed His grace on thee,**

_6. **And crown Thy good with brotherhood**

_7. **from sea to shining sea.**

Verse 4:

_8. **O! beautiful for patriot dream**

_9. **that sees beyond the years.**

_10. **Thine alabaster cities gleam**

_11. **undimmed by human tears.**

_12. **America! America! God shed His grace on thee,**

_13. **And crown thy good with brotherhood**

_14. **from sea to shining sea.**

Glossary: *America The Beautiful*

_1. **alabaster**	- marble		_8. **patriot**	- fighter for a country
_2. **amber**	- tan *(grain color)*		_9. **plain**	- flat land
_3. **crown** (v.)	- add to		_10. **shed** (v.)	- give off
_4. **gleam**	- shine		_11. **spacious**	- large, roomy
_5. **grace**	- favor		_12. **thee**	- you
_6. **majesties**	- royal, special		_13. **thine, thy**	- your
_7. **O** (Oh!)			_14. **undimmed**	- not clouded

◇ *amber waves of grain* - tan colored fields of grain
◇ *from sea to shining sea* - from the Atlantic to the Pacific Oceans
◇ *sees beyond the years* - looks to the future

Statue of Liberty

~ **Presented in Paris on July 4, 1884, a Symbol of Freedom** ~
~ **Dedicated on October 28, 1886** ~
Located on Liberty Island (formerly Bedloe's Island), New York Harbor.
A smaller copy is in Paris, France.

Statue of Liberty: *The "Goddess of Liberty" Holding a Torch.*

_1. *What is it?*   - A large statue. A symbol of Freedom.

_2. *Where is it?*   - Liberty Island, New York Harbor.

_3. *Where did it come from?*   - A gift from the people of France.

_4. *Its title is?*   - *Liberty Enlightening the World.*

_5. *When was it dedicated?*   - October 28, 1886.

_6. *Who made it?*   - Frederic Auguste Bartholdi, in France.

_7. *It was in honor of the?*   - American Revolution & French Revolution.

_8. *Details?*   - 152 feet high, copper, on an 11 pointed star.
    - A spiral stairway inside goes to the crown.

_9. *What poem is on the base?* - *The New Colossus;* on a bronze plaque (1903).

_10. *Who wrote the poem?*   - American Poet, Emma Lazarus, 1883.

_11. **A tablet in her left hand has on it?** - "July 4th, 1776" (in Roman numerals).

> ### Statue of Liberty: **The New Colossus, poem** - *Excerpts*
> by **Emma Lazarus**, 1883
> American poet Emma Lazarus wrote this poem about the Statue of Liberty in 1883.
> It was put on a bronze plaque on the base of the monument in 1903.

_1. **Give me your tired, your poor,**

_2. **Your huddled masses**

_3. **yearning to breathe free,**

_4. **The wretched refuse**

_5. **of your teeming shore.**

_6. **Send these, the homeless,**

_7. **tempest-tost, to me,**

_8. **I lift my lamp**

_9. **beside the golden door!**

Glossary: *The New Colossus,* **poem**

_1. **breathe**	_8. **lamp**	_15. **teem** (ing) - crowded
_2. **beside** - next to	_9. **lift**	_16. **tempest** - storm
_3. **door**	_10. **mass** (es)	_17. **tired** - weary
_4. **free**	_11. **poor**	_18. **tost** - tossed
_5. **gold** (en)	_12. **refuse** *(n)* - discards	_19. **wretched** - miserable
_6. **homeless**	_13. **send**	_20. **yearn** (ing) - want
_7. **huddle** (d) - crowded	_14. **shore**	

Note: **Colossus** - A statue much bigger than life size. Ex: The Colossus of Rhodes.

Excerpts: **The Gettysburg Address**

Speech given by President Abraham Lincoln

November 19, 1863 - Gettysburg, Pennsylvania - Civil War

_1. **Four score and seven years ago** *(4 x 20 + 7 = 87) = 1776

_2. **our fathers brought forth on this continent,**

_3. **a new nation, conceived in Liberty,**

_4. **and dedicated to the proposition**

_5. **that all men are created equal. . . .**

_6. **The world will little note, nor long remember what we say here,**

_7. **. . . we here highly resolve that these dead shall not have died in vain**

_8. **- that this nation, under God,**

_9. **shall have a new birth of freedom**

_10. **- and that government**

_11. **of the people, by the people, for the people,**

_12. **shall not perish from the earth.**

Glossary: The Gettysburg Address

_1. **conceive** (d) - begin   _5. **forth**   - here   _9. **proposition** - idea

_2. **continent**   - United States   _6. **liberty** - freedom   _10. **resolve**   - decide

_3. **create** (d)   - born   _7. **note**   - take notice   _11. **score**   - 20

_4. **dedicate** (d) - pledge   _8. **perish** - die   _12. **in vain** - without cause

*Note: _ *four <u>score</u>*   =   4 x 20 = 80   (score = 20)
 _ *and <u>seven</u> years ago* =   + 7   (years)
 _ <u>80</u> + 7   =   87 years ago (from 1863)
 _ <u>1863</u> - <u>87</u> years   =   1776   (year the country gained independence)

ABR: YOU CAN READ!

Adult Beginning Reader Program

Index and Supplements

by

Frederick J. Zorn, Ed.D.

Principal, Teacher, Adjunct Professor, Literacy Tutor

Topics: By Academic Categories (Check Index for Page Numbers)

Language Arts:
- ☐ Basic Sight Words / Phrases
- ☐ Blenders
- ☐ Compound Words
- ☐ Consonants, Vowels
- ☐ Contractions
- ☐ Homonyms
- ☐ Letters: Cursive / Manuscript
- ☐ Parts of Speech
- ☐ Prepositions
- ☐ Punctuation
- ☐ Root Words, Prefix, Suffix
- ☐ Sentence, Subject / Predicate
- ☐ Syllables
- ☐ Weird Words: Pronunciation
- ☐ Word Enders: -s, -ed, -ing, -ion
- ☐ Word Pictures

Science:
- ☐ Birds
- ☐ Body
- ☐ Chemistry / Elements
- ☐ Colors
- ☐ Fruits & Nuts
- ☐ Mammals
- ☐ Sea Animals
- ☐ Simple Machines
- ☐ Solar System
- ☐ Vegetables & Grains

Mathematics:
- ☐ Calendar
- ☐ Checks
- ☐ Decimals, Fractions, Percent (%)
- ☐ Geometric Shapes
- ☐ Measurement
- ☐ Money
- ☐ Numbers
- ☐ Roman Numerals
- ☐ Time

Social Studies:
- ☐ Branches of Government
- ☐ Citizen
- ☐ 13 Colonies
- ☐ Congress
- ☐ Constitution
- ☐ Flag
- ☐ Geography
- ☐ *Gettysburg Address*
- ☐ Independence Hall, Liberty Bell
- ☐ National Observances
- ☐ Patriotic Songs
- ☐ *Pledge of Allegiance*
- ☐ President
- ☐ Statue of Liberty
- ☐ Supreme Court
- ☐ 50 United States
- ☐ Voting, Registration

Health / Wellness:
- ☐ Check Up / Symptoms
- ☐ Digestion
- ☐ Doctors
- ☐ Food Groups
- ☐ Grooming
- ☐ Prescription, Labels, Terms
- ☐ Teeth

Practical / Functional Literacy:
- ☐ Buildings: Furniture, Furnishings
- ☐ Clothing
- ☐ Containers
- ☐ Directions, Opposites
- ☐ Family
- ☐ Greeting Cards
- ☐ Ice Cream
- ☐ Mail
- ☐ Menu
- ☐ Music: Instruments, Symbols
- ☐ Occupations, Jobs, Application
- ☐ Signs
- ☐ Sports: Terms
- ☐ Symbols
- ☐ Table Settings
- ☐ Tools

Index: Alphabetical by Topic

Index: Alphabetical by Topic

Story Suggestions: Interesting Lesson Enders

Ending each tutoring session with a story at appropriate reading levels gives practice and feelings of accomplishment. The following are interesting selections found in varied sources.

Aesop's Fables:

Short, interesting and have a moral.

- ☐ Lion and the Mouse
- ☐ Milkmaid & Her Pail (Don't Count your Chickens Before They're Hatched)
- ☐ Boy Who Cried Wolf
- ☐ Goose and the Golden Eggs
- ☐ Miller, His Son, & a Donkey
- ☐ Hare & the Tortoise
- ☐ Fox & the Crow
- ☐ Fox & The Grapes
- ☐ Town Mouse & Country Mouse
- ☐ Belling The Cat
- ☐ Ants & The Grasshopper
- ☐ Two Goats
- ☐ Wolf & The Lamb
- ☐ Fox & The Goat
- ☐ Farmer & His Sons
- ☐ Wolf in Sheep's Clothing
- ☐ Old Lion & The Fox
- ☐ The Miser
- ☐ Two Travelers & A Bear
- ☐ Dog & His Reflection
- ☐ North Wind & The Sun

Myths:

Interesting; historical.

- ☐ The Trojan Horse
- ☐ Pandora's Box
- ☐ King Midas

Stories / Tales:

Timeless; find illustrated versions.

- ☐ Stone Soup
- ☐ The Porridge Pot
- ☐ The Emperor's New Clothes
- ☐ The Ugly Duckling
- ☐ Rip Van Winkle
- ☐ Paul Bunyan
- ☐ Johnny Appleseed
- ☐ King Arthur
- ☐ Alice in Wonderland

Invention Stories:

Inspiring and informative.

- ☐ Coffee
- ☐ The Sandwich
- ☐ The Shopping Cart
- ☐ Sneakers
- ☐ Levi's / Jeans

Poetry / Nursery Rhymes:

Familiar; can be retold to children.

- ☐ Thirty Days Hath September
- ☐ Hickory, Dickory, Dock
- ☐ Twinkle Twinkle Little Star
- ☐ Humpty Dumpty
- ☐ Little Miss Muffet
- ☐ Jack and Jill
- ☐ Jack Be Nimble
- ☐ Old King Cole
- ☐ Rock a Bye Baby

Use different techniques: Read to. Alternate reading. Give first letter cues. Anticipate difficult words. Read short selections at a time. Explain. Discuss. Use a Story Map. Read to Enjoy!

Story Map: *Who? What? Where? When? Why?*

Title:_____

Author:_____ **Illustrator:**_____

Setting: *Where? What?* Description?	Characters: *Who?*
"Picture Read"	*"Picture Read"*

Story Progression:

First: *What? When?* What happened?

Next? *What? When?* What happened?

Then? *What? When?* What happened?

End: *What? When? Why?* What finally happened?

Sample: **Lesson Plan Form:** *@20 - 30 minutes / lesson*

☐ **Letters**		Pp. 1-137
☐ **Basic Sight Words / Phrases** 3 -5 letter sets		Pp. 144-153
☐ **Words / Let's Learn** *(See Index)*	Pp. 155-271 (Pp. 276-358 - Use later in term)	
◇ **Story** *(Choose your own)*		
◇ **Other**		

Date:_____   **Note: Topic and Page Numbers**

☐ **Letters:** _____

☐ **Basic Sight Words / Phrases:** _____

☐ **Words / Let's Learn:** _____

☐ **Story:** _____

☐ **Other:** _____

Date:_____   **Note: Topic and Page Numbers**

☐ **Letters:** _____

☐ **Basic Sight Words / Phrases:** _____

☐ **Words / Let's Learn:** _____

☐ **Story:** _____

☐ **Other:** _____

Date:_____   **Note: Topic and Page Numbers**

☐ **Letters:** _____

☐ **Basic Sight Words / Phrases:** _____

☐ **Words / Let's Learn:** _____

☐ **Story:** _____

☐ **Other:** _____

Progress Report: Sample

Name: **Date:**

Lessons Covered: **Improved:**

☐ **Letters**   _____

☐ **Basic Sight Words/Phrases** _____

☐ **Words / Let's Learn**   _____

☐ **Story Reading:**
 • **Word Attack**   _____

 • **Grammar, Punctuation**   _____

 • **Comprehension**   _____

 • **Pronunciation**   _____

 • **Read w/Expression, Fluency** _____

Self-Evaluation:

I improved most in:

I need to work on:

What I liked most:

Tutor Evaluation:

Comments:

Made in the USA
Monee, IL
04 March 2024